YOUR CH...
HOROSCOP...
NEIL SOMERVI...

What the Year of the Pig Holds in Store for You

TO ROS, RICHARD AND EMILY

HarperElement
An Imprint of HarperCollins*Publishers*
77–85 Fulham Palace Road
Hammersmith, London W6 8JB

The website address is: www.thorsonselement.com

and *HarperElement* are trademarks of
HarperCollins*Publishers* Limited

Published by HarperElement 2006

2

A catalogue record for this book is
available from the British Library

ISBN-13 978-0-00-721132-6
ISBN-10 0-00-721132-5

Printed and bound in Great Britain by
Clays Ltd, St Ives plc

CONTENTS

———◆———

ABOUT THE AUTHOR

Neil Somerville is one of the leading writers in the West on Chinese horoscopes. He has been interested in Eastern forms of divination for many years and believes that much can be learned from the ancient wisdom of the East. His annual book on Chinese horoscopes has built up an international following and he is also the author of *What's your Chinese Love Sign?* (Thorsons, 2000), *Chinese Success Signs* (Thorsons, 2001) and *The Answers* (Element, 2004).

Neil Somerville was born in the year of the Water Snake. His wife was born under the sign of the Monkey, his son is an Ox and daughter a Horse.

ACKNOWLEDGEMENTS

This marks the twentieth year that *Your Chinese Horoscope* has been published and I would like to thank the splendid team I have worked with at HarperElement over the years for their encouragement and support, in particular Katy Carrington and Lizzie Hutchins. I also thank you, the reader, for your interest and I sincerely hope I have not only whetted your interest in this ancient and fascinating subject but have also provided helpful guidance over the years. To you again I say thank you and send my very best wishes.

I would also like to acknowledge Theodora Lau's *The Handbook of Chinese Horoscopes* (Harper & Row, 1979; Arrow, 1981), which was particularly useful to me in my research.

In addition to Ms Lau's work, I commend the following books to those who wish to find out more about Chinese horoscopes: Kristyna Arcarti, *Chinese Horoscopes for Beginners* (Headway, 1995); Catherine Aubier, *Chinese Zodiac Signs* (Arrow, 1984), series of 12 books; E. A. Crawford and Teresa Kennedy, *Chinese Elemental Astrology* (Piatkus Books, 1992); Paula Delsol, *Chinese Horoscopes* (Pan, 1973); Barry Fantoni, *Barry Fantoni's Chinese Horoscopes* (Warner, 1994); Bridget Giles and the Diagram Group, *Chinese Astrology* (HarperCollins, 1996); Kwok Man-Ho, *Complete Chinese Horoscopes* (Sunburst

Books, 1995); Lori Reid, *The Complete Book of Chinese Horoscopes* (Element Books, 1997); Paul Rigby and Harvey Bean, *Chinese Astrologics* (Publications Division, South China Morning Post Ltd, 1981); Ruth Q. Sun, *The Asian Animal Zodiac* (Charles E. Tuttle Company, Inc., 1996); Derek Walters, *Ming Shu* (Pagoda Books, 1987) and *The Chinese Astrology Workbook* (The Aquarian Press, 1988); Suzanne White, *The New Astrology* (Pan, 1987), *The New Chinese Astrology* (Pan, 1994) and *Chinese Astrology Plain and Simple* (Eden Grove Editions, 1998).

———————◆———————

As we march into a new year
we each have our hopes, our ambitions and our dreams.

Sometimes fate and circumstance will assist us,
sometimes we will struggle and despair,
but march we must.

For it is those who keep going,
and who keep their aspirations alive,
who stand the greatest chance of securing what they want.

March determinedly,
and your determination will, in some way, be rewarded.

Neil Somerville

———————◆———————

INTRODUCTION

The origins of Chinese horoscopes have been lost in the mists of time. It is known that Oriental astrologers practised their art many thousands of years ago and even today Chinese astrology continues to fascinate and intrigue.

In Chinese astrology there are 12 signs named after 12 different animals. No one quite knows how the signs acquired their names, but there is one legend that offers an explanation.

According to this legend, one Chinese New Year the Buddha invited all the animals in his kingdom to come before him. Unfortunately, for reasons best known to the animals, only 12 turned up. The first to arrive was the Rat, followed by the Ox, Tiger, Rabbit, Dragon, Snake, Horse, Goat, Monkey, Rooster, Dog and finally Pig.

In gratitude, the Buddha decided to name a year after each of the animals and that those born during that year would inherit some of the personality of that animal. Therefore those born in the year of the Ox would be hardworking, resolute and stubborn, just like the Ox, while those born in the year of the Dog would be loyal and faithful, just like the Dog. While not everyone can possibly share all the characteristics of a sign, it is incredible what similarities do occur and this is partly where the fascination of Chinese horoscopes lies.

In addition to the 12 signs of the Chinese zodiac there are five elements, and these have a strengthening or moderating influence upon the sign. Details about the effects of the elements are given in each of the chapters on the 12 signs.

To find out which sign you were born under, refer to the tables on the following pages. As the Chinese year is based on the lunar year and does not start until late January or early February, it is particularly important for anyone born in those two months to check carefully the dates of the Chinese year in which they were born.

Also included, in the Appendix, are two charts showing the compatibility between the signs for personal and business relationships, and details about the signs ruling the different hours of the day. From this it is possible to locate your ascendant and, as in Western astrology, this has a significant influence on your personality.

In writing this book, I have taken the unusual step of combining the intriguing nature of Chinese horoscopes with the Western desire to know what the future holds and have based my interpretations upon various factors relating to each of the signs. Over the years in which *Your Chinese Horoscope* has been published I have been pleased that so many have found the sections on the forthcoming year of interest, and hope that the horoscope has been constructive and useful. Remember, though, that at all times you are the master of your own destiny. I sincerely hope that *Your Chinese Horoscope 2007* will prove interesting and helpful for the year ahead.

THE CHINESE YEARS

Goat	13 February	1907	to	1 February	1908
Monkey	2 February	1908	to	21 January	1909
Rooster	22 January	1909	to	9 February	1910
Dog	10 February	1910	to	29 January	1911
Pig	30 January	1911	to	17 February	1912
Rat	18 February	1912	to	5 February	1913
Ox	6 February	1913	to	25 January	1914
Tiger	26 January	1914	to	13 February	1915
Rabbit	14 February	1915	to	2 February	1916
Dragon	3 February	1916	to	22 January	1917
Snake	23 January	1917	to	10 February	1918
Horse	11 February	1918	to	31 January	1919
Goat	1 February	1919	to	19 February	1920
Monkey	20 February	1920	to	7 February	1921
Rooster	8 February	1921	to	27 January	1922
Dog	28 January	1922	to	15 February	1923
Pig	16 February	1923	to	4 February	1924
Rat	5 February	1924	to	23 January	1925
Ox	24 January	1925	to	12 February	1926
Tiger	13 February	1926	to	1 February	1927
Rabbit	2 February	1927	to	22 January	1928
Dragon	23 January	1928	to	9 February	1929
Snake	10 February	1929	to	29 January	1930
Horse	30 January	1930	to	16 February	1931

Goat	17 February	1931	to	5 February	1932
Monkey	6 February	1932	to	25 January	1933
Rooster	26 January	1933	to	13 February	1934
Dog	14 February	1934	to	3 February	1935
Pig	4 February	1935	to	23 January	1936
Rat	24 January	1936	to	10 February	1937
Ox	11 February	1937	to	30 January	1938
Tiger	31 January	1938	to	18 February	1939
Rabbit	19 February	1939	to	7 February	1940
Dragon	8 February	1940	to	26 January	1941
Snake	27 January	1941	to	14 February	1942
Horse	15 February	1942	to	4 February	1943
Goat	5 February	1943	to	24 January	1944
Monkey	25 January	1944	to	12 February	1945
Rooster	13 February	1945	to	1 February	1946
Dog	2 February	1946	to	21 January	1947
Pig	22 January	1947	to	9 February	1948
Rat	10 February	1948	to	28 January	1949
Ox	29 January	1949	to	16 February	1950
Tiger	17 February	1950	to	5 February	1951
Rabbit	6 February	1951	to	26 January	1952
Dragon	27 January	1952	to	13 February	1953
Snake	14 February	1953	to	2 February	1954
Horse	3 February	1954	to	23 January	1955
Goat	24 January	1955	to	11 February	1956
Monkey	12 February	1956	to	30 January	1957
Rooster	31 January	1957	to	17 February	1958
Dog	18 February	1958	to	7 February	1959
Pig	8 February	1959	to	27 January	1960
Rat	28 January	1960	to	14 February	1961
Ox	15 February	1961	to	4 February	1962

Tiger	5 February	1962	to	24 January	1963
Rabbit	25 January	1963	to	12 February	1964
Dragon	13 February	1964	to	1 February	1965
Snake	2 February	1965	to	20 January	1966
Horse	21 January	1966	to	8 February	1967
Goat	9 February	1967	to	29 January	1968
Monkey	30 January	1968	to	16 February	1969
Rooster	17 February	1969	to	5 February	1970
Dog	6 February	1970	to	26 January	1971
Pig	27 January	1971	to	14 February	1972
Rat	15 February	1972	to	2 February	1973
Ox	3 February	1973	to	22 January	1974
Tiger	23 January	1974	to	10 February	1975
Rabbit	11 February	1975	to	30 January	1976
Dragon	31 January	1976	to	17 February	1977
Snake	18 February	1977	to	6 February	1978
Horse	7 February	1978	to	27 January	1979
Goat	28 January	1979	to	15 February	1980
Monkey	16 February	1980	to	4 February	1981
Rooster	5 February	1981	to	24 January	1982
Dog	25 January	1982	to	12 February	1983
Pig	13 February	1983	to	1 February	1984
Rat	2 February	1984	to	19 February	1985
Ox	20 February	1985	to	8 February	1986
Tiger	9 February	1986	to	28 January	1987
Rabbit	29 January	1987	to	16 February	1988
Dragon	17 February	1988	to	5 February	1989
Snake	6 February	1989	to	26 January	1990
Horse	27 January	1990	to	14 February	1991
Goat	15 February	1991	to	3 February	1992
Monkey	4 February	1992	to	22 January	1993

Rooster	23 January	1993	to	9 February	1994
Dog	10 February	1994	to	30 January	1995
Pig	31 January	1995	to	18 February	1996
Rat	19 February	1996	to	6 February	1997
Ox	7 February	1997	to	27 January	1998
Tiger	28 January	1998	to	15 February	1999
Rabbit	16 February	1999	to	4 February	2000
Dragon	5 February	2000	to	23 January	2001
Snake	24 January	2001	to	11 February	2002
Horse	12 February	2002	to	31 January	2003
Goat	1 February	2003	to	21 January	2004
Monkey	22 January	2004	to	8 February	2005
Rooster	9 February	2005	to	28 January	2006
Dog	29 January	2006	to	17 February	2007
Pig	18 February	2007	to	6 February	2008

NOTE

The names of the signs in the Chinese zodiac occasionally differ, although the characteristics of the signs remain the same. In some books the Ox is referred to as the Buffalo or Bull, the Rabbit as the Hare or Cat, the Goat as the Sheep and the Pig as the Boar.

For the sake of convenience, the male gender is used throughout this book. Unless otherwise stated, the characteristics of the signs apply to both sexes.

WELCOME TO THE
YEAR OF THE PIG

———◆·◆———

The Year of the Pig is significant, not only in completing the cycle of animal years but also in marking what can be a time of considerable opportunity and growth. Pig years have potential and this year will be no exception.

One prominent feature of the Pig year is that it favours family values and the home. It is considered an auspicious year for starting a family as well as for spending more time with loved ones. Over the year, much emphasis will be placed on the quality of home life and on leading a more balanced lifestyle.

Economic prospects are also encouraging for the year, with many countries enjoying growth and improved conditions. The leisure, entertainment and construction industries could fare particularly well. The financial sector could also have a good year, with several stock markets recording new highs. It was in the last Pig year that the Dow Jones Industrial Average closed above the 5,000 mark for the first time and the Nasdaq Composite Index first closed above 1,000.

However, while many will benefit from the buoyant conditions, the Pig year also calls for personal restraint. When times feel good, it can be tempting to spend freely and increase credit, and without care, problems could result. This may be an expansive time, but it is also one for realism.

In addition to the growth seen in many economies, certain industries will be enjoying major advances during the year and new products will often make life easier and more efficient. IBM launched the personal computer system in a Pig year (1983) and the transistor and self-starter motor were also invented in Pig years. Pig years are certainly innovative and 2007 will witness more major inventions.

This will also be a year which will see some remarkable feats of human endeavour, with certain individuals capturing the admiration of many with their courage and achievements. It was, for example, in the last Pig year that Steve Fossett became the first person to make a solo flight across the Pacific Ocean in a balloon and in previous Pig years Thor Heyerdahl sailed on a raft from Peru to Polynesia and Roald Amundsen reached the South Pole.

More worrying, though, is that the climate changes seen in recent years will continue. Previous Pig years have been characterized by severe weather patterns and this year will be no exception. The last Pig year saw unprecedented heatwaves in many countries – in America, midwestern states were particularly affected, with temperatures exceeding 40°C (104°F) for five consecutive days. And while it is hoped that 2007 may be spared such extremes or natural catastrophes, this is unlikely to be the case, although with increased monitoring and greater awareness, some of the damage caused by the forces of nature could be mitigated. The Pig year also has a very strong humanitarian element and over the year generous amounts will be raised to help those in need.

Political leaders will also be active in dealing with some long-running disputes and here real progress can be made.

In some areas occupying troops could be withdrawn and treaties negotiated which will bring peace to troubled areas. With this year marking the end of another cycle of Chinese years, it can be a time for completing unfinished business and much can be achieved as a result.

Another feature of the year is that quite a few countries will see political change. In particular, those who have been in power for some time will now make way for others. Several important figures will emerge onto the world stage and usher in change for their respective countries. Britain is one country which could see such change.

The Year of the Pig is certainly one of potential, offering the chance to join together and tackle world problems as well as help everyone to benefit from the latest advances, whether technological, medical or social. For the individual, the Pig year places great emphasis on the family and relationships. Valuing those who are important to you and making the most of your situation – and personal hopes – can make this a positive and encouraging year. While some signs will fare better than others, I hope that you will both enjoy and make the most of the next 12 months and wish you every good fortune.

YOUR CHINESE
HOROSCOPE 2007

18 FEBRUARY 1912 ～ 5 FEBRUARY 1913   *Water Rat*

5 FEBRUARY 1924 ～ 23 JANUARY 1925   *Wood Rat*

24 JANUARY 1936 ～ 10 FEBRUARY 1937   *Fire Rat*

10 FEBRUARY 1948 ～ 28 JANUARY 1949   *Earth Rat*

28 JANUARY 1960 ～ 14 FEBRUARY 1961   *Metal Rat*

15 FEBRUARY 1972 ～ 2 FEBRUARY 1973   *Water Rat*

2 FEBRUARY 1984 ～ 19 FEBRUARY 1985   *Wood Rat*

19 FEBRUARY 1996 ～ 6 FEBRUARY 1997   *Fire Rat*

THE
RAT

THE PERSONALITY OF THE RAT

'The great secret of success in life is for a man to be ready
when his opportunity comes.'

Benjamin Disraeli, a Rat

The Rat is born under the sign of charm. He is intelligent,
popular and loves attending parties and large social gatherings. He is able to establish friendships with remarkable ease
and people generally feel relaxed in his company. He is a very
social creature and is genuinely interested in the welfare and
activities of others. He has a good understanding of human
nature and his advice and opinions are often sought.

The Rat is a hard and diligent worker. He is also very
imaginative and is never short of ideas. However, he does
sometimes lack the confidence to promote his ideas and
this can often prevent him from securing the recognition
he deserves.

The Rat is very observant and many Rats have made
excellent writers and journalists. The Rat also excels at
personnel and PR work and any job which brings him into
contact with people and the media. His skills are particularly appreciated in times of crisis, for the Rat has an
incredibly strong sense of self-preservation. When it comes
to finding a way out of an awkward situation, the Rat is
certain to be the one who comes up with a solution.

The Rat loves to be where there is a lot of action, but
should he ever find himself in a very bureaucratic or
restrictive environment he can become a stickler for discipline and routine.

He is also something of an opportunist and is constantly on the lookout for ways in which he can improve his wealth and lifestyle. He rarely lets an opportunity go by and can become involved in so many plans and schemes that he sometimes squanders his energies and achieves very little as a result. He is also rather gullible and can be taken in by those less scrupulous than himself.

Another characteristic of the Rat is his attitude towards money. He is very thrifty and to some he may appear a little mean. The reason for this is purely that he likes to keep his money within his family. He can be most generous to his partner, his children and close friends and relatives. He can also be generous to himself, for he often finds it impossible to deprive himself of any luxury or object he fancies. He is very acquisitive and can be a notorious hoarder. He also hates waste and is rarely prepared to throw anything away. He can be rather greedy and will rarely refuse an invitation for a free meal or a complimentary ticket to some lavish function.

The Rat is a good conversationalist, although he can occasionally be a little indiscreet. He can be highly critical of others – for an honest and unbiased opinion, the Rat is a superb critic – and sometimes will use confidential information to his own advantage. However, as he has such a bright and irresistible nature, most people are prepared to forgive him his slight indiscretions.

Throughout his long and eventful life the Rat will make many friends and will find that he is especially well suited to those born under his own sign and those of the Ox, Dragon and Monkey. He can also get on well with those born under the signs of the Tiger, Snake, Rooster, Dog and

Pig, but the rather sensitive Rabbit and Goat will find the Rat a little too critical and blunt for their liking. The Horse and Rat will also find it difficult to get on with each other – the Rat craves security and will find the Horse's changeable moods and rather independent nature a little unsettling.

The Rat is very family-orientated and will do anything to please his nearest and dearest. He is exceptionally loyal to his parents and can himself be a very caring and loving parent. He will take an interest in all his children's activities and will see that they want for nothing. The Rat usually has a large family.

The female Rat has a kindly, outgoing nature and involves herself in a multitude of different activities. She has a wide circle of friends, enjoys entertaining and is an attentive hostess. She is also conscientious about the upkeep of her home and has good taste in home furnishings. She is most supportive to the other members of her family and, due to her resourceful, friendly and persevering nature, can do well in practically any career.

Although the Rat is essentially outgoing, he is also a very private individual. He tends to keep his feelings to himself and while he is not averse to learning what other people are doing, he resents anyone prying too closely into his own affairs. He also does not like solitude and if he is alone for any length of time he can easily get depressed.

The Rat is undoubtedly very talented, but he does sometimes fail to capitalize on his many abilities. He has a tendency to become involved in too many schemes and chase after too many opportunities all at once. If he can slow down and concentrate on one thing at a time, he can become very successful. If not, success and wealth can elude him. But, with his tremendous ability to charm, the Rat will rarely, if ever, be without friends.

THE FIVE DIFFERENT TYPES OF RAT

In addition to the 12 signs of the Chinese zodiac there are five elements and these have a strengthening or moderating influence on the sign. The effects of the five elements on the Rat are described below, together with the years in which the elements were exercising their influence. Therefore those Rats born in 1960 are Metal Rats, those born in 1912 and 1972 are Water Rats, and so on.

Metal Rat: 1960
This Rat has excellent taste and certainly knows how to appreciate the finer things in life. His home is comfortable and nicely decorated and he likes to entertain and mix in fashionable circles. He has considerable financial acumen and invests his money well. On the surface the Metal Rat appears cheerful and confident, but deep down he can be troubled by worries that are quite often of his own making. He is exceptionally loyal to his family and friends.

Water Rat: 1912, 1972
The Water Rat is intelligent and very astute. He is a deep thinker and can express his thoughts clearly and persuasively. He is always eager to learn and is talented in many different areas. He is usually very popular, but his fear of

loneliness can sometimes lead him into mixing with the wrong sort of company. He is a particularly skilful writer, but he can get sidetracked very easily and should try to concentrate on just one thing at a time.

Wood Rat: 1924, 1984

The Wood Rat has a friendly, outgoing personality and is popular with his colleagues and friends. He has a quick, agile brain and likes to turn his hand to anything he thinks may be useful. His one fear is insecurity, but given his intelligence and capabilities, this fear is usually unfounded. He has a good sense of humour, enjoys travel and, due to his highly imaginative nature, can be a gifted writer or artist.

Fire Rat: 1936, 1996

The Fire Rat is rarely still and seems to have a never-ending supply of energy and enthusiasm. He loves being involved in the action – be it travel, following up new ideas or campaigning for a cause in which he fervently believes. He is an original thinker and hates being bound by petty restrictions or the dictates of others. He can be forthright in his views, but can sometimes get carried away in the excitement of the moment and commit himself to various undertakings without thinking through all the implications. Yet he has a resilient nature and with the right support can often go far in life.

Earth Rat: 1948

This Rat is astute and very level-headed. He rarely takes unnecessary chances and while he is constantly trying to improve his financial status, he is prepared to proceed slowly and leave nothing to chance. The Earth Rat is probably not as adventurous as the other types of Rat and prefers to remain in familiar territory rather than rush headlong into something he knows little about. He is talented, conscientious and caring towards his loved ones, but at the same time can be self-conscious and worry a little too much about the image he is trying to project.

PROSPECTS FOR THE RAT IN 2007

The Year of the Dog (29 January 2006 to 17 February 2007) will have been a mixed one for the Rat and he will have faced some pressures and disappointments. However, there is good reason for him to take heart. The closing months of the year will be a much improved time and while care is still needed, the Rat's prospects will become much brighter.

At work he could now benefit from some of the hard work and commitment he has been putting in over the year, and for those Rats keen to advance their career, there could be the opportunity to take on greater responsibilities. Those seeking work could also see some positive developments, with October and November being particularly encouraging months.

The friendly and outgoing Rat sets great store by his relations with others, but during the Dog year these may not always have gone as smoothly as he would have liked. As the year draws to a close the Rat would find it helpful to spend more time with those who are special to him and to talk over plans and ideas. He will achieve more as a result. His social life can also pick up at this time and he will often have the opportunity to go out and enjoy himself.

The Dog year may not have been the easiest of years for the Rat, but with care he will still have accomplished a great deal and will be able to build on this in the next Chinese year.

The Year of the Pig starts on 18 February and will be an encouraging one for the Rat. This is a year for him to move forward, and although he will need to work hard for results, it can be a rewarding time.

The Rat is born under the sign of charm and his amiable manner and wide interests can lead to his social life enjoying quite a fillip this year. Those Rats who would welcome new friendships and perhaps romance could see quite a transformation in their situation. For those who have experienced problems in their relationships recently and are alone, this is a time to draw a line under past disappointments and make a new start. There are excellent romantic possibilities and some Rats will meet someone who will become truly special. For socializing and meeting others March, April, August and October are favoured, but new friendships and romance can occur at almost any time.

For those Rats who are settled in their relationships, this will also be a rewarding year. By spending time with their loved ones and sharing plans and activities, these Rats can strengthen their rapport with those around them and enjoy many pleasurable moments. Shared interests or home projects can be particularly satisfying and whenever the Rat has any ideas for joint activities, he should put them forward.

The Rat will also value the support he is given over the year and if he is perhaps considering a change of work or has a particular problem to deal with, he will benefit from the advice and encouragement of those around him. In some cases more senior relations could be especially helpful and assist in ways he had not envisaged.

Travel is also favourably aspected over the year and even though some Rats may decide not to go too far away from home, a change of scene can still do them a lot of good. In addition the Rat should take up any invitations he receives to visit family and friends. Such visits can go well and lead to some enjoyable occasions.

Another positive area concerns the Rat's own personal interests and although he will often have many demands on his time, it is important that he allows time for recreational pursuits. These will not only allow him to relax and unwind but can sometimes bring social opportunities too.

As far as the Rat's work prospects are concerned, this is a year of encouraging developments. However, unlike some years, when the Rat's luck and resourcefulness can pay off handsomely, 2007 calls for effort, discipline and hard work. Whenever the Rat has objectives to meet or projects to complete, he will need to remain focused and committed. This is no year for half-hearted efforts or slacking. However, what the Rat is able to accomplish over the year can open up some important possibilities for the future.

For those Rats who are seeking work or hoping to broaden their experience by moving to other areas, this can be a year of opportunity. However, they too will need to remain determined and persistent. As many will find, extra effort *can* make a difference. Anything these Rats can do to enhance their knowledge and prospects – whether through taking advantage of training (or retraining) opportunities or seeking advice from agencies – can help. Results will have to be worked for, but with determination many Rats will be successful in securing the opportunity they want. April, June and the period from late August to November could see some interesting developments.

As far as money matters are concerned, this is a year for care and good management. The Rat should be particularly wary of taking risks or making major purchases without sufficient thought. Also, if entering into any financial agreement, he should take the time to check the terms and implications. This is very much a year to remain thorough and vigilant. The Rat could also find it helpful to plan ahead for any more substantial outgoings, including accommodation costs, family expenses and travel.

Generally, however, this can be a positive and encouraging year for the Rat. In his work there will be some excellent opportunities to develop his skills, although results will need to be worked for. The Rat will also enjoy his recreational pursuits, but the most rewarding aspect of the year will concern his relations with others. Throughout the year family and friends will be important and will offer valued support. And for some currently unattached Rats the year will bring new love into their life. Overall, this is a year for effort, hard work and commitment, but on a personal level it can be a special time.

The Metal Rat

This will be a year of interesting developments for the Metal Rat and it will usher in some important changes.

Over recent years the Metal Rat will have seen considerable changes take place, especially in his work. However, this period of transition is far from over. His experience, contacts and keen nature will lead to important opportunities opening up for him. In some cases this could mean a substantial change in what he does or in his location, and he would do well to think carefully about what is involved and to discuss the implications with those close to him. Important decisions should not be rushed. Also, should the Metal Rat (or others) have any misgivings about any of the openings or proposals put to him, he must resolve these before proceeding. As he will soon discover, the Pig year can bring surprising developments and should he decide one particular opportunity is not for him, another will often arise in its place.

This also applies to those Metal Rats seeking work. By considering the various possibilities open to them, many will secure a position which will be a change from what they have previously been doing. Although becoming familiar with a new range of duties and sometimes adjusting to a different working pattern may initially be daunting, by rising to the challenge and showing commitment, these Metal Rats will soon settle into their new role.

Another important feature of the year will be the way in which the Metal Rat is able to extend his skills. Whenever he has the chance of further training or sees a course he feels could be useful to him, even if this is something he has to pursue in his own time, he should make the most it.

The knowledge and skills he can develop over the year will not only be helpful to him now but can also widen his scope for later on. Late March and April could see some interesting possibilities, but the key openings will occur in the second half of the year, notably from mid-August to November.

The progress the Metal Rat makes in his work will often lead to an increase in income and he could also benefit from a bonus, gift or maturing policy over the year. However, he does still need to manage his money well, including keeping a watchful eye over his outgoings. Without care, his spending could creep up and prevent him from pursuing other activities, including travel. The more the Metal Rat can plan ahead and the greater the control he can exert over his purse-strings, the more he will find he can ultimately enjoy. This can be a positive year financially, but it does require careful management and good discipline.

Another pleasingly aspected area of the year concerns the Metal Rat's relations with others. With his sincere and amiable nature he gets on well with many and during the year his family and social life will be of great value to him.

In his home life the Metal Rat can look forward to some particularly pleasing times, with the year marking some important family events. The Metal Rat himself will give considerable support to his loved ones, and his judgement, advice and time will be much appreciated. Also, with some of the decisions he will face over the year, especially concerning his work situation, it is important that he lets others help him in return. Openness and the willingness to discuss matters will often make it easier to take decisions and will result in greater support.

Joint family activities will also go well over the year. Whether these are interests that can be shared, domestic projects or holidays and breaks, they will not only lead to some pleasing occasions but also help with rapport and understanding. As the Metal Rat will find, spending time with his loved ones will make his home life all the more rewarding.

The Metal Rat's social life is also favourably aspected and is set to become busier as the year progresses. He will often have invitations to go out as a result of his work or interests and some weeks could be especially active. His circle of friends and acquaintances is set to increase over the year and for those Metal Rats who have experienced recent disappointments in their personal life the Pig year can mark a major upturn in their fortunes. With the prospects so encouraging for socializing and meeting others, now is a time to draw a line under the past and look to move forward. By making the most of social opportunities and perhaps considering joining a special interest or social group in their area, these Metal Rats will enjoy quite a change their situation. The months from late February to mid April and August and October will be the most active socially, but such is the nature of the Pig year that opportunities could arise at almost any time, and in surprising ways too!

The prospects are certainly encouraging for the Metal Rat, particularly in terms of moving his career forward and developing his skills. In addition his relations with others will often go well over the year, with his home and social life bringing pleasure and many meaningful times. With the support of others, the openings that become available and his willingness to make the most of himself, in many ways this can be a rewarding and successful year for the Metal Rat.

TIP FOR THE YEAR
At times of change, do consult others. This will not only help clarify your options and feelings in your own mind, but will often result in useful advice being offered. In this important year do not forget those who are willing to help and support you.

The Water Rat

This will be a year of opportunity for the Water Rat, with much going in his favour. However, to benefit, the Water Rat will need to be flexible in his outlook as well as prepared to adapt to situations as they arise.

The Water Rat is about to enter a significant phase of his career and the Pig year is a time to seize the initiative. This is particularly true for those Water Rats who are feeling unfulfilled or in a rut. By taking action, making enquiries and following up any areas that appeal to them, they can find some important new possibilities opening up. This year can be an exciting transitional period, but to make things happen the Water Rat does need to take that all-important initial step.

This also applies to those Water Rats seeking work. This is a year of considerable opportunity and many will be given the chance to become involved in a different and more fulfilling type of work. By embracing any opportunities that come their way, even if initially daunting or not quite what they were expecting, they will find that important consequences can follow. This is a year that can set many on a new and potentially rewarding career path. Late March and April are particularly likely to see work opportunities, with interesting possibilities also becoming available in the second half of the year, especially from mid-August to November.

For those Water Rats who are established in their career, again the Pig year can bring the chance to move forward. As senior colleagues move on, new projects are launched or openings created, these Water Rats will often find themselves with the right experience and skills to benefit. By putting themselves forward and indicating their desire to take on greater responsibilities, many will be successful in advancing their career. Should any application not go his way, the Water Rat should not lose heart. Events in the Pig year can move in curious ways and a rejection could prove a blessing as other openings appear in its wake.

The progress the Water Rat makes in his work will also help his financial position and many Water Rats will enjoy a noticeable rise in their income over the year. However, to benefit the Water Rat does need to manage his finances well. This includes budgeting for forthcoming expenses and, if he has large borrowings, to consider reducing these. With care and prudence he can do much to improve his financial position. However, should he be tempted by any speculative transaction at any time, it is important that he checks the details and obligations carefully. This is not a year for risks or pushing his luck too far. Water Rats, do take note.

This will also be an important year as far as the Water Rat's relations with others are concerned. With his widespread interests and many friends, he will often find himself in demand. Some new people he meets during the year could become important and offer valued friendship and advice. The months from late February to April and August and October could be the most active socially.

For those Water Rats who would welcome new friends and perhaps a more fulfilling social life, the Pig year offers real hope, and by going out more and becoming involved in new interests and activities, they could enjoy quite a transformation in their situation. For some, a wonderful new romance could blossom. In addition a holiday these Water Rats take could lead to some good social opportunities. As with so much in 2007, positive action on the Water Rat's part can bring significant results.

As far as the Water Rat's domestic life is concerned, this will be a busy and rewarding year. Those close to him will often seek out his help and advice and while this could sometimes take up much of his time, the assistance and support he gives will often be of more value than he may realize. Both senior and younger relations will have particularly good reason to be grateful to him over the year. Also, if the Water Rat has certain domestic plans he would like to get underway, he should allow plenty of time for them. Projects and tasks *will* get done, but they should not be rushed. The Water Rat does need to make allowance for any pressures he and others may be under and be flexible when planning more time-consuming activities.

Another area the Water Rat would do well to give some consideration to over the year is his well-being. With his often demanding lifestyle it is important that he takes good care of himself, takes sufficient exercise and has a healthy and balanced diet. To make the most of this encouraging year he needs to keep himself in good form.

The Pig year certainly holds good opportunities for the Water Rat and by taking action he can both enjoy success now and pave the way for some significant developments in the future. This is a year for action and progress.

TIP FOR THE YEAR

Give some thought to what you want to achieve over the year and discuss your plans with those close to you. With some clear aims and objectives in mind, you will find the year will be that much more successful.

The Wood Rat

This will be an encouraging year for the Wood Rat, giving him an excellent chance to improve on his present position and look forward to some exciting developments in his personal life. There will certainly be a lot going his way in the Pig year.

In the Wood Rat's personal life there could be celebrations in store, as some Wood Rats will get married, settle down with a partner or see an addition to their family. As far as relationships are concerned, this can be a special year. In addition many Wood Rats will change their accommodation over the year and will spend a lot of time settling into their new home and getting it as they want. For these Wood Rats this will be a busy and exciting time.

For those Wood Rats who are unattached, the Pig year can mark a transformation in their situation. A chance introduction or event they attend could lead to meeting someone who will quickly become special. For those who may have had a relationship flounder recently, this is a year to move forward and a new and exciting romance may well change their situation.

The Wood Rat's social life is also likely to be busy. Wood Rats who move house or change their work will often be brought into contact with a new circle of people, some of whom will quickly become friends. Attending courses, going on holiday or pursuing personal interests can also lead to new friendships and contacts. The Pig year will certainly see the Wood Rat living life to the full and enjoying himself. For socializing and key personal developments late February to April, August and October are particularly favourable times, but those who are unattached could feel the effects of Cupid's arrow at almost any time.

Another positive area concerns the Wood Rat's personal interests. Although his spare time may be limited, it is important that he sets time aside to develop interests he enjoys. Whether these are creative, practical or sporting, by extending his skills and knowledge, he will not only gain more satisfaction from what he does but may also see new possibilities opening up.

In addition the Wood Rat should not neglect his well-being over the year and should aim to have a healthy and balanced diet as well as the occasional chance to rest and catch up, especially after demanding and arduous weeks. This may be an exciting and busy year, but he can only do so much and to keep himself on good form he does need to take care of himself. Wood Rats, do take note.

As far as work is concerned, the aspects are promising. As a result of the experience they have built up, many

Wood Rats will have the chance to take on further duties and secure promotion. And while many will remain with their present employer and make good progress there, those who want to extend their skills in other areas or feel that their prospects could be better elsewhere should be active in following up openings that interest them. They will find their experience and recent achievements will stand them in good stead. This is certainly a year for the Wood Rat to look to build on what he has accomplished so far and to move his career forward.

For those Wood Rats who are seeking work or not feeling fulfilled in their present employment, again the Pig year can be one of significant opportunity. To benefit, however, these Wood Rats will need to make the most of the opportunities available to them. In some cases, consulting employment advisers, agencies or professional organizations may help, as it will give them ideas or alert them to possibilities worth considering. By taking the initiative and remaining active, many Wood Rats will be able to set their career off on a rewarding new path. April, June and late August to November could see some interesting developments.

Although the year will hold many possibilities for the Wood Rat, one area which could be problematic is finance. With his often busy social life and all the activities he wishes to pursue, as well as accommodation and other costs, his finances will often be stretched. As a result it is important that he keeps a close watch on his position. Also, if at any time he enters into a financial agreement or commitment, he should check the terms and obligations. Financial matters do need close and thorough attention this year and when appropriate, the Wood Rat would do well to seek professional advice. This is not a year for risks or giving insufficient attention to matters that could have long-term implications. Wood Rats, do take careful note.

Overall, in many respects the Pig year holds excellent prospects for the Wood Rat. On a personal level he will be much in demand, with affairs of the heart and an often lively social life leading to many happy occasions and sometimes personal celebrations. At work the aspects are also encouraging, with the Wood Rat being able to build on his experience and move his career forward. This is a year when he can really benefit from his many strengths and talents.

TIP FOR THE YEAR
Persevere. This is a good year for you, but sometimes plans may not quite work out as you intended. Learn what you can from any disappointments and *do keep going*. Your willpower and personal strengths can lead to success.

The Fire Rat

This will be a year of change and opportunity for the Fire Rat and although a lot will be asked of him, the events of the year will often be to both his present and future advantage.

Many of those Fire Rats born in 1996 will change their school during the year and while they may feel ready for this, there will be times when they will be anxious as they adjust to a new routine and environment. However, with a willing attitude, these Fire Rats will soon settle down and enjoy the chance to extend their skills and make new friends as well as try out some of the new facilities available. Indeed, over the year a wealth of opportunities will open up for the young Fire Rat, making this an interesting and satisfying time.

Also, if the Fire Rat has a particular skill or interest he would like to take further, he should let others know about it. Whether this involves learning an instrument or developing sporting or creative skills, by making the most of the opportunities available, including after-school clubs, the Fire Rat will find his interests bringing him a lot of fun.

Those Fire Rats who remain at their present school will also find new opportunities opening up, and whether this is through new subjects or becoming involved in a wider range of activities, by showing willingness they will again find this an interesting time.

The Fire Rat will also be encouraged by his close band of friends and by the knowledge that many share similar apprehensions and concerns to his own. The comradeship and support young Fire Rats can offer each other will often mean a great deal. And with their lively nature and wide interests, they may well make new friends over the year.

The young Fire Rat will also welcome the support of those around him, whether his family at home or his tutors at school. If at any time there are any matters concerning him, it is important that he lets others know about them. By being forthcoming, he will often find that problems can be put into perspective and dealt with satisfactorily.

Those Fire Rats born in 1936 will also find this an interesting and often eventful year. With the aspects indicating change, quite a few Fire Rats will decide to move to accommodation that better suits their requirements. This could entail considerable upheaval. However, by allowing plenty of time for any move and drawing on the support and assistance of others, these Fire Rats will be pleased with their decision and the benefits their new home brings.

It is, however, important that when tackling anything of a strenuous nature, whether in the home, garden or elsewhere, the Fire Rat proceeds carefully. A strain could cause considerable discomfort and curtail some of his activities. Help will often be available and he should draw on it where necessary. Also, if at any time he feels below par or lacking his usual energy, it is important that he seeks advice. The care and attention that he pays to his own wellbeing can make a difference.

Over the year the Fire Rat will take a great deal of satisfaction from his personal interests, particularly more expressive pursuits. The keen writer, artist or photographer could find his talents bringing especial pleasure as well as an encouraging response from others. Some Fire Rats may also decide to learn or develop a skill by enrolling on a course. This will not only give them an interesting new challenge but sometimes also bring a pleasing social element to their lives. The Pig year is an encouraging time for the Fire Rat and especially supportive of his talents.

In much of what he does the Fire Rat will enjoy the support of those close to him and there could also be several family events that will mean a great deal to him. These could include a wedding, the birth of a great-grandchild or the success of someone dear to him. For some there could also be the prospect of a house-warming party. Domestically, this will often be a special time.

The Pig year will also offer some excellent travel opportunities and whether these involve visiting places the Fire Rat has long wanted to see or taking up an invitation to stay with family and friends, he will often enjoy his times away. Many of his travels will also have a pleasing social element.

The one area in which the Fire Rat will need to be particularly careful is money matters. This is not a year for taking risks and when entering into important commitments he does need to check all the terms and implications. If he has any doubts or questions about a financial matter, he would do well to obtain professional guidance. He should be especially wary if he is tempted into anything of a more speculative nature. With the aspects as they are, this is no year to push his luck too far. Fire Rats, do take note.

In most respects, though, this will be a positive year for the Fire Rat. Whether born in 1936 or 1996, he will find that the changes that occur will often bring new opportunities. With a willing attitude and the determination to make the most of his chances, he will find the year satisfying, pleasurable and successful.

TIP FOR THE YEAR

In view of the changes that the year will bring and the important decisions that will need to be taken, it is important to talk to others. That way you will be able to benefit from their advice and support. A greater openness will also help maintain the often close understanding you enjoy with those around you.

The Earth Rat

This will be an important year for the Earth Rat and one which will bring significant change.

As the Pig year starts the Earth Rat would find it helpful to think about his hopes and plans and discuss them with those close to him. Clear ideas will not only give him something positive to aim for but also make it more likely that they will be realized. Just mentioning some of his ideas can set the wheels in motion, especially as others will often give him the encouragement he needs to get started.

The Earth Rat's planning can extend to several areas of his life, but with this being a year of transition and change, quite a few Earth Rats will consider moving, perhaps to a location they have long favoured. Such plans will involve a lot of time and effort, but preparing well in advance – including sorting through storage areas and clearing away unwanted items – will not only help get the moving process underway but also ease some of the pressure at the time of the actual move.

Those Earth Rats who remain where they are will also pay a lot of attention to their home during the year, with many making changes they have long been considering. This may include altering the décor and furnishings of certain rooms as well as sorting through various accumulated items. The Pig year certainly has a strong practical element to it and by following through their plans these Earth Rats will often be satisfied with what they are able to accomplish. Tackling projects with others will also help to get things done – and that much faster too.

In addition to the considerable activity that will be seen in many Earth Rat homes over the year, there will also be family occasions that will mean a great deal. The progress of a younger relation could be especially pleasing. Over the year the Earth Rat will do much to help and encourage those dear to him, with younger relations in particular valuing the support and advice he is able to give. Although there may sometimes be a considerable gap in years, the rapport that the Earth Rat enjoys with those around him can often be strong and special.

The Pig year will also bring some good travel opportunities, sometimes at short notice. These could be surprise invitations to visit others, last-minute offers or decisions to go away on the spur of the moment. Whatever the nature of their travels, the Earth Rat will often find them leading to some enjoyable occasions. Some Earth Rats will especially appreciate the social opportunities that their travels will bring.

Another positive area concerns the Earth Rat's personal interests, and with this being a year of opportunity, he should aim to develop these in some way. This could be by setting himself new challenges, furthering his skills or even taking up a new interest. If he does not get much regular exercise, he could consider taking up an activity that could help his well-being, perhaps some additional walking, cycling or swimming. Whatever he does, he will find his personal interests a valuable part of the year.

As with all Rats, the one area in which the Earth Rat will need to be vigilant this year concerns finance. This is no time for taking risks or being lax when dealing with financial matters. If the Earth Rat moves or is involved in any major financial transaction, it is essential that he checks all the details and implications first. Also, with the expensive plans and purchases he may have in mind, it would be helpful for him to keep watch over his general spending. With discipline and self-control (and the Earth Rat *is* usually careful in money matters), he will be pleased with how his plans work out, but this is a year for thoroughness and careful budgeting.

With this also being a year of change, many Earth Rats will face important decisions concerning their work. Some will choose to take advantage of early retirement opportunities while others will be keen to build on what they are currently doing, either by switching to other duties, opting for a more supervisory role or taking on greater responsibilities. With the aspects as they are, the Earth Rat is likely to make the most of his new role or the additional time available to him. Interesting work developments are likely in April, June and the second half of the year, especially from August to November.

The Pig year certainly holds good prospects for the Earth Rat and will allow him to do a great deal as well as enjoy some positive changes. To benefit fully he does need to give careful thought to his plans for the year and liaise closely with others. With support and care, however, he can make this a pleasing and often significant year.

TIP FOR THE YEAR
While this will be a year of considerable activity it is important that you do not neglect your personal interests or recreational pursuits. These can be a source of much pleasure and often open up other possibilities as well. In this full year, do give time to yourself.

FAMOUS RATS

Ben Affleck, Ursula Andress, Louis Armstrong, Lauren Bacall, Shirley Bassey, Kathy Bates, Irving Berlin, Silvio Berlusconi, Kenneth Branagh, Marlon Brando, Charlotte Brontë, Jackson Browne, George H. W. Bush, Glen Campbell, David Carradine, Jimmy Carter, Aaron Copland, Cameron Diaz, David Duchovny, T. S. Eliot, Queen Elizabeth the Queen Mother, Eminem, Colin Firth, Clark Gable, Liam Gallagher, Hugh Grant, Geri Halliwell, Thomas Hardy, Prince Harry, Haydn, Charlton Heston, Buddy Holly, Mick Hucknall, Henrik Ibsen, Jeremy Irons, Samuel L. Jackson, Jean-Michel Jarre, Scarlett Johansson, Gene Kelly, Avril Lavigne, Lawrence of Arabia, Jude Law, Gary Lineker, Lord Andrew Lloyd Webber, Katie Melua, Claude Monet, Richard Nixon, Ozzy Osbourne, Sean Penn, Terry Pratchett, Ian Rankin, Lou Rawls, Vanessa Redgrave, Burt Reynolds, Rossini, William Shakespeare, Donna Summer, James Taylor, Leo Tolstoy, Henri Toulouse-Lautrec, Spencer Tracy, Carol Vorderman, the Prince of Wales, George Washington, the Duke of York, Emile Zola.

---

6 FEBRUARY 1913 ⁓ 25 JANUARY 1914   *Water Ox*

24 JANUARY 1925 ⁓ 12 FEBRUARY 1926   *Wood Ox*

11 FEBRUARY 1937 ⁓ 30 JANUARY 1938   *Fire Ox*

29 JANUARY 1949 ⁓ 16 FEBRUARY 1950   *Earth Ox*

15 FEBRUARY 1961 ⁓ 4 FEBRUARY 1962   *Metal Ox*

3 FEBRUARY 1973 ⁓ 22 JANUARY 1974   *Water Ox*

20 FEBRUARY 1985 ⁓ 8 FEBRUARY 1986   *Wood Ox*

7 FEBRUARY 1997 ⁓ 27 JANUARY 1998   *Fire Ox*

THE
OX

THE PERSONALITY OF THE OX

'I have always believed, and I still believe, that whatever good or bad fortune may come our way we can always give it meaning and transform it into something of value.'

Hermann Hesse, an Ox

The Ox is born under the signs of equilibrium and tenacity. He is a hard and conscientious worker and sets about everything he does in a resolute, methodical and determined manner. He has considerable leadership qualities and is often admired for his tough and uncompromising nature. He knows what he wants to achieve in life and, as far as possible, will not be deflected from his ultimate objective.

The Ox takes his responsibilities and duties very seriously. He is decisive and quick to take advantage of any opportunity that comes his way. He is also sincere and places a great deal of trust in his friends and colleagues. He is, nevertheless, something of a loner. He is a quiet and private individual and often keeps his thoughts to himself. He also cherishes his independence and prefers to set about things in his own way rather than be bound by the dictates of others or influenced by outside pressures.

The Ox tends to have a calm and tranquil nature, but if something angers him or he feels that someone has let him down, he can have a fearsome temper. He can also be stubborn and obstinate and this can lead him into conflict with others. Usually he will succeed in getting his own way, but should things go against him the Ox is a poor loser and will take any defeat or setback extremely badly.

The Ox is often a deep thinker and rather studious. He is not particularly renowned for his sense of humour and does not take kindly to new gimmicks or anything too innovative. He is too solid and traditional for that and prefers to stick to the more conventional norm.

His home is very important to him and in some respects he treats it as a private sanctuary. His family tends to be closely knit and the Ox will make sure that each member does their fair share around the house. The Ox tends to be a hoarder, but he is always well organized and neat. He also places great importance on punctuality and there is nothing that infuriates him more than to be kept waiting, particularly if it is due to someone's inefficiency. The Ox can be a hard taskmaster!

Once settled in a job or house the Ox will quite happily remain there for many years. He does not like change and he is also not particularly keen on travel. He does, however, enjoy gardening and other outdoor pursuits and he will often spend much of his spare time out of doors. He is usually an excellent gardener and whenever possible will make sure he has a large area of ground to maintain. He usually prefers to live in the country rather than the town.

Due to his dedicated and dependable nature the Ox will usually do well in his chosen career, providing he is given enough freedom to act on his own initiative. He invariably does well in politics, agriculture and in careers which need specialized training. He is also very gifted artistically and many Oxen have enjoyed considerable success as musicians or composers.

The Ox is not as outgoing as some and it often takes him a long time to establish friendships and feel relaxed in another person's company. His courtships are likely to be long, but once he is settled he will remain devoted and loyal to his partner. The Ox is particularly well suited to those born under the signs of the Rat, Rabbit, Snake and Rooster. He can also establish a good relationship with the Monkey, Dog, Pig and another Ox, but he will find that he has little in common with the whimsical and sensitive Goat. He will also find it difficult to get on with the Horse, Dragon and Tiger – the Ox prefers a quiet and peaceful existence and those born under these three signs tend to be a little too lively and impulsive for his liking.

The female Ox has a kind and caring nature, and her home and family are very much her pride and joy. She always tries to do her best for her partner and can be a most conscientious and loving parent. She is an excellent organizer and also a very determined person who will often succeed in getting what she wants in life. She usually has a deep interest in the arts and is often a talented artist or musician.

The Ox is a very down-to-earth character. He is sincere, loyal and unpretentious. He can, however, be rather reserved and to some he may appear distant and aloof. He has a quiet nature, but underneath he is very strong-willed and ambitious. He has the courage of his convictions and is often prepared to stand up for what he believes to be right, regardless of the consequences. He inspires confidence and trust and throughout his life he will rarely be short of people who are ready to support him.

THE FIVE DIFFERENT TYPES OF OX

In addition to the 12 signs of the Chinese zodiac there are five elements and these have a strengthening or moderating influence on the sign. The effects of the five elements on the Ox are described below, together with the years in which the elements were exercising their influence. Therefore those Oxen born in 1961 are Metal Oxen, those born in 1913 and 1973 are Water Oxen, and so on.

Metal Ox: 1961
This Ox is confident and very strong-willed. He can be blunt and forthright in his views and is not afraid of speaking his mind. He sets about his objectives with a dogged determination, but he can become so involved in his various activities that he can be oblivious to the thoughts and feelings of those around him, and this can sometimes be to his detriment. He is honest and dependable and will never promise more than he can deliver. He has a good appreciation of the arts and usually has a small circle of very good and loyal friends.

Water Ox: 1913, 1973
This Ox has a sharp and penetrating mind. He is a good organizer and sets about his work in a methodical manner. He is not as narrow-minded as some of the other types of Ox and is more willing to involve others in his plans and aspirations. He usually has very high moral standards and

is often attracted to careers in public service. He is a good judge of character and has such a friendly and persuasive manner that he usually experiences little difficulty in securing his objectives. He is popular and has an excellent way with children.

Wood Ox: 1925, 1985

The Wood Ox conducts himself with an air of dignity and authority and will often take a leading role in any enterprise in which he becomes involved. He is very self-confident and is direct in his dealings with others. He does, however, have a quick temper and has no hesitation in speaking his mind. He has tremendous drive and willpower and an extremely good memory. He is particularly loyal and devoted to the members of his family and has a most caring nature.

Fire Ox: 1937, 1997

The Fire Ox has a powerful and assertive personality and is a hard and conscientious worker. He holds strong views and has very little patience when things do not go his own way. He can also get carried away in the excitement of the moment and does not always take into account the views of those around him. He nevertheless has many leadership qualities and will often reach positions of power, eminence and wealth. He usually has a small group of loyal and close friends and is very devoted to his family.

Earth Ox: 1949

This Ox sets about everything he does in a sensible and level-headed manner. He is ambitious but also realistic in his aims and is often prepared to work long hours in order to secure his objectives. He is shrewd in financial and business matters and is a very good judge of character. He has a quiet nature and is greatly admired for his sincerity and integrity. He is also very loyal to his family and friends and his views and opinions are often sought.

PROSPECTS FOR THE OX IN 2007

The Year of the Dog (29 January 2006 to 17 February 2007) will have been a busy one for the Ox and in the closing months the pace is set to increase. In most areas of his life the Ox will have a lot to do and may sometimes despair of all that is being asked of him, but this can still be a constructive and personally rewarding time.

Many Oxen will face a heavy workload, but although the pressure may at times be great, by using his experience and talents well the Ox will not only accomplish a great deal but also do his reputation and prospects a lot of good. For some there will be the chance to take on greater responsibilities or secure a new position, with September and November seeing interesting developments.

As the year draws to a close the Ox's spending is also likely to increase and wherever possible he should make early provision for his forthcoming expenses as well as spread out his seasonal purchases. Advanced planning can certainly help, especially at times when his outgoings could be high.

The Ox's domestic life will also see much activity, and with so much happening he does need to communicate well with others. This includes putting forward any ideas he may have concerning forthcoming plans and arrangements. In the closing months of the year good communication between family members can make a considerable difference, not only in terms of achieving more but also in preventing possible misunderstandings.

The Ox will certainly enjoy some of the family occasions that take place towards the end of the year, whether he is spending time with loved ones at home, visiting relations or going out to events and functions. In addition, there could be some good travel opportunities in the last quarter of the year.

The Year of the Pig begins on 18 February and will be a pleasing one for the Ox, giving him the chance to make good progress and use his talents well. In addition his personal life is encouragingly aspected. Overall, he will have much in his favour.

At work this will be a significant time for the Ox. In view of his recent activities (including the good work many Oxen will have done in the closing months of the Dog year) and the reputation he has built up, the Ox will often find himself well placed to benefit from opportunities. As more senior colleagues move on or new positions are created, he will find he has the experience and knowledge needed, and by putting himself forward he may well succeed in advancing his career.

While many Oxen will remain with their present employer over the year, for those who feel there may be better opportunities elsewhere or are keen to branch out in other directions, this can be an important year. By remaining alert for opportunities and seeking the advice of others, whether their own contacts or professional organizations, these Oxen will often find their efforts leading to an exciting new opportunity. And once they are in a new role, by immersing themselves in their duties and mastering what they have to do, they will not only find their work more fulfilling but will also increase their scope for the future. The headway the Ox can make in the Pig year can come to be important in the longer term.

This also applies to those Oxen seeking work or feeling discontented with their present position. By giving careful thought to what they would like to do and following up any vacancies that interest them, again they will find that their efforts can often lead to an interesting opportunity opening up for them. Admittedly, this may not always be exactly what they were hoping for, but once they have settled down they will be able to extend their skills and build on their position.

For those Oxen studying for qualifications or undertaking an apprenticeship, this can also be an important time. By showing commitment and working hard they are not only making an investment in their future but also opening the way to other possibilities. March, May, June and October will see the best opportunities workwise, but this is a promising year throughout.

As far as money matters are concerned this will be a reasonable year for the Ox and by being careful when making major purchases, he will generally be pleased with what he is able to do with his money. He would also do well to spend some time looking over his financial situation. In some cases he could find he has policies or outgoings which are no longer needed or savings that could be moved to higher-yielding accounts. He will certainly benefit from keeping watch on his outgoings and managing his situation well.

Another area the Ox should keep an eye on is his own well-being. Although many Oxen keep themselves active with their busy lifestyle, during the Pig year it is important that the Ox has a healthy diet and allows sufficient time for rest and relaxation. The conscientious Ox often drives himself hard and can really benefit from more time to relax and unwind. A few lifestyle modifications (particularly for busy Oxen) can make a considerable difference over the year.

In so much of what he does the Ox will value the love and support of those dear to him and his domestic life will bring him great pleasure. Setting time aside to spend with loved ones and tackling various activities and projects together will bring the Ox many happy moments. And while this year may not contain as many travel opportunities as some, any holiday or short break that he can take with his loved ones can do everyone good and again lead to some enjoyable occasions.

For much of the year the Ox's home life will go well, but as with any year problems and differences of opinion will arise. Sometimes these could be over relatively minor issues and they may not be helped by the pressure the Ox (or others) may be under. At such times the Ox should try to resolve any disagreement as quickly and amicably as he can, before it has a chance to escalate. With discussion and a willingness on everyone's part to come to agreement, any difficulties that do arise can often be quickly dealt with and will rarely mar the rewarding times the Ox's home life will bring.

As far as the Ox's social life is concerned, this will be a pleasant year, although with their busy lives some Oxen will decide to keep this relatively low key. By being selective, the Ox will often appreciate the times he does go out all the more. For unattached Oxen and those who would welcome new friendships, their work or personal interests will often be good ways for them to meet others, and for quite a few the Pig year can mark the start of a significant friendship or romance. April, July, September and December could see the most social activity.

With his redoubtable character, the Ox likes to be in control and in the Pig year his tenacity, belief in his abilities and strong sense of purpose will often be rewarded. This is a year for him to hold true to his aims, to develop his skills and to make the most of his opportunities. By using his talents well and ensuring his life has balance, he can make this a successful and satisfying year.

The Metal Ox
The Metal Ox has a determined and tenacious nature and over the year his efforts and talents will enable him to achieve a great deal.

The prospects are especially encouraging in his work, with the Pig year holding some significant opportunities.

The many Metal Oxen who are well-established in their career will often be given the chance to progress to more specialist work, perhaps by becoming involved in specific projects, assisting with new initiatives or taking on greater responsibilities. The Pig year will certainly bring some opportunities which will allow the Metal Ox to benefit from the experience and skills he has built up, often over many years. Also, as many Metal Oxen will find, the changes that take place over the year can help to make their work more fulfilling and purposeful.

While a great many Metal Oxen will advance in their chosen career, there will be some who will feel they have accomplished all they can in a certain area and will welcome the chance to do something different. For these Metal Oxen, as well as those seeking work, the Pig year can again open up some interesting possibilities. These may arise in surprising ways and the Metal Ox should not be too restrictive in what he is prepared to consider. A new position may lead to him discovering new strengths as well as developing his talents in other ways. Workwise, the Pig year can reward the Metal Ox well. March, May to mid-July and October will see the best opportunities and most interesting work developments.

In addition to the progressive work aspects, this is also an encouraging year as far as the Metal Ox's personal interests are concerned. Over the year he should look to further these in some way, perhaps by adding to his knowledge, setting himself a new project or even taking up a different interest altogether. By giving himself something purposeful to do, he can again derive much pleasure from his interests. Some Metal Oxen could also benefit from joining a group or enrolling on a course in their area. Not only will this be a good way to further their knowledge but it could have a pleasing social element as well.

Another area that would be worth the Metal Ox giving some consideration to is his well-being. If he does not tend to get much exercise, he could make up for this by additional walking or possibly cycling, swimming or starting a mind and body discipline such as yoga or tai chi. And while travel may not figure too prominently, he should make sure he goes away for a holiday or takes a proper break at some time during the year. A change of scene and break from his usual routine could do him a lot of good and he could also get to visit some interesting places.

As far as money matters are concerned this will be a reasonable year, with many Metal Oxen enjoying a rise in income. However, to benefit, the Metal Ox would do well to manage his situation carefully and take his time when considering more substantial purchases. If he does so, he will not only acquire more suitable items but often obtain better value too. If he is able to make any savings or reduce any borrowings over the year, this could also be helpful. With care and control, this can be an improved year financially.

The Metal Ox will value his domestic life over the year and despite the often busy lives both he and his loved ones may lead, if he sets time aside for joint activities, his contribution can make an important difference. Also, by being open with his thoughts and as well as any problems or concerns he may have (including changes relating to his work position), he will be grateful for the advice and encouragement that others can offer. In 2007 openness and good dialogue really can prove very helpful to the Metal Ox. In return he too will give valuable support to family members, with both younger and more senior relations being grateful for his assistance.

While the Metal Ox's home life will generally go well, should he start any major domestic project he does need to allow plenty of time to complete it as well as be prepared for what could be considerable disruption. While he may set about his plans with some relish, sometimes they will need more time, thought and commitment than he initially envisaged. When considering any practical activities, the Metal Ox does need to plan very carefully. Metal Ox, do take note.

Away from the home, the Metal Ox will enjoy the social occasions he decides to attend during the year. As a result of his interests and work he will get to meet many new people over the year, some of whom he will get on with particularly well. For those Metal Oxen keen to build up their social circle, the Pig year is encouragingly aspected, with April, mid-June to July, September and December being favourable months for meeting others.

The Pig year certainly holds good prospects for the Metal Ox and will allow him to make good use of his strengths and talents. By acting on the opportunities that arise and looking to progress, he can make this a satisfying and successful year.

TIP FOR THE YEAR

Value your relations with others, whether family, friends or colleagues. They can all give you much support and assistance over the year. The care you put into your relationships will be rewarded in many ways.

The Water Ox

The Water Ox has a keen and ambitious nature and he knows that to secure his aims and enjoy the success he would like, he will need to strive long and hard. As the Chinese proverb reminds us, 'A long journey will not deter one with high aspirations', and the Water Ox can look forward to making significant strides on his journey in 2007.

His work prospects are particularly encouraging and he is highly likely to further his position and experience over the year. For those Water Oxen who have been in the same position for several years, this is an excellent time to build on existing knowledge and skills and put in for greater responsibilities. By indicating their desire to move on, including seeking advice from more senior colleagues, they can find important doors opening up. These could be in their existing place of work or with another employer, but in either case many Water Oxen will find their experience placing them in a strong position for promotion. Those who do find that applications do not go their way should not let this weaken their resolve. In some cases they could be told where their application form, interview technique or approach could be bettered, and in this way rejections and failures, while disheartening, can prove very instructive.

The many Water Oxen who do change their jobs during the year will often find their new responsibilities will extend their skills and increase their options for the future. March, May to mid-July and October could see some interesting opportunities, but whenever an opening arises the Water Ox should make the most of it. Progress made during the Pig year can have long-term value.

The prospects also are encouraging for those Water Oxen currently seeking work or dissatisfied in their present position. By giving careful thought to what they now want to do and pursuing suitable opportunities, many can set their career off on an interesting new track. These Water Oxen may find retraining or advice from professional organizations helpful, particularly in alerting them to possibilities worth considering. This is a year when the Water Ox's initiative and determination will be well rewarded.

The progress the Water Ox makes in his work will lead to an increase in income over the year and some Water Oxen may be able to supplement this through some additional work or an enterprising idea. To benefit fully, however, the Water Ox will need to manage his situation well. With often large accommodation expenses and all his other commitments, he does need to make allowance for his obligations as well as budget carefully for any major purchases. Should he take on any new financial obligation, particularly relating to his accommodation, he does need to check the terms and seek appropriate advice before proceeding. However, provided he remains his careful and disciplined self, his financial situation can improve over the year and he will be satisfied with his plans and purchases.

Although the Water Ox will often have many demands on his time, it is also important that he sets some aside for recreational pursuits. Those that take him out of doors and give him the chance to get additional exercise could be especially beneficial. Interests that can lead to him meeting others can also be enjoyable. Being the conscientious sort that he is, it is important that the Water Ox does not drive himself so hard that other aspects of his life begin to suffer. The aspects may be encouraging this year, but he does need to maintain a sensible lifestyle balance. He can also benefit by going away for a holiday over the year. Not only will a break from his usual routine do him good but he will also enjoy spending time with others and seeing new sights.

This will be a busy year as far as the Water Ox's domestic life is concerned. For those Water Oxen who are parents or who become parents over the year, much time will be spent attending to the needs of their babies or encouraging their children, and while the year will bring its demanding moments, it can also be a happy and special time. Drawing on the assistance of others can ease some of the pressure. More senior relations can offer good advice, and should any matter be concerning the Water Ox (or he just wants a sympathetic ear), he will find talking to those with experience both helpful and reassuring. Throughout this often busy year, the Water Ox should remember that there are people around him who are keen and able to help.

During the year the Water Ox will derive much satisfaction from some of the more practical projects he tackles, particularly those involved with improving the comfort and décor of his home. Planning carefully, discussing projects with loved ones and allowing plenty of time will lead to some pleasing results. And with accommodation matters featuring prominently over the year, some Water Oxen could decide to move, perhaps to somewhere more convenient for their work or more suited to their requirements. Again, these Water Oxen will need to allow plenty of time for their plans to take shape.

In view of his many commitments the Water Ox will often be selective in his social engagements this year. However, his social life can be a good way for him to unwind and he should still try to go out fairly regularly, whether to meet friends or to attend social events that appeal to him. Again it is important that he strives for a balanced lifestyle.

Any Water Oxen who would welcome more companionship would do well to consider enrolling on a course, joining an interest group or going to places where they can meet those with similar interests to their own. Positive action on their part will be well rewarded and for some unattached Water Oxen the Pig year can mark the start of a special romance. April, mid-June to July, September and December will be the most active months socially.

The Year of the Pig certainly holds promising prospects for the Water Ox. By using his talents and personal qualities well and seizing his opportunities, he can make this a satisfying and highly constructive year.

TIP FOR THE YEAR

Despite the busy nature of the year, do make sure you spend time enjoying your interests and recreational pursuits. In 2007 you do need to strike a sensible balance. Also, draw on the advice and support that others can give. Their input can make a considerable difference to how you fare and can ease the pressure you may be under.

The Wood Ox

There is a Chinese proverb which reminds us 'Constant effort yields certain success' and the Wood Ox would do well to remember this during the Pig year. This is a time of considerable opportunity and by showing commitment and working hard, the Wood Ox can achieve a great deal. And pleasingly, the encouraging aspects extend to most areas of his life.

The Wood Ox's personal life is likely to be especially busy. In view of the various activities he is involved with, he will often have many chances to go out and to enjoy himself. In addition, changes in his circumstances, perhaps through a move or a change in his work, can lead to him meeting others and adding to his social circle. During the Pig year, the Wood Ox will certainly find himself in demand and valuing the friendships, acquaintances and contacts he has built up. Also, many unattached Wood Oxen will meet someone who will become very important and the year could well mark the start of a significant and wonderful romance. April, the months from July to September and December could be the most active socially, as well as bring some interesting developments in the Wood Ox's personal life.

For those Wood Oxen with a partner this can also be an important year and these Wood Oxen will enjoy making plans and setting many of their ideas in motion, particularly concerning their accommodation.

The Wood Ox will also be well supported by family members over the year, and although he may wish to do a lot on his own, he should not let this prevent him from seeking advice or asking for assistance. Throughout the year he should remember that others are keen to support him and he only has to ask.

One area in which the Wood Ox will need to be especially careful, however, is finance. With his various plans, personal and accommodation expenses and other commitments, he will find his outgoings will often be considerable and he will need to budget well. Fortunately his careful Wood Ox nature will help, but he should keep a close watch on his spending as well as check the terms of any agreement(s) he may enter into. If at any time he has uncertainties over any financial matter, it is important that he addresses these before proceeding.

However, while this is a year for financial prudence, many Wood Oxen can look forward to an increase in earnings. And as far as the Wood Ox's work is concerned, this is an encouraging year, particularly as it will give him a greater chance to make the most of his strengths. Those Wood Oxen in work will often find their recent experience will place them in a good position to take on greater responsibilities. And with the aspects as they are, one step forward can often pave the way for others.

For those Wood Oxen who are seeking work or feeling unfulfilled in their present position, the Pig year can also open up important possibilities. By remaining alert, making enquiries and following up any vacancies that interest them, these Wood Oxen will often be successful in securing a position which will provide them with a base from which they can develop. This is, though, a year when commitment and effort can make an important difference. Those Wood Oxen studying for qualifications will also find that commitment and discipline can lead to important results and open up new possibilities. All Wood Oxen will find the effort they put in now can have value both now *and in the future*. Workwise, March, May to mid-July and October could see some good opportunities.

With the year's strong emphasis on development and progress, if the Wood Ox has any interests or recreational pursuits he would like to try or take further, he should follow his ideas through. By making the most of his skills and the facilities in his area he will not only derive much pleasure from what he does but also feel that he is moving himself forward. If he can encourage his friends to join him or can get to know other enthusiasts he will find this can add to the fun as well as result in him learning more. Any skills the Wood Ox can learn or develop over the year can be of value in the future.

Although travel may not feature prominently over the year, those Wood Oxen who do decide to go away would find it worth their while reading up about their destination and checking on their likely requirements while away. The better prepared they are, the more they will get from their travels.

Prospects are certainly promising for the Wood Ox over the year and by making the most of any opportunities to further his own development (including adding to his qualifications), he will be able to improve on his present situation and lay the groundwork for his future success. With his good circle of friends, personal interests and in some cases supportive partner, the Wood Ox can enjoy a happy and often special year.

Aim to further your skills and make the most of any training opportunities. You are still in the early stages of your working life and what you learn now can have far-reaching value. This is a year of exciting opportunities. Use them well.

The Fire Ox

This year the Fire Ox enters a new decade in his life and, whether born in 1937 or 1997, he will find it holds encouraging prospects. However, to get the best from the year and to benefit from the support others can give, both younger and more senior Fire Oxen will need to be open and forthcoming and not keep their thoughts, hopes and ideas to themselves.

Fire Oxen born in 1937 could have wide-ranging plans for the year. However, one area which will bring them considerable pleasure is their personal interests. By devoting time to these and, if possible, setting themselves new projects to complete or skills to master, they will be very satisfied with what they are able to accomplish. Going out and meeting those who share their interests will often add to the pleasure. Fire Oxen who are keen to build up their social life will find their interests a good way to meet others, and by joining a local interest or social group or enrolling on a course, they can find their social life becoming more rewarding and meaningful as the year progresses.

In particular those Fire Oxen who enjoy creative activities should make the most of their talents over the year. What they produce will not only bring them much personal pleasure, but if they are tempted to promote their work in some way, perhaps by entering a competition, they could be encouraged by the response of others. In addition, if the Fire Oxen comes across a subject that intrigues him or sees a course in his area that appeals, he should find out more. The many Fire Oxen who are keen gardeners will also enjoy the time they spend out of doors and will appreciate the results of their hard work.

Many Fire Oxen will also be keen to carry out projects on their home over the year. These could range from redecorating and making improvements to sorting through cupboards and storage areas. Tackling projects with others will make these practical tasks easier to accomplish.

Although travel does not tend to figure prominently for the Ox in Pig years, the Fire Ox should still aim to go away for a holiday or break during the year, even if he does not travel far. His time away can often give him the chance to meet others. Some Fire Oxen may also decide to spend time visiting places in their immediate area, including nearby towns or places of interest. Going with loved ones and friends can make such visits all the more enjoyable.

As far as money matters are concerned this will be a reasonable year, with some Fire Oxen benefiting from additional funds, including the possible fruition of a savings or investment policy. However, to get the best from his resources, the Fire Ox will need to watch his situation carefully and budget in advance for any large purchases. In addition, if entering into a new commitment or agreement, it is important that he checks the terms and, where necessary, seeks appropriate advice. This may be a fairly good year financially, but he should not let his usual vigilance slip, especially when there could be long-term implications. Fire Oxen, take note and do be thorough.

The Fire Ox's domestic life is encouragingly aspected and as well as enjoying any celebrations to mark his 70th year, he will also enjoy many of the family activities that take place. These include plans and ideas he can pursue with loved ones. Taking part in activities together (rather than setting about things too independently) can not only lead to better rapport and understanding but also help make his home life more rewarding. In addition the Fire Ox could do much to support a younger relation who may be facing an important decision or feeling under pressure.

For those Fire Oxen born in 1997, again the Pig year holds encouraging prospects, and by making the most of the opportunities the year will bring, they will often enjoy themselves and manage to do a great deal. One particularly promising area concerns the way the Fire Ox will be able to develop some of his interests, and if there is something he particularly wants to do, it is important that he lets others know about it.

In so many respects 2007 offers all Fire Oxen considerable scope. And the more the Fire Ox is willing to involve others in his activities, the greater the pleasure he will obtain from them.

TIP FOR THE YEAR
If you have ideas and plans you are keen to act upon, seize the moment. There is no time like the present and this is no time to delay or put things off. By making the most of your ideas and opportunities, and the support of others, you can make this a fulfilling year.

The Earth Ox

This will be a pleasant year for the Earth Ox, with much going in his favour.

At work many Earth Oxen will be content to continue in a position they know well. With the considerable experience they have behind them, they will often find their advice being sought and valued by colleagues. Workwise, this can be a constructive and fulfilling year.

For Earth Oxen who are keen to progress in their career or currently looking for work, the Pig year can open up some interesting possibilities. Again the Earth Ox's experience and specialist knowledge will serve him well, and in many cases he will be successful in advancing his career.

There will, however, be some Earth Oxen who will now welcome a less demanding position, perhaps one involving fewer hours or less commuting. Again, by making enquiries and following up positions that appeal to them, these Earth Oxen will often be successful in making the change. March, May, June and October could see some interesting developments regarding the Earth Ox's work situation.

Another encouraging aspect of the year is the way it will allow the Earth Ox time to enjoy his interests. Some Earth Oxen may also consider enrolling at a gym, taking a fitness course or starting a discipline such as yoga or tai chi. They will often feel better as a result.

Although travel is not strongly aspected over the year, if the Earth Ox should see an offer that appeals to him he would do well to follow it up. Similarly, if he sees a social event or form of entertainment which appeals, again he should mention it to others and see what can be arranged. The Pig year will certainly contain a great many pleasurable occasions and the Earth Ox should make the most of it by putting forward his ideas and suggestions.

As far as the Earth Ox's domestic life is concerned, this will be a rewarding year. Doing things with others and pooling talents and ideas will also help with rapport and understanding. However, while so much will go well, the Earth Ox should be wary of tackling too many activities all at once. As always, though, he will play a central role in his domestic life, with his talents, good sense and caring nature being much appreciated. During the Pig year, he will do a lot to help and advise others, particularly younger relations.

The Earth Ox's social life is also pleasingly aspected and he will appreciate going out and meeting up with friends. Any Earth Oxen who may be lonely and would welcome more companionship will find that going out more and becoming involved in activities and interests can lead to quite a transformation. Some of these Earth Oxen may also consider giving time to charity work or helping others in the community, and this too can add something extra to their lives.

As far as financial matters are concerned, the Earth Ox can enjoy some pleasing developments. In addition to a possible increase in income, he could benefit from a bonus, the fruition of a policy or something extra from some additional work. Financially, he can fare well this year, although to benefit fully he does need to manage his situation in his usual careful and thorough way. This includes taking his time when considering more expensive purchases as well as making provisions for forthcoming expenses. Also he would do well to set something aside for the longer term.

Generally, this will be a satisfying year for the Earth Ox and by acting upon his ideas and plans and using his talents well, he will derive much pleasure from his activities. He will also be greatly encouraged by the support he receives from those around him and his domestic and social life will often mean a great deal to him.

TIP FOR THE YEAR
Look to develop your interests in some way or consider taking up a new one. You may discover new talents as well as come into contact with others. Your interests can also be an excellent way to relax and unwind.

FAMOUS OXEN

Hans Christian Andersen, Johann Sebastian Bach, Warren Beatty, Kate Beckinsale, Napoleon Bonaparte, Rory Bremner, Albert Camus, Jim Carrey, Charlie Chaplin, Diana, Princess of Wales, Marlene Dietrich, Walt Disney, Harry Enfield, Jane Fonda, Richard Gere, Ricky Gervais, Handel, Adolf Hitler, Dustin Hoffman, Anthony Hopkins, Saddam Hussein, Billy Joel, Mark Knopfler, Burt Lancaster, Jessica Lange, Kate Moss, Alison Moyet, Eddie Murphy, Paul Newman, Jack Nicholson, Leslie Nielsen, Gwyneth Paltrow, Oscar Peterson, Colin Powell, Paula Radcliffe, Robert Redford, Lionel Richie, Wayne Rooney, Tim Roth, Rubens, Meg Ryan, Jean Sibelius, Sissy Spacek, Bruce Springsteen, Meryl Streep, Lady Thatcher, Alan Titchmarsh, Scott F. Turow, Vincent van Gogh, Gore Vidal, Minette Walters, Zoë Wanamaker, Sigourney Weaver, the Duke of Wellington, Arsène Wenger, W. B. Yeats.

26 JANUARY 1914 ～ 13 FEBRUARY 1915   *Wood Tiger*

13 FEBRUARY 1926 ～ 1 FEBRUARY 1927   *Fire Tiger*

31 JANUARY 1938 ～ 18 FEBRUARY 1939   *Earth Tiger*

17 FEBRUARY 1950 ～ 5 FEBRUARY 1951   *Metal Tiger*

5 FEBRUARY 1962 ～ 24 JANUARY 1963   *Water Tiger*

23 JANUARY 1974 ～ 10 FEBRUARY 1975   *Wood Tiger*

9 FEBRUARY 1986 ～ 28 JANUARY 1987   *Fire Tiger*

28 JANUARY 1998 ～ 15 FEBRUARY 1999   *Earth Tiger*

THE
TIGER

THE PERSONALITY OF THE TIGER

'Not knowing when the dawn will come, I open every door.'

Emily Dickinson, a Tiger

The Tiger is born under the sign of courage. He is a charismatic figure and usually holds very firm views. He is strong-willed and determined, and sets about most of his activities with tremendous energy and enthusiasm. He is very alert and quick-witted and his mind is forever active. He is a highly original thinker and is nearly always brimming with new ideas or full of enthusiasm for some new project or scheme.

The Tiger adores challenges and loves to get involved in anything which he thinks has an exciting future or which catches his imagination. He is prepared to take risks and does not like to be bound either by convention or the dictates of others. He likes to be free to act as he chooses and at least once during his life he will throw caution to the wind and go off and do the things he wants to do.

The Tiger does, however, have a somewhat restless nature. Even though he is often prepared to throw himself wholeheartedly into a project, his initial enthusiasm can soon wane if he sees something more appealing. He can also be rather impulsive and there will be occasions in his life when he acts in a manner he later regrets. If the Tiger were to think things through or be prepared to persevere in his various activities, he would almost certainly enjoy a greater degree of success.

Fortunately the Tiger is lucky in most of his enterprises, but should things not work out as he hoped, he is liable to suffer from severe bouts of depression and it will often take him a long time to recover. His life often consists of a series of ups and downs.

The Tiger is, however, very adaptable. He has an adventurous spirit and rarely stays in the same place for long. In the early stages of his life he is likely to try his hand at several different jobs and he will also change his residence fairly frequently.

The Tiger is very honest and open in his dealings with others. He hates any sort of hypocrisy or falsehood. He is also well known for being blunt and forthright and has no hesitation in speaking his mind. He can be rebellious at times, particularly against any form of petty authority, and while this can lead him into conflict with others, he is never one to shrink from an argument or avoid standing up for what he believes is right.

The Tiger is a natural leader and can invariably rise to the top of his chosen profession. He does not, however, care for anything too bureaucratic or detailed, and he does not like to obey orders. He can be stubborn and obstinate and throughout his life he likes to retain a certain amount of independence in his actions and be responsible to no one but himself. He likes to consider that all his achievements are due to his own efforts and he will not ask for support from others if he can avoid it.

Ironically, despite his self-confidence and leadership qualities, the Tiger can be indecisive and will often delay making a major decision until the very last moment. He can also be sensitive to criticism.

Although the Tiger is capable of earning large sums of money, he is rather a spendthrift and does not always put his money to its best use. He can also be most generous and will often shower lavish gifts on friends and relations.

The Tiger cares very much for his reputation and the image that he tries to project. He carries himself with an air of dignity and authority and enjoys being the centre of attention. He is very adept at attracting publicity, both for himself and for the causes he supports.

The Tiger often marries young and he will find himself best suited to those born under the signs of the Pig, Dog, Horse and Goat. He can also get on well with the Rat, Rabbit and Rooster, but will find the Ox and Snake a bit too quiet and serious for his liking, and he will be highly irritated by the Monkey's rather mischievous and inquisitive ways. He will also find it difficult to get on with another Tiger or a Dragon – both partners will want to dominate the relationship and could find it difficult to compromise on even the smallest of matters.

The Tigress is lively, witty and a marvellous hostess at parties. She takes great care over her appearance and is usually most attractive. She can be a very doting mother and while she believes in letting her children have their freedom, she makes an excellent teacher and will ensure that her children are well brought up and want for nothing. Like her male counterpart, she has numerous interests and likes to have sufficient independence and freedom to go off and do the things she wants to do. She has a most caring and generous nature.

The Tiger has many commendable qualities. He is honest, courageous and often a source of inspiration to others. Providing he can curb the wilder excesses of his restless nature, he is almost certain to lead a fulfilling and satisfying life.

THE FIVE DIFFERENT TYPES OF TIGER

In addition to the 12 signs of the Chinese zodiac there are five elements, and these have a strengthening or moderating influence on the sign. The effects of the five elements on the Tiger are described below, together with the years in which the elements were exercising their influence. Therefore those Tigers born in 1950 are Metal Tigers, those born in 1962 are Water Tigers, and so on.

Metal Tiger: 1950
The Metal Tiger has an assertive and outgoing personality. He is very ambitious and while his aims may change from time to time, he will work relentlessly until he has obtained what he wants. He can, however, be impatient for results and become highly strung if things do not work out as he would like. He is distinctive in his appearance and is admired and respected by many.

Water Tiger: 1962
This Tiger has a wide variety of interests and is always eager to experiment with new ideas or satisfy his adven-

turous nature by going off to explore distant lands. He is versatile, shrewd and has a kindly nature. He tends to remain calm in a crisis, although he can be annoyingly indecisive at times. He communicates well with others and through his many capabilities and persuasive nature usually achieves what he wants in life. He is also highly imaginative and is often a gifted orator or writer.

Wood Tiger: 1914, 1974

The Wood Tiger has a friendly and pleasant personality. He is less independent than some of the other types of Tiger and is more prepared to work with others to secure a desired objective. However, he does have a tendency to jump from one thing to another and can easily become distracted. He is usually very popular, has a large circle of friends and invariably leads a busy and enjoyable social life. He also has a good sense of humour.

Fire Tiger: 1926, 1986

The Fire Tiger sets about everything he does with great verve and enthusiasm. He loves action and is always ready to throw himself wholeheartedly into anything which catches his imagination. He has many leadership qualities and is capable of communicating his ideas and enthusiasm to others. He is very much an optimist and can be most generous. He has a likeable nature and can be a witty and persuasive speaker.

Earth Tiger: 1938, 1998
This Tiger is responsible and level-headed. He studies everything objectively and tries to be scrupulously fair in all his dealings. Unlike other Tigers, he is prepared to specialize in certain areas rather than get distracted by other matters, but he can become so involved in what he is doing that he does not always take into account the opinions of those around him. He has good business sense and is usually very successful in later life. He has a large circle of friends and pays great attention to both his appearance and his reputation.

PROSPECTS FOR THE TIGER IN 2007

The Year of the Dog (29 January 2006 to 17 February 2007) will have been a generally positive one for the Tiger and in the closing months the aspects are encouraging. However, as the Tiger will have found, it does require commitment to get results in the Dog year and the closing months will be no time for him to ease up either in effort or resolve.

In the Tiger's work there will be good opportunities for him to use his talents and by giving his best he will not only be helping his present situation but also his standing and prospects. For those Tigers keen to progress, September to mid-October and January 2007 could see some chances worth pursuing.

The Tiger can also look forward to some good financial news as the year draws to a close. Many Tigers will receive a bonus or gift at this time. However, while anything extra will be welcome, with much spending likely in the final Dog months, the Tiger should keep a watchful eye on his outgoings and think carefully about any more expensive purchases and spur of the moment temptations. Without care, he could end up spending more than he anticipated. Also, there will be some excellent travel opportunities in the closing months of the Dog year and anything that the Tiger can set aside for travel could be helpful.

The Tiger's personal life is also favourably aspected at this time, although with so much happening it is important that he regularly consults those around him. That way things can be planned, arranged and enjoyed, rather than left to the last moment and rushed.

The Tiger's social life will also become busier as the year draws to a close. September, December and January will be especially active months, and for some Tigers, affairs of the heart and new friendships can help make this a special time.

The Year of the Pig starts on 18 February and will be an interesting one for the Tiger. Over the year he will have some excellent chances to improve on his present position and will find much going his way. However, while the aspects may be encouraging, they also signal a need for care. This is not a year for risky undertakings or for throwing caution to the wind, and at times it would be wise for the Tiger to watch his sometimes impulsive and over-zealous nature.

In his work the aspects are promising and will give the Tiger the opportunity to benefit from the skills and experience he has built up. If he learns of an opening worth considering, by putting himself forward he may well be able to advance his career. This is very much a year to make the most of opportunities as they arise and to act swiftly.

In addition, with his talent for coming up with ideas (the Tiger is well known for his inventive and resourceful nature), whenever he feels he can make a positive contribution, he should do so. In some cases his suggestions and initiative will be taken further and do his reputation a lot of good. Those Tigers whose work is of a more creative or expressive nature can especially benefit from promoting their talents. As the Tiger will find, enterprise, commitment and good work will be recognized and rewarded in the Pig year.

The aspects are also encouraging for those Tigers who would like to move on from what they are currently doing, as well as for those seeking work. Although some of these Tigers may have become disheartened by their situation, the Pig year can herald an upturn in their fortunes. However, to benefit, they do need to take positive action, otherwise there is a risk that opportunities could slip by and they could remain in a rut. As the Pig year begins, these Tigers would do well to consider what it is they now want to do. Some innovative thinking can lead to new possibilities, and by following up their ideas and not being too restrictive in what they are prepared to consider, these Tigers can find some exciting opportunities can open up for them. February, and as the Pig year begins, March, May and November could see the best opportunities, but with the aspects as they are, interesting possibilities could arise at almost any time. Similarly, any ideas and proposals that the Tiger is able to put forward can lead to positive developments throughout the year.

However, while the aspects are favourable, the Pig year also requires a certain care. In particular, the Tiger does need to be careful about becoming complacent, letting his standards slip and pushing his luck or the goodwill of others too far. The Pig year can provide some sharp reminders for those who take a risk too many. Tigers, take note!

This cautionary advice also applies to financial matters. Although many Tigers will, through their work and success, enjoy a rise in income, this is not a year for risky undertakings or speculations. Should the Tiger be tempted by any scheme, opportunity or investment, it would be worth him seeking advice and checking the details and implications first. Without such care, money could be lost and mistakes made. Where important financial matters are concerned, this is very much a year for care and vigilance.

More positively, there will be some good travel opportunities for the Tiger over the year, sometimes arising at short notice. And whether he is visiting family and friends some distance away or indulging in last-minute holidays, he will often enjoy his times away. For some Tigers, new friendships can be made too, and the unattached may find their travels leading to romance.

The Tiger will also enjoy his social life over the year and in addition to keeping in contact with his existing circle of friends, he will have good opportunities to meet others. Not only travel but also his interests and recreational pursuits will bring him into contact with new people. Those Tigers who would welcome new friends or a more fulfilling social life will find that by joining social or special interest groups in their area, their prospects can enjoy a pleasing upturn. April, May, August and September will see the most social activity.

The Tiger's domestic life can generally go well in the Pig year, although there is one important caveat. Sometimes when pressures are great, patience wears thin and tempers become frayed. It is important that the Tiger recognizes such times and is prepared to talk about any pressures or concerns. By being open and forthcoming, he will enable others to understand – and to help. Fortunately the Tiger is usually mindful in this respect, but to prevent differences of opinion or some heated exchanges during the year, a certain care will be needed. However, in spite of the cautionary aspects, with good communication and shared activities, there will be much in his home life for him to appreciate.

The Pig year certainly holds some encouraging prospects for the Tiger, particularly in terms of developing his skills and advancing his career. His personal interests, travel and the activities he shares with family and friends can also bring much pleasure. However, financial matters do need care. Also, when busy and under pressure the Tiger does needs to be mindful of others and allow those around to help him more. Provided he remains aware of these trickier aspects, though, the Pig year can go well and be to his benefit.

The Metal Tiger
This will be a pleasing year for the Metal Tiger and by setting about his plans and activities in his usual earnest way he can look forward to accomplishing a great deal.

In his work the aspects are especially encouraging and during the year many Metal Tigers will have opportunities to make more of their strengths and concentrate on the areas they find most satisfying. Sometimes these Metal Tigers will be offered the chance to take on more specialist responsibilities or will see vacancies or promotion opportunities which they will be well qualified to put in for. This is certainly a year when the Metal Tiger can move his career forward and enjoy some sometimes overdue success. Also, if he is engaged in work which is creative, expressive or involves communication, this is very much a time to make the most of his skills and ideas. His originality and commitment will again meet with a good response.

The Metal Tiger will also be helped by the good working relations he enjoys with so many people. In some cases colleagues and contacts could alert him to possibilities worth considering or offer important support and advice. In return the Metal Tiger will often assist less experienced colleagues and his guidance and instruction will again be valued. His good working relations can be an important factor in the success and progress he enjoys during the year.

Many Metal Tigers will decide to remain with their existing employer over the year and build on their current position, but for those who are keen to change or looking for a position, the Pig year can open up some exciting possibilities. In particular, by considering other ways in which they can draw on their experience as well as by talking to those able to offer good advice (here again their contacts could be especially helpful), these Metal Tigers will often be successful in securing a new position which offers fresh challenges and suits them well. February, March, May and November could see some good openings.

In addition to the encouraging aspects concerning his work, the Metal Tiger's personal interests can develop well over the year, with creative and more expressive pursuits again being favoured. If there is a skill or technique the Metal Tiger feels it could be helpful to learn or improve on, he should follow this up. By doing so, he can increase the pleasure his interests bring him. Those Metal Tigers who, because of their many commitments, have let their interests lapse recently should aim to rectify this over the year. The Metal Tiger's personal interests can not only give his lifestyle a greater balance but sometimes bring other benefits too, including the chance to get some additional exercise or get out of doors more.

Many Metal Tigers will enjoy an increase in their earnings over the year and some may also be successful in supplementing their income through a skill or some freelance work. However, while any increase will be welcome, the Metal Tiger will need to be careful in money matters. This is no year for risks or complacency. In particular, when considering any large purchase or if entering into an agreement, it is important that he checks the details and implications. This is particularly important if he is tempted by what could be a more risky or speculative investment. Also, if there is an expensive purchase that he is keen to make, it could be worth checking various sources as well as waiting for favourable opportunities. This way he could save himself some unnecessary outlay as well as obtain better value.

Despite the need for financial care, the Metal Tiger will enjoy the travel opportunities the year will bring. Many

Metal Tigers will be attracted by an offer they see and they could also receive invitations to stay with family or friends. The Metal Tiger can again look forward to some enjoyable times away.

The Metal Tiger's home life can also give rise to some pleasing occasions. For many Metal Tigers, the progress of a younger relation will bring especial delight and there could also be good cause for a family celebration. During the year the Metal Tiger will often be involved in a great many activities and whether carrying out jobs around his home or helping and advising loved ones, he will generally be satisfied with what he is able to do.

However, while home life will generally go well, the Pig year does have its more cautionary aspects. If problems or disagreements arise the Metal Tiger should try to deal with them as quickly and amicably as possible, otherwise there is a risk they could start to cast a shadow over his home life and take on greater proportions than they warrant. Similarly, after busy and demanding days or weeks, the Metal Tiger should be careful not to take his feelings, weariness and irritations out on others. Fortunately he is usually careful in this respect, but it is something he would do well to watch over the year.

As far as the Metal Tiger's social life is concerned, this will again be an interesting year. As a result of his personal interests, his work and his existing circle of friends, he will often have opportunities to go out. Those Metal Tigers who are members of a society or interest group will often find their knowledge and skills leading to them playing a greater role. On a social level the Metal Tiger will definitely find himself in demand, and those who are keen to make more of their social life and meet others should aim to get involved in various activities over the year. If they do so, their situation can improve markedly. April, May, August and September will be the best and busiest months socially.

Overall, the Pig year can be a pleasing and satisfying one for the Metal Tiger, particularly as he will be able to use, develop and benefit from his skills and talents. He will also be helped by the support and goodwill of others. This is a year for action and for moving forward.

TIP FOR THE YEAR
Concentrate on your natural strengths. It is in these areas that you will enjoy the greatest success.

The Water Tiger

This will be a year of opportunity for the Water Tiger, although to benefit from the prevailing trends he will need to be flexible in his outlook as well as prepared to make the most of chances *as they arise*. Even if this involves looking again at existing plans or modifying some of his aims, he will find events over the year opening up new possibilities for him as well as bringing some deserving success.

In his work the aspects are especially encouraging, and for those Water Tigers who are keen to build on their present situation, the year will bring some excellent chances. In some cases, as more senior colleagues move on the Water Tiger will be well placed to take over. Equally, if he feels the time is now right to broaden his career and gain experience in another area, he should make enquiries and follow up positions that interest him. As he will find, by looking to advance and making the most of the chances that arise, he is likely to be successful in moving his career forward.

This is also a year of opportunity for those Water Tigers who feel unfulfilled in their present situation, consider themselves in a rut or are seeking work. By being prepared to consider different types of work as well as other ways in which they can use their skills, many will be successful in gaining a position which will not only give them an exciting new challenge but also set their career off on a more rewarding path. To benefit, though, these Water Tigers will need to show a certain flexibility as well as the willingness to adapt to their new duties. With effort and commitment, however, many will succeed in laying the groundwork for a much brighter future.

The Water Tiger will also benefit from the advice and support he receives over the year and whenever he is thinking over new possibilities, he will find it helpful to speak to those who are qualified to give advice or information. These could be colleagues, contacts or professional organizations, but whoever he consults, the Water Tiger will find that he can really benefit from the assistance he is given. February, March, May to mid-June and November could see the best opportunities as far as his work is concerned.

The progress the Water Tiger makes in his work will often bring a welcome increase in income during the year. In addition, some Water Tigers can look forward to receiving a bonus payment or some additional funds. However, while money may flow into the Water Tiger's account, without care it could flow out again all too easily, and he does need to keep a watchful eye over his spending. If he has any large expenses coming up, whether for his home, family or travel, he should make allowances well in advance. By managing his situation well and remaining disciplined in his approach (including avoiding too many impulse and often expensive purchases), he will fare well and appreciate what he is able to do with his money. However, with the aspects as they are, this is not a year for risks, and should he be tempted by any investment, venture or speculation, the Water Tiger would do well to seek further advice as well as check the details and implications carefully. Without care, money could be lost. Water Tigers, do take note and treat anything of a risky nature with caution.

While money matters need care, the Pig year will bring some good travel opportunities and whether the Water Tiger is going away for short breaks or on a special holiday, he will often enjoy his time away and the places he visits. Also, some Water Tigers may be tempted to find out about areas near to them, including places of interest, or just enjoy the facilities their area offers. This is an excellent year for making the most of travel ideas and opportunities.

This will also be an active year in the Water Tiger's home life. With his own commitments and others in his household being similarly busy, it is also a time when good organization and communication can make a real difference. Talking to loved ones, making plans and discussing ideas will not only lead to things proceeding more smoothly but will also help rapport and understanding. Similarly, should any problems or differences of opinion arise, the Water Tiger will find that talking things over will be to the benefit of all. In addition many Water Tigers will be grateful for the time and support more senior family members are able to give. Should they have uncertainties or perhaps need assistance, they should not forget that others are often willing to help. Domestically, this can be a busy and sometimes demanding year, but it can a rewarding one too.

Although the Water Tiger will have many demands on his time it is also important that he does not allow his social life to lapse. By keeping in contact with friends and going to events that appeal to him, he will often enjoy himself as well as benefit from the chance to relax and unwind. His social life will also help to bring balance to his often busy lifestyle. Over the year many Water Tigers will find that changes in their work or the interests they pursue can lead to some good social opportunities. April, May, August and September will be the best months for social activities.

The Pig year certainly holds encouraging prospects for the Water Tiger, particularly as it will give him the chance to make more of his potential. By looking to move forward and following up any opportunities that arise, he can make important headway. This may be a busy year, but it can be a significant and rewarding one too.

TIP FOR THE YEAR
In view of all the activity of the year, do draw on the support of others and be prepared to talk over your hopes and concerns. Also, when changes occur, particularly in your work, be flexible and willing to adapt. This way your level of success can be that much greater.

The Wood Tiger

This year holds good prospects for the Wood Tiger, although just how well he fares is very much in his own hands. Over the year he can make important headway, but to benefit from the opportunities that will open up for him he will need to put himself forward as well as be prepared for change. Change does bring uncertainty and pressure, but these are almost inevitable on the path of progress. The Pig year will ask a lot of the Wood Tiger, but it *can* reward him well.

The area which is likely to see the greatest change is the Wood Tiger's work. For those Wood Tigers who feel that they could be making more of their talents, this is a year to seize the initiative and look to move on. If not, the rut some are in will not only become more difficult to break out of, but their feelings of discontent will continue. Those who have been in the same position for some time also need to be careful that they do not become staid or lose some of their ambition. This is a year when the Wood Tiger can make some significant career moves, but the call to action does rest with him.

Once the Wood Tiger does take action – and the early months of the Pig year can be a positive time for it – he will find possibilities quickly opening up. Enquiries made to companies, agencies and other organizations can often give him useful information and important developments can soon take place. February, March, May and November will see some good opportunities.

This is also a year of progress for those Wood Tigers already established in their career. As a result of their commitment and expertise, many will find themselves with the chance to move on to more specialist areas. Although what is offered can be daunting and bring increased pressure, if the Wood Tiger rises to the challenge he will find it will not only represent an important stage in his development but also prepare him for greater responsibilities later on. The Pig year is one of considerable opportunity, although much does rest with the Wood Tiger's willingness to put himself forward and make the most of his talents.

The encouraging aspects also extend to the Wood Tiger's personal interests and despite the many demands on his time it would be worth him setting a regular time aside for recreational pursuits he enjoys. This is an excellent year for self-development and any new knowledge and skills the Wood Tiger acquires will add to the pleasure his interests bring.

He can also benefit from any attention he can give to his well-being over the year. In particular if he does not tend to get much regular exercise or is reliant on convenience foods, he could find that a few modifications can make a real difference to how he feels.

The Wood Tiger will also enjoy the travel opportunities that the year will bring and should aim to go away for a break or holiday at some time. With his adventurous nature and desire to explore new places, he could get to visit some impressive areas. In addition some short breaks or even day trips that are arranged almost on a whim could particularly delight him. This is certainly a year for making the most of opportunities.

As with all Tigers, though, the Wood Tiger will need be careful when dealing with money matters. Although many will enjoy an increase in income, with all their existing obligations and some of the plans and purchases they are considering, it would be worth them keeping a close watch on their spending. With care and good management the Wood Tiger can fare well, but should he become lax in his financial dealings, some purchases could have to be postponed or economies called for. This is very much a year for planning, control and the avoidance of risks. In addition, the Wood Tiger will need to be thorough and attentive when dealing with paperwork.

As far as the Wood Tiger's home life is concerned, this will be a full and active year. At busy times it is important that the Wood Tiger and his loved ones support one another and talk over any concerns and plans. The better the communication, the smoother home life will be. Setting aside time to pursue joint interests or tackle home or garden projects can also lead to some enjoyable occasions. Those Wood Tigers who are parents will find that time spent encouraging their children can again bring some special moments. As with all Tigers in the Pig year, the Wood Tiger's home life does call for a certain care and mindfulness. But if he can be aware of this and give time to his loved ones, this will be a busy but gratifying year for him.

The Wood Tiger's social life is pleasingly aspected and while this may not be such an active year as some (particularly as other commitments and responsibilities will take up much time), the Wood Tiger will often appreciate the chances he has to go out and meet up with friends. Also, as a result of his interests, travel and changes in his work, he may well have the chance to get to know others over the year and extend his social circle.

The Year of the Pig certainly holds good prospects for the Wood Tiger but to get the best from it he will need to pursue his aims and objectives with determination. This is very much a year to further his often special talents. Positive action will be well rewarded.

TIP FOR THE YEAR

This is a year of considerable opportunity, but to make things happen you will need to be clear about what you want and take the relevant action. With focus and effort, this can be a successful and rewarding time. Also, do make sure that your lifestyle has balance and that you set time aside to be with your loved ones.

The Fire Tiger

This is a year of considerable potential for the Fire Tiger, although to benefit from its encouraging trends he will need to show both commitment and enterprise. This is a time to rise to challenges and opportunities. By doing so, the Fire Tiger can look forward to making pleasing progress.

For those Fire Tigers studying for qualifications this can be an important year. While sometimes, with student life and the many activities the Fire Tiger is involved with, there will be much to do and many distractions, by working well and giving proper attention to their situation, they can make important progress. To help keep themselves motivated, these Fire Tigers could find it helpful to think of the possibilities that could open up as a result of the qualifications they may gain. What they are working towards now can have considerable value in the future.

This also applies to those Fire Tigers in work. Any training they can do and skills they can acquire can open up other possibilities later on. Accordingly, throughout the year these Fire Tigers should take full advantage of any ways in which they can further their development.

Those Fire Tigers who are seeking work and are not yet sure of what they want to do could find it helpful to talk over possibilities with advisers and employment agencies as well as contact professional organizations. By obtaining information and following up openings that interest them, many will be successful in securing a position and getting that all-important foothold on the employment ladder. The actions these Fire Tigers take now can often shape the next few years.

For work developments and openings the early months of the Pig year are favoured, especially February to May, and opportunities will also arise from mid-October to November. However, the success and progress the Fire Tiger enjoys over the year is very dependent on his effort, attitude and determination.

One factor in the Fire Tiger's favour is his ability to relate so effectively with others and over the year he should aim to use his personal strengths and make the most of his chances to meet others. This can result in some enjoyable social occasions, new friendships and contacts.

Over the year the Fire Tiger's efforts can lead to an increase in earnings and some Fire Tigers may also be able to supplement this through an enterprising idea they have or some additional work they are able to do. The Pig year will reward the Fire Tiger well and his often greater income will lead to him being able to do much more. However, he would still be wise to keep a watchful eye on his outgoings and everyday spending. Also, as with all Tigers in the Pig year, he should be wary of risks. If considering anything of a more speculative nature, he would do well to get advice and check the implications. If he wants to make the most of his resources, he should aim to be both careful and thorough.

More positively, the Fire Tiger's social life is well aspected and he will often have chances to go out and enjoy himself. In addition some of his personal interests could lead to him meeting new people and making new friends. For some Fire Tigers romance can figure prominently, although a few will find the path of true love will not always run smoothly and the Fire Tiger should be wary of building up his expectations in the early stages of any romance. However, while affairs of the heart will need care and consideration, these can still be pleasing times and the Fire Tiger will often enjoy himself and be able to add to his social circle. For those already in an established relationship, this can be a special year, and time spent getting to know and understand each other better will be both enjoyable and worthwhile.

Over the year the Fire Tiger will also be helped by the support of those around him. If he is ever in a dilemma or facing a big decision, talking to senior relations can often be of value. As he will find, the support of others can make a real difference to his level of success.

In many respects this will be an important year for the Fire Tiger, particularly as it will prepare the way for the greater progress that awaits in following years. Accordingly the Fire Tiger should aim to make the most of any chances to add to his experience and qualifications. On a personal level, with the friendship and support of so many, he will not only be encouraged but also enjoy himself.

TIP FOR THE YEAR
Be determined and have faith in yourself and your skills. With resolve and willingness, this can be an important year and the experience you gain can be far-reaching.

The Earth Tiger

This is a year of interesting possibilities for the Earth Tiger. However, to get the most from the encouraging trends he would do well to decide what he wants to accomplish over the year and make some plans. And, as he thinks about possibilities, he should actively discuss his ideas with those close to him. The support and involvement of others will often lead to more being achieved.

One area which can bring the Earth Tiger considerable pleasure is his personal interests. With his keen and enquiring nature, he will invariably have projects he is keen to tackle or ideas he wants to take further. In addition he will often enjoy the chance to share his knowledge with others, whether these are loved ones or fellow enthusiasts. Many Earth Tigers will also find their hobbies and interests having a positive social element during the year. If he has not done so already, the Earth Tiger could consider getting in contact with a local society or interest group where he can meet fellow enthusiasts. Alternatively, he could correspond with others over the internet.

There will also be some good travel opportunities over the year and whether the Earth Tiger is going away for a short break, visiting areas he has long wanted to see or following up invitations to visit family and friends, he will often enjoy his times away. However, before setting off on any journey, time spent going through the details could save problems or delays. Earth Tigers, do bear this in mind.

In addition to going away, the Earth Tiger will also enjoy the chances he has to visit places of interest in his area. These could range from local attractions to exhibitions or beauty spots, but by making the most of what is relatively close to him the Earth Tiger can enjoy some particularly pleasing times.

The Earth Tiger's domestic life is also well aspected over the year and he will value the good rapport he enjoys with those around him. Should any concerns ever be troubling him, he will find that talking things over with others can do a lot to help. The Earth Tiger will also follow the activities of family members with fond interest and will be glad to give additional help to any who may be under pressure, even if this is simply by lending a listening ear. Others do value his opinions and judgement, and his support and empathy will be appreciated.

Although a lot can go well over the year, the one area which could be problematic is paperwork. The Earth Tiger should take particular care over completing paperwork carefully and on time. If not, a delay could be to his detriment – and cost. Similarly, if there is ever a question or part of a form that is not clear to him or gives him concern, he should seek advice. Paperwork – especially any with financial implications – does need careful and thorough attention this year. Also, whenever the Earth Tiger is considering any more expensive purchases or undertakings, he needs to check the details, costs and implications. Financially, this is a year for care and vigilance.

However, in most respects, this will be a positive year for the Earth Tiger and by following through his ideas and spending time on interests and pursuits he enjoys, he will be satisfied with what he is able to do. Involving others in his plans and activities can help add to the pleasure.

TIP FOR THE YEAR

Make some plans for the year. With something definite in mind, you will be able to do more and enjoy more as a result. And whenever possible, do try to involve others.

FAMOUS TIGERS

Kofi Annan, Sir David Attenborough, Victoria Beckham, Beethoven, Chuck Berry, Jon Bon Jovi, Sir Richard Branson, Emily Brontë, Mel Brookes, Isambard Kingdom Brunel, Agatha Christie, Charlotte Church, Phil Collins, Robbie Coltrane, Sheryl Crow, Tom Cruise, Penelope Cruz, Leonardo DiCaprio, Emily Dickinson, David Dimbleby, Queen Elizabeth II, Enya, Jodie Foster, Germaine Greer, Tim Henman, William Hurt, Ray Kroc, Stan Laurel, Jay Leno, Groucho Marx, Karl Marx, Marilyn Monroe, Demi Moore, Alanis Morissette, Jeremy Paxman, Marco Polo, Beatrix Potter, John Prescott, Renoir, Kenny Rogers, the Princess Royal, Dame Joan Sutherland, Dylan Thomas, Liv Ullman, Jon Voight, Julie Walters, H. G. Wells, Oscar Wilde, Robbie Williams, Dr Rowan Williams, Tennessee Williams, Sir Terry Wogan, Stevie Wonder, William Wordsworth.

14 FEBRUARY 1915 ～ 2 FEBRUARY 1916   *Wood Rabbit*

2 FEBRUARY 1927 ～ 22 JANUARY 1928   *Fire Rabbit*

19 FEBRUARY 1939 ～ 7 FEBRUARY 1940   *Earth Rabbit*

6 FEBRUARY 1951 ～ 26 JANUARY 1952   *Metal Rabbit*

25 JANUARY 1963 ～ 12 FEBRUARY 1964   *Water Rabbit*

11 FEBRUARY 1975 ～ 30 JANUARY 1976   *Wood Rabbit*

29 JANUARY 1987 ～ 16 FEBRUARY 1988   *Fire Rabbit*

16 FEBRUARY 1999 ～ 4 FEBRUARY 2000   *Earth Rabbit*

THE
RABBIT

THE PERSONALITY OF THE RABBIT

'Let us then be what we are, and speak what we think, and
in all things keep ourselves loyal to the truth.'
Henry Wadsworth Longfellow, a Rabbit

The Rabbit is born under the signs of virtue and prudence.
He is intelligent, well-mannered and prefers a quiet and
peaceful existence. He dislikes any sort of unpleasantness
and will try to steer clear of arguments and disputes. He is
very much a pacifist and tends to have a calming influence
on those around him. He has wide interests and usually a
good appreciation of the arts and the finer things in life. He
also knows how to enjoy himself and will often gravitate to
the best restaurants and nightspots in town.

The Rabbit is a witty and intelligent speaker and loves
being involved in a good discussion. His views and advice
are often sought by others and he can be relied upon to be
discreet and diplomatic. He will rarely raise his voice in
anger and will even turn a blind eye to matters which
displease him just to preserve the peace. He likes to remain
on good terms with everyone, but he can be rather sensitive and takes any form of criticism very badly. He will also
be the first to get out of the way if he sees any form of
trouble brewing.

The Rabbit is a quiet and efficient worker and has an
extremely good memory. He is very astute in business and
financial matters, but his degree of success often depends
on the conditions that prevail. He hates being in a situation
which is fraught with tension or where he has to make

sudden decisions. Wherever possible he will plan his various activities with the utmost care and a good deal of caution. He does not like to take risks and does not take kindly to change. Basically, he seeks a secure, calm and stable environment, and when conditions are right he is more than happy to leave things as they are.

The Rabbit is conscientious and because of his methodical and ever-watchful nature he can often do well in his chosen profession. He makes a good diplomat, lawyer, shopkeeper, administrator or priest, and he excels in any job where he can use his superb skills as a communicator. He tends to be loyal to his employers and is respected for his integrity and honesty, but if he ever finds himself in a position of great power he can become rather intransigent and authoritarian.

The Rabbit attaches great importance to his home and will often spend a lot of time and money maintaining and furnishing it and fitting it with all the latest comforts – the Rabbit is very much a creature of comfort! He is also something of a collector and there are many Rabbits who derive much pleasure from collecting antiques, *objets d'art* or anything else which catches their eye or particularly interests them.

The female Rabbit has a friendly, caring and considerate nature, and will do all in her power to give her home a happy and loving atmosphere. She is also very sociable and enjoys holding parties and entertaining. She has a great ability to make the maximum use of her time and although she involves herself in numerous activities, she always manages to find time to sit back and enjoy a good read or a chat. She has a great sense of humour, is very artistic and is often a talented gardener.

The Rabbit takes considerable care over his appearance and is usually smart and well turned out. He also attaches great importance to his relations with others and matters of the heart are particularly important to him. He will rarely be short of admirers and will often have several serious romances before he settles down. The Rabbit is not the most faithful of signs, but he will find that he is especially well suited to those born under the signs of the Goat, Snake, Pig and Ox. Due to his sociable and easy-going manner he can also get on well with the Tiger, Dragon, Horse, Monkey, Dog and another Rabbit, but he will feel ill at ease with the Rat and Rooster as both these signs tend to speak their mind and be critical in their comments, and the Rabbit just loathes any form of criticism or unpleasantness.

The Rabbit is usually lucky in life and often has the happy knack of being in the right place at the right time. He is talented and quick-witted, but he does sometimes put pleasure before work and wherever possible will tend to opt for the easy life. He can at times be a little reserved and suspicious of the motives of others, but generally will lead a long and contented life and one which – as far as possible – will be free of strife and discord.

THE FIVE DIFFERENT TYPES OF RABBIT

In addition to the 12 signs of the Chinese zodiac there are five elements and these have a strengthening or moderating influence on the sign. The effects of the five elements on the Rabbit are described below, together with the years in which the elements were exercising their influence. Therefore those Rabbits born in 1951 are Metal Rabbits, those born in 1963 are Water Rabbits, and so on.

Metal Rabbit: 1951

This Rabbit is capable, ambitious and has very definite views on what he wants to achieve in life. He can occasionally appear reserved and aloof, but this is mainly because he likes to keep his thoughts to himself. He has a quick and alert mind and is particularly shrewd in business matters. He can also be very cunning in his actions. The Metal Rabbit has a good appreciation of the arts and likes to mix in the best circles. He usually has a small but very loyal group of friends.

Water Rabbit: 1963

The Water Rabbit is popular, intuitive and keenly aware of the feelings of those around him. He can, however, be rather sensitive and tends to take things too much to heart. He is very precise and thorough in everything he does and has an exceedingly good memory. He tends to be quiet and at times rather withdrawn, but he expresses his ideas well and is highly regarded by his family, friends and colleagues.

Wood Rabbit: 1915, 1975

The Wood Rabbit is likeable, easy-going and very adaptable. He prefers to work in a group rather than on his own and likes to have the support and encouragement of others. He can, however, be rather reticent in expressing his views and it would be in his own interests to become a little more open and let others know how he feels on certain matters. He usually has many friends, enjoys an active social life and is noted for his generosity.

Fire Rabbit: 1927, 1987

The Fire Rabbit has a friendly, outgoing personality. He likes socializing and being on good terms with everyone. He is discreet and diplomatic and has a very good under-standing of human nature. He is also strong-willed and provided he has the necessary backing he can go far in life. He does, not, however, suffer adversity well and can become moody and depressed when things are not working out as he would like. He has a particularly good manner with children, is very intuitive and there are some Fire Rabbits who are even noted for their psychic ability.

Earth Rabbit: 1939, 1999

The Earth Rabbit is a quiet individual, but he is neverthe-less very astute. He is realistic in his aims and is prepared to work long and hard in order to achieve his objectives. He has good business sense and is invariably lucky in financial matters. He also has a most persuasive manner and usually experiences little difficulty in getting others to fall in with his plans. He is held in high esteem by his friends and colleagues and his views are often sought and highly valued.

PROSPECTS FOR THE RABBIT IN 2007

The Year of the Dog (29 January 2006 to 17 February 2007) holds interesting prospects for the Rabbit, with the closing months being an active and generally pleasant time.

The Rabbit's domestic and social life are both set to become busier as the year draws to a close. At home the Rabbit will often have a lot to deal with, including supporting loved ones and arranging various activities as well as finishing certain household projects. Some weeks could be especially busy and whenever possible the Rabbit would find it helpful to spread out his commitments. With good planning and the co-operation of others, however, he can enjoy himself a great deal at this time. November could see some particularly interesting social occasions and in the closing months of the Dog year the Rabbit will not only find his social circle widening but will also make friends and contacts that could come to be helpful in the future.

The Rabbit's outgoings will be fairly high as the Dog year draws to a close, although he could be particularly fortunate in some acquisitions he makes. In particular, if there is something he is keen to buy, by keeping alert he could obtain it at a favourable price. The Rabbit's eye for quality and a good buy will certainly serve him well at this time.

As far as the Rabbit's work is concerned he would do well to concentrate on the areas where he has most experience and can best use his skills. Good work done now can help his prospects in the new Chinese year.

Overall, the closing months of the Dog year will be a time of considerable activity for the Rabbit, but by being well-organized and liaising with others, he will enjoy himself and be satisfied with most of what he does.

The Year of the Pig starts on 18 February and is a well-aspected one for the Rabbit. During it he will have the opportunity to use his personal strengths and qualities to advantage and as a result will enjoy positive developments in many areas of his life. This is a year of considerable good fortune and promise for the Rabbit.

With his genial nature and good personal skills, the Rabbit always sets great store by his relations with others, and throughout the year he will be in demand. His social life is especially favourably aspected and he will have many invitations and opportunities to go out. Those Rabbits who would like to build up their social life, perhaps having recently moved, can see quite an improvement in their situation during the Pig year. New interests, work and recreational pursuits can all be excellent ways to meet others and March, June, August and December will be particularly busy months.

In addition to an active social life, the affairs of the heart are splendidly aspected and, for those enjoying romance, many will settle down with their partner or marry over the year. For those who would perhaps welcome romance, the chances of finding true love are excellent. Sometimes such a meeting will come about in a totally unexpected way. The Pig year can certainly bring a wonderful transformation in the unattached Rabbit's life, with love changing everything. In 2007 romance will definitely be in the air!

For those Rabbits who may have had recent disappointments in their personal life and would welcome new friends, again this is an encouraging year. By drawing a line under what has happened and looking to move forward, they will find they can do a great deal to improve their situation. Going out more, taking up new interests, joining social groups and helping with local activities will all help and can lead to meeting others and making new friends. Travel can also bring some enjoyable social opportunities. With the aspects as they are, the Rabbit's social life can bring much happiness.

The Rabbit's home life is also splendidly aspected and for many there will be memorable occasions and celebrations in store. On a personal level this can be a special and meaningful year. Also, throughout, the Rabbit will value the encouragement of his loved ones, and whenever he has decisions to make or is considering new ideas, he will find those around him glad to offer advice as well as give assistance in ways he might not have anticipated.

The Rabbit will also be pleased with some of the plans he carries out on his home over the year and here again his sense of style will be to the fore. Whether he is choosing new items or furnishings for his home, altering the layout of rooms or carrying out other home projects, he will be satisfied with what he is able to achieve. His knack of finding useful items to enhance the home will also prove valuable and during the year many Rabbits will delight in the treasures, souvenirs or more aesthetic items they acquire for their home.

This will also be an encouraging year as far as the Rabbit's work is concerned and he will be able to make good use of his strengths. Those Rabbits already established in their career will often have the chance to take on greater responsibilities and make more satisfying use of their skills, while those who would welcome fresh challenges will find this a year of interesting possibilities. By remaining alert for openings that interest them and would help to advance their career, these Rabbits can make important progress in their overall career development. April, May, September and November could see some interesting opportunities.

Those Rabbits seeking work should also make the most of any chances they are given. Even though these may sometimes be different from what they were considering, by making the most of their situation and showing commitment, many could soon find other possibilities opening up. Events in the Pig year can go in the Rabbit's favour and prove a useful stepping-stone to further progress. For those Rabbits engaged in or interested in the creative arts, this too is a year to promote their talents. The Pig year does favour creativity and the Rabbit's often innovative approach can be recognized and well rewarded.

Although the Rabbit's progress and success will often lead to a rise in income, he will need to remain his careful self when dealing with money matters. With his existing commitments and the plans he wants to carry out, his spending will sometimes be considerable, and without some watchfulness, his outgoings could creep up and be greater than he anticipated. Also, if he should have any misgivings over any transaction or important form he may be required to complete, it is important that he seeks advice. Where financial or bureaucratic matters are concerned, this is a year for care and vigilance.

In most respects, though, this will be a pleasing year for the Rabbit. In his work he will have the chance to make greater use of his strengths and what he achieves now will often be useful in the longer term. On a personal level, this will be a year when he will truly value the good relations he has with so many, and for some Rabbits, particularly the unattached, there could be celebrations in store. Overall, the Pig year certainly holds good prospects for the Rabbit and in true Rabbit style he will often make the most of the opportunities and pleasures it will bring.

The Metal Rabbit

This will be an interesting year for the Metal Rabbit, with many of his plans and activities working out well.

In view of the changes many Metal Rabbits will have seen in their work in recent years, many will be content to remain where they are and concentrate on duties they perform so well. For these Metal Rabbits, their work will often bring them much personal satisfaction. In addition, through their seniority and expertise, some may take on a more supervisory role, mentoring and training junior colleagues, and they will often find this another enjoyable and worthwhile aspect of their work.

For those Metal Rabbits who would welcome the chance to take on new challenges or are seeking work, this can also be an encouraging year. By making enquiries, including talking to contacts, friends and employment agencies, many will be alerted to possibilities worth following up. With initiative and persistence, the Pig year will see many of these Metal Rabbits taking on a new position which will give them the chance to both use and extend their skills. For work opportunities and developments, April to early June, September and November are particularly favourable times.

Whether the Metal Rabbit remains where he is or changes his work over the year he will find his ability to enjoy good working relations with others a great asset. And many colleagues and associates will value his judgement and support.

Many Metal Rabbits are also blessed with a creative streak and those whose work involves the creation of ideas or communication or presentation should make the most of their talents. Over the year they can look forward to some heartening successes. This is very much a time to use their talents to advantage and to promote what they do.

In addition to the positive aspects concerning the Metal Rabbit's work, his personal interests are also favoured. Again those Metal Rabbits who take pleasure in more creative and expressive pursuits should aim to develop their skills, perhaps by setting themselves new projects. Some may also consider taking up something different over the year, feeling the time is now right for a new personal challenge, and if they can encourage a loved one or friend to join them, this can often add to the pleasure.

Many Metal Rabbits will also be attracted to outdoor pursuits, and whether this involves following a particular sport, gardening or travelling, they will again enjoy what they do as well as the social element many of their activities will bring.

However, with all the Metal Rabbit's activities, commitments and family expenses, as well as the purchases he will be keen to make (particularly for his home), his outgoings will be fairly considerable over the year. Although he is usually careful in money matters, this is very much a time for careful budgeting. Setting funds aside for future requirements will often help, and if the Metal Rabbit is able to use any increase in income to reduce borrowings and interest payments, this can also be to his advantage. In the Pig year he does need to manage his resources carefully and keep a watch on his spending levels. Also, when entering into any agreement, it is important that he checks the terms and obligations carefully. Where money matters are concerned, this is a year to remain vigilant and to avoid risks or complacency. Metal Rabbits, do take note.

More positively, the Metal Rabbit can look forward to an often lively home life during the Pig year. By spending time with his loved ones and carrying out plans and projects with them, he will often find his home life particularly rewarding. He will also do much to help and advise both younger and more senior relations during the year and here his good judgement and caring nature will mean a great deal. When difficulties and pressures arise, as they do in any year, his ability to deal tactfully with differing viewpoints will also count for a lot. As far as the Metal Rabbit's home life is concerned, this will be an active and pleasing year.

The Metal Rabbit will also find himself in demand on a social level, with many invitations to go out. For those Metal Rabbits who enjoy going to concerts, the cinema or the theatre, the Pig year will bring some memorable events. And with the aspects as they are, unattached Metal Rabbits or those who would welcome a more fulfilling social life can see a great improvement in their situation over the Pig year. Where the Metal Rabbit's relations with others are concerned, this is a particularly favourable year. For socializing, May, June, August and the period from mid-November to December will be the most active times.

The Pig year certainly holds encouraging prospects for the Metal Rabbit and by making the most of his talents and the opportunities that the year will bring, he can make this a successful and satisfying time.

TIP FOR THE YEAR
With the aspects on your side, this is a year to act upon your aims and make the most of your strengths. By doing so, you will reap some fine and deserved rewards.

The Water Rabbit

This will be a satisfying year for the Water Rabbit, particularly as it will allow him to build on his strengths. However, to do well, he does need to concentrate on the areas he knows well rather than take risks or venture into less familiar territory.

In his work this will be a year of steady rather than spectacular progress. However, by setting about his duties in his usual committed and conscientious way, the Water Rabbit will not only achieve some impressive results but also do his prospects much good. Also, whenever opportunities do arise, he should act smartly. Anything he can do to develop his skills, whether through taking up the chance of additional training or taking on other responsibilities, can be to his future benefit. It is very much a case of building steadily on his current situation, with his efforts leading to rewards later on, especially in the closing months of the Pig year.

Throughout the year the Water Rabbit will be helped by his ability to relate well with others and whether this involves working as part of a team, building up new contacts or putting forward ideas, by using his strengths to advantage he will again lay the groundwork for future success. Those Water Rabbits whose work involves communication or allows them to draw on their ideas and creative talents should aim to promote their skills. They will not only impress others but could also find interesting possibilities opening up as a result.

For those Water Rabbits who are particularly anxious to move on from their present position or are seeking work, the Pig year can bring some interesting opportunities. However, to do well, these Water Rabbits should aim for positions which draw on their existing experience rather than look to make major changes. In their quest they would also find it helpful to draw on the support and advice available to them rather than remaining isolated or acting too independently. Talking to colleagues and contacts, contacting employment agencies and taking advantage of training or refresher courses can all be to their benefit. Results and progress *will* need to be worked for in the Pig year, but with his experience, drive and personal qualities, the Water Rabbit has a lot in his favour. By remaining persistent, many will succeed in gaining a new position which will allow them to both use and develop their skills. Work opportunities are particularly likely to arise in April, May, September and November 2007 and January 2008.

As with all Rabbits, though, the Water Rabbit will need to be careful in money matters during the Pig year. With all his commitments and plans, his outgoings will need careful control and at times it would be prudent for him to keep a tight control on his purse-strings rather than be tempted by impulse buys. If he can make early provision for some of his larger outgoings, including travel and accommodation, he could find this helpful. Fortunately the Water Rabbit is usually careful in money matters, but this is very much a year when good management and control can make a noticeable difference.

The Pig year is more positively aspected as far as the Water Rabbit's relations with others are concerned and he will find himself much in demand.

In his domestic life he will do much to encourage loved ones and his interest and support will often be much appreciated. Although the Water Rabbit will have many demands on his time, by ensuring time is set aside to spend with others and on general family activities, he can make his home life all the more rewarding. Domestically, this can be a fine and meaningful year.

The positive aspects also extend to the Water Rabbit's social life and he can look forward to going to an often wide variety of events. There will be good opportunities for him to add to his social circle, and for the unattached, affairs of the heart are especially well aspected, with many finding love over the year. Again, with the Water Rabbit's fine personal qualities and the positive aspects that prevail, the Pig year can be a happy time. March, June, August and December will be the busiest and most eventful months socially.

The Water Rabbit will also derive much pleasure from his personal interests, especially any that take him out of doors or allow him to draw on his more creative talents. In addition, if he is sedentary for much of the day he could find it helpful to give some consideration to his well-being. Some medical advice on suitable exercise to take and, if appropriate, modifications to his diet could be to his benefit

In so many respects this will be a positive and encouraging year for the Water Rabbit and by making the most of his personal strengths he will be satisfied with the progress he makes. This may not be a year for dramatic breakthroughs, but it can be a fulfilling one. And personally, the love, friendship and support he will enjoy will mean a lot to the Water Rabbit. The Pig year can certainly bring him some special times.

TIP FOR THE YEAR
Further your knowledge and expertise. What you learn during the Pig year can have long-term value. In addition, make the most of your chances to meet others. Again, contacts made now can be important in the future.

The Wood Rabbit

This will be a year of important developments for the Wood Rabbit, although to benefit he will need to take positive action. As the proverb reminds us, 'Nothing ventured, nothing gained.' This is very much a year for the Wood Rabbit to venture.

The Wood Rabbit will be encouraged by the support he receives from those around him and whenever he is considering an idea or perhaps making plans, he would do well to talk things over with those who have the knowledge and experience to advise. By being forthcoming and listening to what others say, he will not only benefit from their guidance but could find that just by mentioning certain ideas he can set important wheels in motion. In the Pig year, the input of others can make a real difference to how the Wood Rabbit fares.

In addition to the helpfulness of others, the Wood Rabbit will value the good relations he enjoys with so many. Domestically, this can be an especially pleasing year, and by spending time with his loved ones and encouraging joint activities and pursuits, the Wood Rabbit will find his home life meaning a great deal to him. Also, by assisting his loved ones, whether his partner or younger or more senior relations, he can do much to help the rapport and understanding he shares with those close to him. Whenever any pressures or tensions arise, as they do in any year, by being willing to address them, the Wood Rabbit can often help to ease them. Positive input and a willingness to act will help him (and others) a lot.

Although the Wood Rabbit will be kept fairly busy over the year, he may well spend some time carrying out home improvements, particularly adding new furnishings and other features. However, while he will be pleased with what he accomplishes, he should be careful not to rush decisions or hurry plans just to get them completed. More time spent considering, discussing and selecting purchases will often lead to better decisions – and better value too. In addition, if tackling any difficult or strenuous tasks himself it is important that the Wood Rabbit takes care and follows all the safety procedures, otherwise accidents or mishaps could result. If in doubt, he should obtain help or ask a professional. Wood Rabbits, do take careful note.

The Wood Rabbit would also do well to consider taking a holiday with his loved ones over the year. Discovering new areas together can lead to a good deal of fun.

This will also be a positive year as far as the Wood Rabbit's social life is concerned, and despite the many demands on his time he should try to keep in regular contact with his friends as well as go to any social occasions or events that appeal to him. Not only can his social life be a source of pleasure, but it can also help keep his lifestyle in balance. And with the prevailing aspects, any Wood Rabbits who may desire more companionship or perhaps romance will find this a year of wonderful opportunity. By going out and involving themselves in new activities, these Wood Rabbits will not only enjoy a more fulfilling social life but can also make important new friends and even find new love. The Pig year is a particularly good one for relations with others, with March, June, August and December being especially favourable.

As far as the Wood Rabbit's work prospects are concerned, this is a year of steady progress. Many Wood Rabbits will be keen to build on their present position rather than make major changes. By putting themselves forward whenever suitable openings become available, however, they will often have the chance to take on greater responsibilities as well as gain further (often invaluable) experience. This is also very much a year when the Wood Rabbit should make the most of his creative talents. Once again, by being active and venturing, he will find success can often result.

Those Wood Rabbits seeking work will find, however, that their quest will often demand a lot of them. With competition sometimes high and positions limited, the job-seeking process could at times be disheartening. However, these Wood Rabbits should remember that one of the positive features of the Pig year is the effect the input of others can have, and by contacting those who are able to give informed advice or who may know of possible openings, they can do much to help their situation. Once they do succeed in gaining a position, they may well find it is a useful platform to build on. As all Wood Rabbits will find, results will need to be worked for, but what is achieved now can have important long-term value. April, May and the period from September to November could see some interesting developments workwise.

Although many Wood Rabbits will enjoy an increase in income over the year, this is, however, still a time for financial prudence and the Wood Rabbit would do well to keep track of his outgoings and budget carefully. As some of his purchases and plans will involve much outlay, he needs to be especially careful if taking on new loans and should check the terms and obligations of any agreement carefully. This is very much a year for vigilance and good financial management.

In most respects this will be a pleasing year for the Wood Rabbit. In his work the prospects are encouraging and by putting himself forward and making the most of his strengths, he can make useful headway as well as gain experience which will be helpful to him both now and in the future. However, the real plus of the year will be his relations with others, with the love, friendship, support and advice he receives making a real difference to his life. On a personal level, this can be a happy and meaningful year.

TIP FOR THE YEAR

Draw on the support of others. Consult, ask, talk – the more you contact others, the more help you will get. And that way important developments can be set in motion.

The Fire Rabbit

This year marks the start of a new decade in the Fire Rabbit's life and as he enters his twenties he will certainly have many hopes and plans for the decade ahead. With his keen nature, strengths and many fine personal qualities, he knows he has it within him to accomplish many things. Fire as his element helps to reinforce the more active and determined side of his nature, and in the Pig year he will fare well. While his actual progress may not always meet his (high) expectations, the experience he gains now can have great long-term value. Also, his personal life will flourish, helping to make his twentieth year both an interesting and exciting one.

The Pig year very much favours affairs of the heart and for many Fire Rabbits romance will play a big part during the year. Those currently enjoying the love of another could find their relationship becoming more meaningful, while those who are unattached may be hit by Cupid's arrow at almost any moment. For many this will be a year of romance and one they will thoroughly enjoy. March, June, August and the months from mid-November to mid-January could be the busiest months socially, but such are the aspects that the Fire Rabbit will nearly always have something happening. And while sometimes the path of true love may not always run smoothly, with some romances floundering, with the aspects as positive as they are, new relationships could quickly take their place. On a personal level this really is a special and often happy time.

The Fire Rabbit will also value the companionship of his close circle of friends over the year and their support can be another pleasing aspect of his life. For those Fire Rabbits who move, whether for work or education, there will be chances to build up a new social circle and the year could see quite a transformation in their situation.

The Fire Rabbit will also get much pleasure from his personal interests over the year and by furthering his knowledge and skills he will often find his interests becoming more meaningful to him. Those Fire Rabbits who have thoughts of turning an interest or skill into a vocation will find that the knowledge they acquire and practice they put in over the year can serve them well in the future. Again, the lessons and legacy of the Pig year can be far-reaching.

For those Fire Rabbits who are involved in education this can also be a significant year, and by concentrating on what they need to do and remaining disciplined in their approach, many will achieve the results they have been hoping for. However, as all Rabbits will find, this is a year which rewards commitment, and should the Fire Rabbit be tempted to slack or become complacent, this could affect his more immediate prospects. Fire Rabbits, do take note and do not waste current opportunities.

For those Fire Rabbits in work this will be an important year. Although some may feel disenchanted by the routine nature of what they are currently doing, by showing commitment and being prepared to put in the effort many will find their attitude leading to more rewarding responsibilities. This is a year for making the most of their situation, even though they may not consider it ideal. The Fire Rabbit is still at an early stage in his career and what he learns now can be a necessary and important stage in his development.

For those Fire Rabbits seeking work the Pig year can offer the opportunity they want, but again they will need to remain persistent as well as show the determined side of their Fire Rabbit nature. Progress in the Pig year *will* need to be worked for. Similarly, once the Fire Rabbit is offered a chance, he does need to make the most of it. Again, however, progress made now can be significant in the future.

As far as financial matters are concerned, this is a year for care and watchfulness. With his various activities and often busy social life the Fire Rabbit's spending will often be high and he would do well to keep track of his outgoings and manage his finances carefully. While he may be keen to supplement his earnings, he also needs to be wary of getting involved in any 'get rich quick' schemes or taking unnecessary risks. The Pig year can trip up the unwary and is a time for careful financial management. Fire Rabbits, do take note.

One expense many Fire Rabbits will have over the year will be travel. While these Fire Rabbits will often thoroughly enjoy their time away – including the social opportunities their travels can bring – wherever possible they should try to save up in advance for any travel plans. Also, by managing their resources carefully, they will often get to do more while away.

In many respects this will be a pleasing year for the Fire Rabbit. His personal life is especially well aspected, and with good prospects of friendship and romance, he will often greatly enjoy himself. Also, if he is prepared to put in the effort in his work or study, what he accomplishes now can be an important factor in his future success.

TIP FOR THE YEAR
Work hard. The effort you put in now and the experience (and qualifications) you gain can be far-reaching. Also, do draw on the help and advice that is available to you. This too can make a difference in how you fare.

The Earth Rabbit

This will be a special year for the Earth Rabbit and, with his genial nature and wide interests, he will find himself much in demand.

In the Earth Rabbit's family life there could be several good causes for celebration, including a possible marriage or the birth of a great-grandchild. During the year, the Earth Rabbit will follow the progress of family members with keen interest and, in some cases, be pleased to assist any who may be under time pressure or facing key decisions. Here his good advice and listening ear will be appreciated.

In addition the Earth Rabbit will enjoy the various activities he can share with his loved ones. Whether these involve pursuing mutual interests, travelling or undertaking projects in the home or garden, by liaising with others, he will find what is accomplished can be satisfying to all concerned. The emphasis during the year is very much on sharing, planning and doing things together rather than acting too independently.

In this regard, those Earth Rabbits who may be alone will value the very good friends they have, and by meeting up regularly and sharing thoughts, activities and interests, they will find the support of others will often give added meaning to the year. The aspects are also encouraging for those who would welcome new friends and a more active social life. By taking up new interests, enrolling in classes or on courses or joining societies or interest groups, they may well meet others whose company they will especially appreciate. The initiative rests with the Earth Rabbit himself, but with the aspects as they are, positive action can often lead to some new and sometimes special friendships, as well as an enriched social life. As far as the Earth Rabbit's relations with others are concerned, this is a positive and encouraging time.

The aspects are also favourable for travel and the Earth Rabbit should take up any invitations he may have to visit family and friends as well as take advantage of any special offers that appeal to him. If there is a particular place that he would like to visit (or revisit), again he would do well to discuss this with others. There could also be travel surprises in store for some Earth Rabbits, with opportunities to go away at short notice.

Another aspect of the year that the Earth Rabbit will appreciate is in the way he is able to use his more creative talents. Those Earth Rabbits who have interests that allow them to express themselves in some way, whether through writing, art, photography or another form, will find their activities a source of great personal pleasure.

As with all Rabbits, though, the Earth Rabbit will need be careful when dealing with money matters. When considering any major purchase or transaction, he would do well to take the time to check various options rather than act too hastily. Impulse buys could be regretted later. Also, when dealing with paperwork, the Earth Rabbit needs to be thorough and check up on anything that is unclear. Without extra attention, mistakes or oversights could be made which could be to his detriment. Earth Rabbits, do take note. In addition if the Earth Rabbit is worried over any matter, whether financial or otherwise, he would do well to seek the advice of those in a position to help. With expert guidance, any worries can often be eased. However, the Earth Rabbit should remember that help is there should he need it.

Overall, the aspects are encouraging for the Earth Rabbit and his family, social life and interests will bring him much pleasure. The year will contain many rewarding moments and possibly celebrations too.

TIP FOR THE YEAR

If there are any ideas you are keen to put into practice, do discuss them with others. This is very much a year when the support you receive can make a difference to what you are able to do.

FAMOUS RABBITS

Bertie Ahern, Margaret Atwood, Drew Barrymore, David Beckham, Harry Belafonte, Pope Benedict XVI, Ingrid Bergman, St Bernadette, Jeff Bezos, Gordon Brown, James Caan, Nicolas Cage, Lewis Carroll, Fidel Castro, John Cleese, Confucius, Marie Curie, Johnny Depp, Albert Einstein, George Eliot, W. C. Fields, James Fox, Sir David Frost, Cary Grant, Edvard Grieg, Oliver Hardy, Seamus Heaney, Tommy Hilfiger, John Howard, Bob Hope, Whitney Houston, Helen Hunt, John Hurt, Anjelica Huston, Chrissie Hynde, Enrique Inglesias, Clive James, Henry James, Sir David Jason, Angelina Jolie, Michael Jordan, Michael Keaton, John Keats, Lisa Kudrow, Danny La Rue, Cheryl Ladd, Gina Lollobrigida, George Michael, Colin Montgomerie, Sir Roger Moore, Andrew Murray, Mike Myers, Brigitte Nielsen, Graham Norton, Jamie Oliver, George Orwell, Edith Piaf, Sidney Poitier, Romano Prodi, Ken Russell, Mort Sahl, Elisabeth Schwarzkopf, Neil Sedaka, Jane Seymour, Maria Sharapova, Neil Simon, Frank Sinatra, Sting, Quentin Tarantino, J. R. R. Tolkien, Tina Turner, Luther Vandross, Queen Victoria, Muddy Waters, Orson Welles, Walt Whitman, Robin Williams, Kate Winslet, Tiger Woods.

3 FEBRUARY 1916 ～ 22 JANUARY 1917		*Fire Dragon*
23 JANUARY 1928 ～ 9 FEBRUARY 1929		*Earth Dragon*
8 FEBRUARY 1940 ～ 26 JANUARY 1941		*Metal Dragon*
27 JANUARY 1952 ～ 13 FEBRUARY 1953		*Water Dragon*
13 FEBRUARY 1964 ～ 1 FEBRUARY 1965		*Wood Dragon*
31 JANUARY 1976 ～ 17 FEBRUARY 1977		*Fire Dragon*
17 FEBRUARY 1988 ～ 5 FEBRUARY 1989		*Earth Dragon*
5 FEBRUARY 2000 ～ 23 JANUARY 2001		*Metal Dragon*

THE
DRAGON

THE PERSONALITY OF THE DRAGON

'Formula of my happiness: a yes, a no, a straight line, a goal …'

Friedrich Nietzsche, a Dragon

The Dragon is born under the sign of luck. He is a proud and lively character and has a tremendous amount of self-confidence. He is also highly intelligent and very quick to take advantage of any opportunities. He is ambitious and determined and will do well in practically anything he attempts. He is also something of a perfectionist and will always try to maintain the high standards he sets himself.

The Dragon does not suffer fools gladly and will be quick to criticize anyone or anything that displeases him. He can be blunt and forthright in his views and is certainly not renowned for being either tactful or diplomatic. He does, however, often take people at their word and can occasionally be rather gullible. If he ever feels that his trust has been abused or his dignity wounded, he can sometimes become very bitter and it will take him a long time to forgive and forget.

The Dragon is usually very outgoing and is particularly adept at attracting attention and publicity. He enjoys being in the limelight and is often at his best when he is confronted by a difficult problem or tense situation. In some respects he is a showman and he rarely lacks an audience. His views are highly valued and he invariably has something interesting – and sometimes controversial – to say.

He has considerable energy and is often prepared to work long and unsocial hours in order to achieve what he wants. He can, however, be rather impulsive and does not always consider the consequences of his actions. He also has a tendency to live for the moment and there is nothing that riles him more than to be kept waiting. The Dragon hates delay and can get extremely impatient and irritable over even the smallest of hold-ups.

The Dragon has an enormous faith in his abilities, but he does run the risk of becoming over-confident and unless he is careful he can sometimes make grave errors of judgement. While this may prove disastrous at the time, he does have the tenacity and ability to bounce back and pick up the pieces again.

The Dragon has such an assertive personality, so much willpower and such a desire to succeed that he will often reach the top of his chosen profession. He has considerable leadership qualities and will do well in positions where he can put his own ideas and policies into practice. He is usually successful in politics, show business, as the manager of his own department or business, and in any job which brings him into contact with the media.

The Dragon relies a tremendous amount on his own judgement and can be scornful of other people's advice. He likes to feel self-sufficient and there are many Dragons who cherish their independence to such a degree that they prefer to remain single throughout their lives. However, the Dragon will often have numerous admirers and many will be attracted by his flamboyant personality and striking looks. If he does marry, he will usually marry young, and will find himself particularly well suited to those born under the signs of the Snake, Rat, Monkey and Rooster. He will also find that the Rabbit, Pig, Horse and Goat make ideal companions and will readily join in with many of his escapades. Two Dragons will also get on well together, as they understand each other, but the Dragon may not find things so easy with the Ox and Dog, as both will be critical of his impulsive and somewhat extrovert manner. He will also find it difficult to form an alliance with the Tiger, for the Tiger, like the Dragon, tends to speak his mind, is very strong-willed and likes to take the lead.

The female Dragon knows what she wants in life and sets about everything she does in a determined and positive manner. No job is too small for her and she is often prepared to work extremely hard to secure her objective. She is immensely practical and somewhat liberated. She hates being bound by routine and petty restrictions and likes to have sufficient freedom to be able to go off and do what she wants to do. She will keep her house tidy, but is not one for spending hours on housework – there are far too many other things that she prefers to do. Like her male counterpart, she has a tendency to speak her mind.

The Dragon usually has many interests and enjoys sport and other outdoor activities. He also likes to travel and often prefers to visit places that are off the beaten track rather than head for popular tourist attractions. He has a very adventurous streak in him and providing his financial circumstances permit – and the Dragon is usually sensible with his money – he will travel considerable distances during his lifetime.

The Dragon is a very flamboyant character and while he can be demanding of others and in his early years rather precocious, he will have many friends and will nearly always be the centre of attention. He has charisma and so much confidence that he can often become a source of inspiration to others. In China he is the leader of the carnival and he is also blessed with an inordinate share of luck.

THE FIVE DIFFERENT TYPES OF DRAGON

In addition to the 12 signs of the Chinese zodiac there are five elements and these have a strengthening or moderating influence on the sign. The effects of the five elements on the Dragon are described below, together with the years in which the elements were exercising their influence. Therefore those Dragons born in 1940 and 2000 are Metal Dragons, those born in 1952 are Water Dragons, and so on.

Metal Dragon: 1940, 2000
This Dragon is very strong-willed and has a particularly forceful personality. He is energetic, ambitious and tries to be scrupulous in his dealings with others. He can also be blunt and to the point and usually has no hesitation in speaking his mind. If people disagree with him or are not prepared to co-operate, he is more than happy to go his own way. The Metal Dragon usually has very high moral values and is held in great esteem by his friends and colleagues.

Water Dragon: 1952

This Dragon is friendly, easy-going and intelligent. He is quick-witted and rarely lets an opportunity slip by. However, he is not as impatient as some of the other types of Dragon and is prepared to wait for results rather than expect everything to happen at once. He has an understanding nature and is prepared to share his ideas and co-operate with others. His main failing is a tendency to jump from one thing to another rather than concentrate on the job in hand. He has a good sense of humour and is an effective speaker.

Wood Dragon: 1964

The Wood Dragon is practical, imaginative and inquisitive. He loves delving into all manner of subjects and can quite often come up with some highly original ideas. He is a thinker and a doer and he has the drive and commitment to put many of his ideas into practice. He is more diplomatic than some of the other types of Dragon and has a good sense of humour. He is very astute in business matters and can also be most generous.

Fire Dragon: 1916, 1976

This Dragon is ambitious, articulate and has a tremendous desire to succeed. He is a hard and conscientious worker and is often admired for his integrity and forthright nature. He is very strong-willed and has considerable leadership qualities. He can, however, rely a bit too much on his own judgement and fail to take into account the views and feelings of others. He can also be rather aloof and it would certainly be in his own interests to let others join in more with his various activities. The Fire Dragon usually enjoys music, literature and the arts.

Earth Dragon: 1928, 1988

The Earth Dragon tends to be quieter and more reflective than some of the other types of Dragon. He has a wide variety of interests and is keenly aware of what is going on around him. He also has clear objectives and usually has no problems in obtaining support and backing for any of his ventures. He is very astute in financial matters and is often able to accumulate considerable wealth. He is a good organizer, although he can at times be rather bureaucratic and fussy. He mixes well with others and has a large circle of friends.

PROSPECTS FOR THE DRAGON IN 2007

The Year of the Dog (29 January 2006 to 17 February 2007) can be a demanding one for the Dragon and in the remaining months he will need to proceed with care and caution.

One of the trickier areas concerns his relations with others, and in the remaining Dog months the Dragon will need to take careful note of the views and feelings of his family, friends and colleagues. This is no time for him to adopt too independent an approach. Also, despite his many commitments, he should make sure he devotes time to those who are special to him. To remain continually occupied or appear inattentive could lead to disagreements. Dragons, do take note – the closing months of the Dog year may bring some happy times, but care is still needed.

More positively, there could be some good travel opportunities as the year draws to a close and the Dragon will often enjoy going away, whether he is visiting others or taking a holiday. He will also benefit from the rest and change.

In his work the Dragon should aim to make good use of his experience as well as take advantage of any opportunities to extend his knowledge and skills. With the encouraging aspects that await in the following Pig year, good work now can help his prospects considerably.

Generally, the Dog year is a time for care and mindfulness, especially with regard to others. However, with the approach of the Pig year, many Dragons will sense their prospects are on the upturn and will look forward to the new Chinese year with optimism, determined to really make the most of the next 12 months.

The Year of the Pig begins on 18 February and almost immediately it will herald an upturn in the Dragon's fortunes. This is a year of considerable promise.

In view of the improved aspects, those Dragons who may start 2007 in low spirits should draw a firm line under the past and look to move on. Indeed, for many, the dawning of the Pig year will mark the opening of an exciting chapter in their life.

The aspects are especially encouraging as far as the Dragon's work is concerned, and with his enterprise and drive, he is destined to achieve a lot over the year. If his more recent progress has disappointed him or his present situation leaves him unfulfilled, he should not be discouraged. This is a year for moving forward, and by making the decision to do something positive, very soon he will find the wheels of fortune moving in his favour. This is a time when the Dragon should seize the initiative, make enquiries and follow up any openings that interest him. Even though there may be disappointments along the way, with persistence, backed by the reputation and experience he has built up, he will find that doors *will* open for him. Over the year many Dragons will succeed in obtaining a position which can mark a new and important stage in their career, whether through promotion or through taking their career in a new direction.

For those Dragons seeking work, either as the Pig year begins or during it, this is an excellent time to give serious thought to what it is they really want to do. By making enquiries and seeking the advice of professional organizations, they will not only be given useful information but also alerted to new possibilities worth considering. In addition, some could find it helpful to consider training or refresher courses. Again, by taking positive action these Dragons will be helping both their present situation and future prospects. In this favourable year, effort and initiative can certainly pay off.

The months from February to April could bring some excellent work opportunities, and with the aspects as encouraging as they are, progress made in the first half of the year could lead to other possibilities later in 2007. This is very much a time for the Dragon to use his skills, talents and opportunities to advance his career.

The aspects are also positive as far as the Dragon's financial situation is concerned, with many Dragons enjoying an improvement in their situation during the year. In addition to an increase in income, some could benefit from an interest they have, additional work they do or a bonus or gift they receive. Financially, this is an encouraging year and the Dragon could find it helpful to consider reducing any borrowings he may have and making some savings for the longer term as well as setting money aside for forthcoming plans and activities. By managing his finances well, rather than proceeding on too much of an ad hoc basis, he can make a real difference to his financial situation over the year.

The Dragon should also make the most of the travel opportunities that the year will bring and if there is a particular area he is keen to visit, he should make enquiries and follow this up. Not only can he visit some particularly interesting destinations over the year but he will also enjoy some of the activities he may try out while away, as well as the chance to just relax. While most Dragons enjoy travel, those who are less inclined to go away may well enjoy setting aside time to visit places in their own area.

Although the Dragon will have many demands on his time, it is also important that he does not allow his recreational pursuits to suffer. Making time for activities he enjoys will not only help him to lead a more balanced lifestyle but can sometimes give him the chance to get additional exercise or enjoy the social elements his interests can bring. In this full and busy year, recreational pursuits can bring a variety of benefits.

The Dragon's domestic and social life will also benefit from the improved aspects of the Pig year. In his home life the Dragon will often find himself at the centre of activity, both helping those close to him and arranging many of the activities that take place. Sharing activities and discussing ideas, rather than setting about plans too independently, will lead to better rapport and understanding and also result in more being achieved. Similarly, if any differences of opinion or problems arise, as they do in any year, by being willing to address these and talk them over, the Dragon can find his input of great benefit to all concerned. Domestically, this will be a generally rewarding year and some of the family occasions and successes can give an added lift to the year.

The Dragon's social life will also see much activity, and in addition to regularly meeting up with his friends, he could have social opportunities connected with his work or interests. On a personal level, he will find himself in demand, with April, June, August and December being the busiest months. Also, as a result of some of the changes that occur over the year, whether in the Dragon's work or due to some new activities he has taken up, he will often have the chance to widen his social circle. The aspects are also encouraging for those Dragons who may start the Pig year in low spirits. The Pig year *is* a time for moving forward, and by going out and remaining active, these Dragons will find this a good year for meeting others, making new friends and, importantly, enjoying a happier and more fulfilling personal life. In the Pig year the aspects are firmly on the Dragon's side.

There is a Chinese proverb which reminds us 'Diligence leads to riches.' In 2007 this will be very true for the Dragon and by using his time, talents and opportunities well, his efforts and enterprise will often be recognized and rewarded. This is a particularly favourable year for him.

The Metal Dragon

The Pig year holds encouraging prospects for the Metal Dragon, although to get the best from it he will need to decide on what he wants to do and then act on his ideas. If he sets about his activities in his usual keen and earnest way, however, he will not only accomplish a great deal but enjoy the year as well.

Many Metal Dragons have a practical side to their nature and over the year the Metal Dragon will often busy himself with projects on his home and, if he has one, garden. If he has a clear idea of what he wants to do, he will be satisfied with how much he is able to get done and pleased by the benefits that follow. In addition some Metal Dragons may decide to mount an efficiency drive and sort through accumulated items and papers and so rid themselves of things they no longer need or are required to keep. As a result the Metal Dragon will again be pleased with what is accomplished as well as with how much neater and better organized certain areas have become. In addition, in their sorting many Metal Dragons could find items of personal value they did not realize they had.

The Metal Dragon will also derive much pleasure from his personal interests during the year and by furthering his knowledge or giving himself a satisfying project to do, he can make these all the more fulfilling. In addition, some interests could have a good social element and by meeting other enthusiasts or joining a local group or society, the Metal Dragon will often have the opportunity to widen his social circle. If there is a new interest that appeals to him or a certain skill he feels it may be useful to acquire (including computer or software-related skills), he should follow this up. Something he starts during the year could become an absorbing new interest and allow him to discover strengths he never realized he had. In this respect, too, this is a year for acting on ideas.

The Pig year will also bring some splendid travel opportunities and several times over the year the Metal Dragon could be tempted by travel offers or decide to take a break at short notice. He could also receive invitations to visit family and friends living some distance away. By taking up his invitations and following up his ideas, he will often enjoy his travels, and they could have some good social opportunities too.

As far as the Metal Dragon's home life is concerned, some memorable occasions will be in store, particularly as younger relations celebrate certain achievements or good personal news. By following the activities of those who are special to him and helping whenever possible, the Metal Dragon will find his family life meaning a great deal to him. He will also appreciate the support he is given for many of his own activities, although to achieve all he wants, he does need to consult those around him and listen to their views. The more he involves others, the more smoothly many of his activities will go, and as someone who can at times be independent-minded, this is something he would do well to bear in mind!

The Metal Dragon's social life is also encouragingly aspected and he will often have the chance to go out and enjoy the company of others. In addition some Metal Dragons may decide to give some of their free time to helping with a charitable cause or community activity. With his ideas, broad interests and many friends and acquaintances, the Metal Dragon will have a full social life, and new friendships can add much to the year. April, June, August and December will see the most social activity.

While so much can go well, no year is without its problems, however, and 2007 will be no exception. When problems or differences of opinion do arise, the Metal Dragon does need to deal with them swiftly, otherwise there is a risk that what started in a trivial and minor way could suddenly escalate and prove an unwelcome distraction. In certain situations, too, the Metal Dragon should be wary of appearing stubborn. Such an attitude could lead to difficulties, whereas a greater flexibility on his part could be to the advantage of all. The strong-minded Metal Dragon should take note!

Also, while the Pig year is generally positive for financial matters, the Metal Dragon does need to be thorough when completing any financially-related forms or entering into any agreements. This is a year to study the small print and avoid unnecessary haste.

In so many respects this will, though, be a fine year for the Metal Dragon, and by seeking the support of others and acting upon his ideas, he will often enjoy the wide-ranging nature of his accomplishments.

TIP FOR THE YEAR

Set yourself a challenge, something you will enjoy and feel is worthwhile. It could be learning a skill, taking up a new interest or something else that you feel has value, but a specific and purposeful activity can bring much personal satisfaction.

The Water Dragon

In recent years the Water Dragon will have undertaken a great deal, but while he will have enjoyed some success, there will also have been occasions when the results of his efforts will have fallen short of what he was hoping for and left him dispirited and unfulfilled. However, his prospects in the Pig year are far more promising and as the new Chinese year starts he can look forward to a distinct improvement in his fortunes.

In his work this is a year of change and progress. For those Water Dragons who may have been in the same position for some time, this is a year to seek out new challenges. Some, as a result of their considerable knowledge, will be well placed to take on greater responsibilities in their present place of work, while others will decide to further their skills in other ways. The Pig year can present these Water Dragons with some excellent opportunities as well as reward them for their previous commitment and good work. Also, despite the pressure that taking up new responsibilities can bring, the Water Dragon will often revel in his new duties and the events of the year will help to give his career new impetus. From the beginning of the Pig year to April will be a good time for work developments, and September and October could also see some good opportunities.

The prospects are also encouraging for those Water Dragons seeking work. In recent times some will have become disillusioned with their situation, but this is a year which will give many the chance they have been wanting for some time. These Water Dragons would do well to register with various employment agencies, talk to those in a position to advise and actively pursue vacancies that interest them. By seizing the initiative and showing the tenacious side of their Water Dragon character, many will be successful in gaining a position in which they can both use *and* extend their skills. As far as the Water Dragon's work prospects are concerned, this is an encouraging year which will bring fresh challenges and allow him to use his talents.

The progress that the Water Dragon makes in his work will also lead to an increase in income, and financially, the Water Dragon's prospects are promising. Some Water Dragons may even be able to supplement their earnings through some extra work. This is very much a year when the Water Dragon's enterprise and good work will be recognized and often well reimbursed. However, to benefit from this the Water Dragon does need to manage his finances with care and should consider setting some funds aside for the future. By using his money wisely, he will not only benefit in the short term but can, with any long-term savings or pension contributions he makes, reap the rewards of his actions in years to come.

One major outlay many Water Dragons will have over the year will be home improvements. Although the Water Dragon may be keen for these to go ahead, he would benefit from taking the time to consider the various options available and to look at the costs involved. Where major projects are concerned, too much haste could lead to problems and possible regrets. Water Dragons, do take note. Careful planning will definitely be worthwhile.

There will also be some excellent travel opportunities for the Water Dragon during the year. He will have several chances to go away, either for a holiday, to visit others or in connection with his work. With travel so well aspected, a holiday taken with his loved ones could be one of the best he has had in years. Here again, time spent planning could pay off handsomely.

The Water Dragon will also take much pleasure in his domestic life over the year. In addition to any practical home or garden projects he may initiate, he will enjoy many of the family activities that take place. Many Water Dragons will do much to assist close relations over the year, especially if they are under pressure or facing difficult decisions, and here the Water Dragon's experience, views and judgement will be particularly appreciated. The Water Dragon sets much store by his family life, and domestically this can be a pleasing and often meaningful year.

The aspects are also promising for the Water Dragon's social life. Travel, his various activities and changes in his work can all lead to him meeting new people, some of whom may well become friends. For any Water Dragon who may start 2007 in low spirits, the Pig year can mark the beginning of a brighter chapter. Many of these Water Dragons will appreciate the social opportunities the year will bring, and for the unattached, a new and often special friendship may result. On a social level this can be an active and pleasing year, with the period from April to June and August and December seeing much activity.

The Pig year certainly holds encouraging prospects for the Water Dragon and will give him the chance to benefit from his strengths and talents. If there are certain objectives he is keen to reach, this is a year to act. In 2007 fortune *will* favour the bold.

TIP FOR THE YEAR
So much can go your way this year, but avoid being too hasty or impulsive. Do take time to think through your plans and consult others. The better prepared you are, the more you can achieve.

The Wood Dragon

There is a well-known saying about being in 'the right place at the right time', and this will happen several times this year to the Wood Dragon. Not only will he benefit from some of the very good opportunities that will come his way, but he will also find many of the events of the year going in his favour.

At work his prospects are especially encouraging, and with the reputation and experience he has built up, he will often find himself well placed to benefit from opportunities. In some cases, promotion which he has been waiting for for some time will now become available. Alternatively, he may see an offer of work elsewhere which will enable him to advance his career and further his skills in the way he wants. By putting himself forward, the Wood Dragon can look forward to making important headway. Many Wood Dragons will also benefit from the good relations they have with their colleagues and the contacts they have built up. Not only will they be well supported in their activities, but they may also be alerted to new possibilities worth considering or may benefit from personal recommendations. Much can go the Wood Dragon's way this year, and by making the most of his opportunities he can enjoy some well-deserved and some-times overdue success.

Those Wood Dragons who may be disillusioned with their current position or seeking work as the Pig year starts can also take heart. However, to benefit these Wood Dragons will need to act determinedly as well as draw a line under any recent disappointments. This is a year for moving forward. These Wood Dragons will, however, need to remain persistent. There may be some disappointments in their quest, but many will find events moving in fortu-itous ways. Sometimes, following a rejection, they could be advised of a different vacancy or offered something else or again benefit from being 'in the right place at the right time' with new companies opening or expanding and offering positions they are ideally suited for. The Pig year can bring some exciting opportunities, with February (and as the Pig year starts) to April and September and October seeing important career developments.

The Wood Dragon's progress in his work will also lead to a rise in his income and for those with a more enterprising nature, there could be the chance to supplement this with some extra work or a profitable idea. The Wood Dragon's earning abilities will certainly be on good form over the year and as a result many Wood Dragons will decide to go ahead with plans for their home as well as for travel. The Wood Dragon could also benefit from spending time reviewing his financial position and making a few modifications, perhaps reducing borrowings, placing money in higher-yielding accounts or making some provision for the longer term.

With his wide interests and outgoing nature the Wood Dragon usually enjoys an active social life and this will again bring him much pleasure over the year. He will rarely be short of things to do! Any Wood Dragons who, because of changed circumstances, would welcome new friendships or a livelier social life will find that by going out more and pursuing their interests they can meet new people and make some good friends. In this respect too the Pig year is encouraging and supportive of the Wood Dragon and will reward positive action. The period from April to June and August and December will see the most social activity.

This will also be a busy year domestically, with many calls on the Wood Dragon's time, including helping both younger and more senior relations. In addition, his practical nature will often get the better of him and he will decide to go ahead with improvements to his home, or even to move somewhere which better suits his requirements. Some of the decisions taken over the year will involve considerable upheaval and the earlier the Wood Dragon can plan for these the better. While parts of the year will be busy and sometimes disruptive, however, the Wood Dragon will be pleased with the results of his efforts and will value the support of his loved ones. Domestically, this will be a busy but meaningful year.

The Pig year will certainly contain plenty of activity and by making most of his situation and opportunities, the Wood Dragon can look forward to doing well. This is a year for moving forward and for enjoying positive developments in many areas of his life.

TIP FOR THE YEAR
Seize the initiative. Pursue your aims and ambitions and use your experience and talents well. Positive, enthusiastic action can lead to success.

The Fire Dragon

This is a year of considerable potential for the Fire Dragon and by using his strengths and seizing his opportunities, he can look forward to accomplishing a great deal.

In his personal life this promises to be a full and eventful year. For those Fire Dragons with a partner there could be exciting news to celebrate, including a possible addition to their family or, for some, the chance to move to more suitable accommodation. In addition, by sharing hopes and ideas with those close to him, the Fire Dragon will benefit from the encouragement and support given. In 2007 the Fire Dragon's loved ones really can help him a great deal. Being forthcoming about his ideas will also help him to clarify in his own mind what he is hoping to achieve. When considering important decisions, he will also find it helpful to draw on the advice of more senior relations. With the experience they have behind them, their views can be useful. In this important and eventful year the Fire Dragon should not forget that there are many who are keen and willing to support him.

In addition to any plans he has regarding his home (and for many Dragons accommodation matters do figure prominently in the Pig year), the Fire Dragon will appreciate the activities he can share with those close to him. Whether these involve pursuing and developing mutual interests, carrying out plans together or just enjoying time in each other's company, there will be much to value. In addition, with travel favourably aspected, the Fire Dragon would do well to consider taking a holiday over the year, and with careful planning, this will be something both he and his loved ones will enjoy.

However, while domestically this is a fine year, as with any year, problems and tensions will sometimes raise their head. With an often busy schedule, as well as all his plans and activities, there will be times when the Fire Dragon will feel under pressure, tired and possibly irritable. At such times, a willingness to talk will help, and at particularly busy times he could find it helpful to defer certain plans rather than try to do too much at once. Also, if any differences of opinion do occur, the Fire Dragon would do well to deal with these before they have chance to escalate. In this often special year, good communication is important.

The positive aspects of the year also extend to the Fire Dragon's social life. While sometimes, with his commitments, he may not feel able to go out as often as he used to, by keeping in contact with his friends as well as going to events that appeal to him, he will find his social life (while sometimes reduced) can still bring him a great deal of pleasure. In addition, with the various interests and activities he is involved with, there will also be opportunities for him to meet others and, for those Fire Dragons who would welcome new friendships, the Pig year can see quite an upturn in their fortunes. April, June, August and December will see the greatest level of social activity.

As far as the Fire Dragon's work is concerned, this will be a significant year. The Fire Dragon knows he has it within him to achieve a great deal, and with his resolve and experience, together with the chances that are about to open up for him, he can look forward to making important progress. He should also not allow himself to be held back by any recent disappointments, as this is a year to move forward and show his true talents. Whether he chooses to stay in his current place of work or look elsewhere, by putting himself forward and applying for positions that interest him, he will find his initiative and determination leading him to greater and often more fulfilling responsibilities.

This is also a year of progress for those Fire Dragons seeking work. While they may feel disheartened by the lack of opportunities or when certain applications do not go their way, by remaining resolute and taking advantage of any training courses and support that may be available, many will be successful in getting back on the employment ladder. Workwise, this is a year of important and often encouraging developments, with February to April, September and October seeing the best chances.

The Fire Dragon's progress in his work will also lead to a rise in income, and for many this will be a considerably improved year. However with his commitments, often expensive accommodation plans and the other purchases he is keen to make, it is important that the Fire Dragon watches his outgoings closely, otherwise his spending could creep up and certain plans have to be delayed or cut back. This is very much a year when good budgeting will help. Fire Dragons, do take note. However, with the aspects as they are, many Fire Dragons will enjoy some strokes of good fortune over the year. If they see a competition that appeals to them, especially if it is related to one of their interests, they would do well to enter it. Similarly, if the Fire Dragon is keen to put an interest or special talent he has to more profitable use, he should do so. The Pig year can reward enterprise and determination with some surprising and lucky developments.

Overall, this is a year of considerable promise for the Fire Dragon and by making the most of his skills and opportunities, he can look forward to making important progress, particularly in terms of his career. In addition he will be greatly encouraged by the love and support of those close to him. In many ways, a special and rewarding year.

TIP FOR THE YEAR
This can be a wonderful year for you, but you do need to remain focused on your aims and be wary of spreading your energies too widely. Decide on your priorities and

concentrate on those. With focus, determination and goodwill, much can be accomplished and enjoyed over the year.

The Earth Dragon

This will be a year of important developments for the Earth Dragon, and with belief in himself and his abilities, he will fare well.

For those Earth Dragons in education this will be an important year, especially as many will take examinations which can have an important bearing on their future. In view of this, it would be worth these Earth Dragons remaining focused and disciplined as well as remembering the benefits that can follow on from the results and qualifications they can gain. It really *is* worth making the effort. Those Earth Dragons who decide to take their education further and start more advanced courses should embrace the challenge and opportunity before them and resolve to give of their best, even though what lies ahead may initially seem daunting. In the Pig year willingness and application on the Earth Dragon's part can make a real difference and, with his future ahead of him, what he does now can have long-term value.

This will also be a significant year for those Earth Dragons in or seeking work, as there will be some excellent opportunities to develop their skills and learn more about their working environment. While the Earth Dragon may feel some of his duties are unchallenging, by putting in the effort, he could find himself being selected for a more rewarding position. He is still in the early stages of his career, but his commitment and willingness to learn can help him move forward quickly.

Those Earth Dragons seeking work will find there is often a lot of competition for certain jobs, but by taking care over their applications and preparing well for any interviews, they will also find that extra effort and initiative can make a difference. If the Earth Dragon is offered the chance of training or a position which allows him both to work and study, he should look on it as a good opportunity. Any skills and qualifications he can obtain now will not only help his present position but also open up possibilities for later. Again, as far as the long term is concerned, this can be an important time. For work opportunities, the period from February to mid-April is well aspected, and many Earth Dragons could also have chances to build on their position in the last quarter of the year, with November and early December being a time of encouraging developments.

Another favourably aspected area of the year is travel and with his adventurous Dragon nature, the Earth Dragon will often thoroughly enjoy visiting areas new to him. Some of his travels can have a strong social element, too, and this can also help to make his time away all the more fun.

The Earth Dragon will also be fortunate in money matters in the Pig year. Some Earth Dragons will benefit from some strokes of luck, including the chance to put an interest or talent to profitable use. However, while there will be an element of good fortune to the year, the Earth Dragon will need to keep a watch on his spending levels as well as make early provision for large expenses, including travel. Also, although this is a positive year, he should be wary of entering into agreements or more risky undertakings without checking all the implications. When in doubt, he does need to ask.

The Earth Dragon would also do well to set some time aside to enjoy his personal interests. Whether these are of a sporting or more creative nature, he will find that extending his knowledge and skills will often add to the pleasure as well as potential benefit his interests bring.

The Pig year also promises much social activity, and in view of some of the changes that are likely to take place, there will be plenty of opportunities for the Earth Dragon to go out and meet others. During the year he will often forge what can be important friendships. Affairs of the heart can also bring added excitement to the year. April, June, August and the period from mid-November to early January 2008 will be the busiest and often liveliest months socially.

The Earth Dragon will also value his domestic life over the year and while sometimes a gap in years may lead to some differences of opinion arising with more senior relations, by being willing to contribute to family life and helping with domestic activities (including chores!), as well as discussing plans and decisions that need making, the Earth Dragon will be grateful for the help and support he is given and will enjoy some of the family occasions that take place.

In so many respects the Pig year will offer the Earth Dragon excellent chances to develop and progress, but, as always, problems, pressures and some difficult moments will occur. At times of pressure or when facing a daunting workload, the Earth Dragon will need to remain determined and resolute rather than give up too easily or not give his best. Over the year it could be helpful for him to remember what can open up to him as a result of doing well. This really is a year which rewards commitment, and by being prepared to give this, the Earth Dragon can make it a pleasing and successful time, and an often enjoyable one too.

TIP FOR THE YEAR
Be determined and give your best. By making an effort you will not only benefit now but can give *your future* added impetus. Use the present year well and your diligence will reward you handsomely.

FAMOUS DRAGONS

Maya Angelou, Jeffrey Archer, Joan Armatrading, Dan Aykroyd, Joan Baez, Roseanne Barr, Count Basie, Maeve Binchy, Sandra Bullock, Julie Christie, James Coburn, Courteney Cox, Bing Crosby, Russell Crowe, Roald Dahl, Salvador Dali, Charles Darwin, Neil Diamond, Bo Diddley, Matt Dillon, Christian Dior, Placido Domingo, Fats Domino, Kirk Douglas, Faye Dunaway, Bruce Forsyth, Sigmund Freud, Graham Greene, Che Guevara, David Hasselhoff, James Herriot, Paul Hogan, Joan of Arc, Tom Jones, Immanuel Kant, Martin Luther King, John Lennon, Abraham Lincoln, Elle Macpherson, Queen Margrethe II of Denmark, Andrew Motion, Hosni Mubarak, Florence Nightingale, Nick Nolte, Sharon Osbourne, Al Pacino,

Gregory Peck, Pelé, Edgar Allan Poe, Vladimir Putin, Keanu Reeves, Sir Cliff Richard, George Bernard Shaw, Martin Sheen, Alicia Silverstone, Ringo Starr, Princess Stephanie of Monaco, Dave Stewart, Karlheinz Stockhausen, Shirley Temple, Maria von Trapp, Andy Warhol, Johnny Weissmüller, Raquel Welch, the Earl of Wessex, Mae West, Reese Witherspoon.

23 JANUARY 1917 ⌢ 10 FEBRUARY 1918		*Fire Snake*
10 FEBRUARY 1929 ⌢ 29 JANUARY 1930		*Earth Snake*
27 JANUARY 1941 ⌢ 14 FEBRUARY 1942		*Metal Snake*
14 FEBRUARY 1953 ⌢ 2 FEBRUARY 1954		*Water Snake*
2 FEBRUARY 1965 ⌢ 20 JANUARY 1966		*Wood Snake*
18 FEBRUARY 1977 ⌢ 6 FEBRUARY 1978		*Fire Snake*
6 FEBRUARY 1989 ⌢ 26 JANUARY 1990		*Earth Snake*
24 JANUARY 2001 ⌢ 11 FEBRUARY 2002		*Metal Snake*

THE
SNAKE

THE PERSONALITY OF THE SNAKE

'Talents are best nurtured in solitude; character is best
formed in the stormy billows of the world.'
Johann Wolfgang von Goethe, a Snake

The Snake is born under the sign of wisdom. He is highly
intelligent and his mind is forever active. He is always
planning and always looking for ways in which he can use
his considerable skills. He is a deep thinker and likes to
meditate and reflect.

Many times during his life he will shed one of his
famous Snake skins and take up new interests or start a
completely different job. The Snake enjoys a challenge and
he rarely makes mistakes. He is a skilful organizer, has
considerable business acumen and is usually lucky in
money matters. Most Snakes are financially secure in their
later years, provided they do not gamble – the Snake has
the distinction of being the worst gambler in the whole of
the Chinese zodiac!

The Snake generally has a calm and placid nature and
prefers the quieter things in life. He does not like to be in a
frenzied atmosphere and hates being hurried into making a
quick decision. He also does not like interference in his
affairs and tends to rely on his own judgement rather than
listen to advice.

At times the Snake can appear solitary. He is quiet,
reserved and sometimes has difficulty in communicating
with others. He has little time for idle gossip and will
certainly not suffer fools gladly. He does, however, have a

good sense of humour and this is particularly appreciated in times of crisis.

The Snake is certainly not afraid of hard work and is thorough in all that he does. He is very determined and can occasionally be ruthless in order to achieve his aims. His confidence, willpower and quick thinking usually ensure his success, but should he fail it will often take a long time for him to recover. He cannot bear failure and is a very bad loser.

The Snake can also be evasive and does not willingly let people into his confidence. This secrecy and distrust can sometimes work against him and it is a trait which all Snakes should try to overcome.

Another characteristic of the Snake is his tendency to rest after any sudden or prolonged bout of activity. He burns up so much nervous energy that he can, if he is not careful, be susceptible to high blood pressure and nervous disorders.

It has sometimes been said that the Snake is a late starter in life and this is mainly because it often takes him a while to find a job in which he is genuinely happy. However, he will usually do well in any position which involves research and writing and where he is given sufficient freedom to develop his own ideas and plans. He makes a good teacher, politician, personnel manager and social adviser.

The Snake chooses his friends carefully and while he keeps a tight control over his finances, he can be particularly generous to those he likes. He will think nothing of buying expensive gifts or treating his friends or loved ones to the best theatre seats in town. In return he demands loyalty. The Snake is very possessive and he can become extremely jealous and hurt if he finds his trust has been abused.

The Snake is also renowned for his good looks and is never short of admirers. The female Snake in particular is most alluring. She has style, grace and excellent (and usually expensive) taste in clothes. A keen socializer, she is likely to have a wide range of friends and a happy knack of impressing those who matter. She has numerous interests and her opinions are often highly valued. She is generally a calm-natured person and while she involves herself in many activities, she likes to retain a certain amount of privacy in her undertakings.

Affairs of the heart are very important to the Snake and he will often have many romances before he finally settles down. He will find that he is particularly well suited to those born under the signs of the Ox, Dragon, Rabbit and Rooster. Provided he is allowed sufficient freedom to pursue his own interests, he can also build up a very satisfactory relationship with the Rat, Horse, Goat, Monkey and Dog, but he should try to steer clear of another Snake as they could very easily become jealous of each other. The Snake will also have difficulty in getting on with the honest and down-to-earth Pig, and will find the Tiger far too much of a disruptive influence on his quiet and peace-loving ways.

The Snake certainly appreciates the finer things in life. He enjoys good food and often takes a keen interest in the arts. He also enjoys reading and is invariably drawn to subjects such as philosophy, political thought, religion or the occult. He is fascinated by the unknown and his enquiring mind is always looking for answers. Some of the world's most original thinkers have been Snakes, and although he may not readily admit it, the Snake is often psychic and relies a lot on intuition.

The Snake is certainly not the most energetic member of the Chinese zodiac. He prefers to proceed at his own pace and to do what he wants. He is very much his own master and throughout his life he will try his hand at many things. He is something of a dabbler, but at some time – usually when he least expects it – his hard work and efforts will be recognized and he will invariably meet with the success and the financial security which he so desires.

THE FIVE DIFFERENT TYPES OF SNAKE

In addition to the 12 signs of the Chinese zodiac there are five elements, and these have a strengthening or moderating influence on the sign. The effects of the five elements on the Snake are described below, together with the years in which the elements were exercising their influence. Therefore those Snakes born in 1941 and 2001 are Metal Snakes, those born in 1953 are Water Snakes, and so on.

Metal Snake: 1941, 2001
This Snake is quiet, confident and fiercely independent. He often prefers to work on his own and will only let a privileged few into his confidence. He is quick to spot opportu-

nities and will set about achieving his objectives with an awesome determination. He is astute in financial matters and will often invest his money well. He also has a liking for the finer things in life and a good appreciation of the arts, literature, music and good food. He usually has a small group of extremely good friends and can be generous to his loved ones.

Water Snake: 1953

This Snake has a wide variety of interests. He enjoys studying all manner of subjects and is capable of undertaking quite detailed research and becoming a specialist in his chosen area. He is highly intelligent, has a good memory and is particularly astute when dealing with business and financial matters. He tends to be quietly spoken and a little reserved, but he does have sufficient strength of character to make his views known and attain his ambitions. He is very loyal to his family and friends.

Wood Snake: 1965

The Wood Snake has a friendly temperament and a good understanding of human nature. He is able to communicate well and often has many friends and admirers. He is witty, intelligent and ambitious. He has numerous interests and prefers to live in a quiet, stable environment where he can work without too much interference. He enjoys the arts and usually derives much pleasure from collecting paintings and antiques. His advice is often highly valued, particularly on social and domestic matters.

Fire Snake: 1917, 1977

The Fire Snake tends to be more forceful, outgoing and energetic than some of the other types of Snake. He is ambitious, confident and never slow in voicing his opinions – and he can be very abrasive to those he does not like. He does, however, have many leadership qualities and can win the respect and support of many with his firm and resolute manner. He usually has a good sense of humour, a wide circle of friends and a very active social life. He is also a keen traveller.

Earth Snake 1929, 1989

The Earth Snake is charming, amusing and has a very amiable manner. He is conscientious and reliable in his work and approaches everything he does in a level-headed and sensible way. He can, however, tend to err on the cautious side and never likes to be hassled into making a decision. He is adept in dealing with financial matters and is a shrewd investor. He has many friends and is very supportive towards the members of his family.

PROSPECTS FOR THE SNAKE IN 2007

The Year of the Dog (29 January 2006 to 17 February 2007) is a generally encouraging one for the Snake and in the closing months, by remaining active and determined, he can look forward to achieving a great deal. This is, though, no time for the Snake to be reticent or hold back. As Virgil declared, 'Fortune will favour the bold.'

In his work the Snake will have good opportunity to use his strengths, and whether dealing with a heavy workload or becoming involved in new initiatives, his drive and resourcefulness will often impress. Those Snakes keen to make headway or seeking a position will find that by remaining alert and following up openings they can make useful progress, with September and November seeing some interesting developments. The Snake should make the most of his ideas at this time and could find some of them bringing a pleasing response.

The Snake will also enjoy positive relations with those around him in the closing months of the Dog year, although to benefit from the support and advice others can give he does need to be prepared to talk over his plans, hopes and ideas. Again, this is no time to hold back. Also, as the Dog year draws to a close the Snake will have an increasing number of chances to go out and his social life will enjoy quite an upturn. For some Snakes, new friendships and romance can add excitement to this time.

Generally, the Dog year will have been a positive one for the Snake and by making the most of his situation and strengths, he will fare well.

The Year of the Pig begins on 18 February and will be a variable one for the Snake. Over the year problems and pressures will arise and the Snake could find progress difficult, but despite the mixed aspects the Pig year will not be without its value or its successes – albeit hard-earned ones. Over the year the Snake will find it helpful to remember the old Chinese saying 'You won't get lost if you frequently ask for directions' and whenever he finds himself in a quandary or facing a complex matter, he would do well to seek the opinions of others rather than keep his concerns to himself. Whether family, friends or colleagues, those he knows can often provide valuable support and advice, and if the Snake 'frequently asks for directions' he will often be helped.

In his work the Snake will need to remain his careful and thorough self. Rather than viewing this as a year for making major changes, he should concentrate his efforts on the areas he knows best. His workload may be considerable and the pressure sometimes great, but he will have a good chance to both use *and* develop his skills. Throughout the year he would do well to work closely with colleagues rather than be too independent. This way he will not only get more done but will also be able to benefit from the support and advice that others are able to give.

Many Snakes will remain with their present employer over the year, but for those who are keen to make a change or who are seeking work, the Pig year will require some careful thought. These Snakes would do well to consider the sort of position they would now like as well as how they can best use and build on their experience. By considering various possibilities and contacting those who are able to advise, these Snakes could identify or be alerted to openings or areas worth pursuing. Progress in the Pig year will need to be worked for, but with the Snake's belief in himself, his efforts may well be rewarded, and his achievements in the Pig year can turn out to be an important stage in his career. March, May, June and September could see some encouraging developments, but generally this is a year for the Snake to build on his experience and proceed carefully.

The Snake also needs to remain his thorough self when dealing with money matters. Again this is no year for risks or for proceeding with large transactions without checking the terms and obligations involved. Fortunately the Snake is usually careful in his financial dealings, but with the aspects as they are, an oversight (sometimes caused by too much haste) could leave him disadvantaged or with a bureaucratic problem to untangle. The Pig year does require the Snake to remain on his guard, and should he have any uncertainties over any financial matter, it would be worth him seeking advice.

Although the Pig year will bring its pressures, the Snake will, however, derive considerable pleasure from his interests and recreational pursuits. With his keen and often enquiring mind, he is likely to set himself some interesting activities and projects to do. He may also benefit from the additional exercise or social opportunities his interests may bring. Some Snakes may decide to take up a new interest or learn a different skill over the year and will enjoy the personal challenge this gives.

The Snake always attaches great importance to his home life and he will again play his usual full part in domestic activities. In particular the progress of close relations will be a source of considerable pride. However, in view of the mixed aspects and the pressures the Snake will sometimes face, it is important that he is prepared to be open and talk over any worries and concerns. This way those around him will be better able to help and, knowing the Snake as well as they do, there will be much wisdom in their words.

Snakes are often selective in their social life, but if the Snake takes up the invitations he receives over the year and goes to the events that appeal to him, he will often enjoy himself. Those Snakes who are keen to build up their social life will find that getting involved in new activities will often introduce them to a new social circle. New activities started in the Pig year can be to the Snake's benefit in several ways. April, May, July and December will be the most active months socially.

The Pig year may not be the easiest of years for the Snake, but by remaining his careful self and avoiding rush, he can gain much from it. In his work, the additional experience he is able to acquire, the objectives he meets and any new responsibilities he is given can often prepare the way for the progress he will make in following years. New interests and skills can also have future value. However, throughout the Pig year the Snake does need to be mindful of others and prepared to talk over important decisions or any worries he may have. By being prepared to 'ask for directions', he will fare better generally.

The Metal Snake

This can be a reasonable year for the Metal Snake, although to achieve all he wants he will need to adapt to prevailing situations as well as remain mindful of others. This is very much a year for proceeding carefully.

One area in which the Metal Snake will need to be especially thorough is his finances. Although, as a Snake, he is generally careful in his financial dealings, this is not a year to take risks or to act in haste. In 2007 impulsiveness or inattention could cost the Metal Snake dear. In addition, where important transactions are involved, the Metal

Snake should check the terms of any agreements he may be entering into and, if applicable, compare ranges, suitability and prices. The more time he spends planning his more substantial purchases the better.

The Metal Snake also needs to be careful when dealing with important forms, especially any related to tax, benefits or other financial matters. To delay or omit essential details could be to his detriment. He should also make sure important policies are kept up to date and documents and guarantees kept safely. In this mixed year, care and thoroughness can often prevent problems from arising. If at any time the Metal Snake does experience problems or has questions over some financial or bureaucratic matter, he would do well to seek advice rather than try to deal with what could be complex matters on his own.

However, while there is an underlying need for care, the Pig year will not be without its successes or memorable times. In particular, interests and projects that the Metal Snake can share with others can go well. In addition, with his enquiring nature, the Metal Snake may be attracted to new interests or recreational pursuits, and here again if he can encourage others to join him, he can make his activities that much more rewarding. Some Metal Snakes may decide to enrol on a course or join a local society, and any way in which the Metal Snake can further his interests can be a satisfying aspect of the year.

The Metal Snake will also do a lot to help family members during the Pig year, and the advice and assistance he gives, especially to those under pressure, will be valued. The year too will contain some memorable family occasions and the Metal Snake can look forward to some particularly pleasing times. However, with the aspects as they are, if he does have any concerns, it is important that he speaks to those close to him so that they are better able to understand and assist. Should any difference of opinion arise or his loved ones have misgivings about some of his thoughts and plans, a willingness to talk these through and a greater flexibility on his part could help. In the Pig year the Metal Snake does need to be wary about being obtuse or intransigent over certain matters.

As with all Snakes, the Metal Snake is often selective in the times he goes out and he also prefers to keep his social circle relatively small. However, in the Pig year it is important that he keeps in regular contact with his friends as well as goes to social occasions that appeal to him, as otherwise there is a risk that some Metal Snakes could become reclusive and so miss out on activities that could benefit them. By making the effort to join social groups in their area, as well as in getting to know others, they *can* make an important difference to their lives. April, May, July and December could be the most active and rewarding months socially.

The Pig year may not be the easiest of years for the Metal Snake and care is needed, especially where finance is concerned. The Metal Snake should also be wary of acting in too much haste. However, provided he remains aware of the trickier aspects of the year and liaises with others, he can do much to minimize some of the more awkward elements and will find many of his activities going well and bringing him considerable pleasure.

TIP FOR THE YEAR

Do consult others. This way more can be agreed and you can gain more from the advice you are given. Also, involve those close to you in your activities. Time spent with others can be helpful *in many ways.*

The Water Snake

The Water Snake has a generally careful and cautious nature and is not one for being hurried. He is a deliberator and a planner, and with the variable aspects of the year, his cautious attitude will serve him well.

In view of the considerable changes many Water Snakes will have experienced in their work in recent years, many will decide to remain in their present position and carry out the duties that they perform so well. Although they will often face increased pressures and a heavy workload, by focusing on their objectives and using their skills well, these Water Snakes will generally be pleased with how they fare. Also, in view of the experience they have behind them, many will do much to help more junior colleagues and their advice will be appreciated.

For those Water Snakes currently seeking a position or feeling unfulfilled in their present role, the Pig year can bring important developments. By deciding on the type of work that they now want to do and paying careful attention to the applications they submit, they can find their extra effort and initiative being noticed and leading to an interesting new position. To succeed, though, *will* require determination. Fortunately, here again the Water Snake's patient and persistent approach will be to his advantage.

For those Water Snakes seeking work or wanting change, March, May, June and September could see some interesting possibilities.

The Water Snake will derive much satisfaction from his personal interests over the year, especially any that allow him to draw on his creative talents. Water Snakes who lead demanding lifestyles will find it particularly beneficial to spend time on pursuits they enjoy and that help them relax. During the Pig year the Water Snake's personal interests can certainly have value and benefit.

Although travel does not tend to figure prominently during the Pig year, the Water Snake should still aim to take a holiday or at least go away for a short break. This will not only give him a valuable break from his usual routine but also the chance to unwind. In this often demanding year, it is important that he has a respite from his often busy lifestyle.

As far as money matters are concerned, this is very much a year for care and thoroughness. The Water Snake does need to pay close attention to his financial position and to keep a watch on his outgoings as well as be careful when dealing with financial paperwork. Without vigilance, mistakes and misjudgements could result in him being disadvantaged. Also, in view of the prevailing aspects, if he does have any problems or is involved in a troubling matter, whether financial or otherwise, it would be worth him obtaining professional guidance. The Pig year is one for care and caution.

The Water Snake will also need to pay close attention to his relations with others. In his home life he should make sure that he spends quality time with those around him rather than being continually busy or preoccupied with his own concerns. Fortunately the Water Snake is usually considerate in this respect, but in this busy and mixed year he does need to remain mindful of others. Whenever he is under pressure or concerned about something, he should aim to talk things over rather than keep his thoughts to himself. That way, those around him will be better able to understand and help. The Water Snake has a tendency to keep things close to his chest, but in the Pig year a greater openness on his part will certainly be to the benefit of all.

However, while there is a need for care, the Water Snake's home life will contain many fine moments, and for many Water Snakes the success of a younger relation will be a source of particular delight.

The Water Snake will also value his close circle of friends over the year. Again, should he be troubled or concerned by any matter, he will find it helpful to talk to those he knows and trusts. Their friendship and support will count for a great deal. In addition the Water Snake will enjoy the social events that he goes to and these can bring an important balance to his lifestyle. For the unattached and/or lonely Water Snake there will be chances to meet others, and for many the Pig year can bring the gift of an important new friendship or even romance. This may be a mixed year, but it will not be without its more positive sides! April, May, July, November and December will be the busiest months socially.

Although the aspects may be variable, the Water Snake can still emerge from the Pig year with much to his credit, and can benefit from the experience he obtains, the skills he acquires and the new interests he takes up. He will be able to build on many of his achievements in the more favourable Rat year that follows. In many respects the Pig year will prepare the way for the success he is soon to enjoy.

TIP FOR THE YEAR
Watch your independent Water Snake tendencies and consult others rather than try to deal with too much on your own. Also make sure that you spend quality time with loved ones and that your personal interests do not suffer amidst all the activity. In the busy and sometimes demanding Pig year it *is* important that you keep your lifestyle in balance.

The Wood Snake

There is a Chinese proverb that is very apt for the Wood Snake this year. It is 'Come prepared and succeed; come unprepared and fail.' In the Pig year the Wood Snake will need to be careful, thorough *and* prepared. If not, he could face disappointments. The Pig year requires him to be alert and on his guard. Provided he remains aware of the trickier aspects, however, he can do much to minimize some of the problems the year could bring.

In his work the Wood Snake will find a lot being asked of him. In some cases he could be set challenging objectives, face a heavy workload or have some complex problems to deal with. In addition he could be concerned about some changes being introduced. However, while the year will have its pressures and the Wood Snake his misgivings, by doing his best and concentrating on what needs to be done, he will manage to accomplish a great deal. In addition, the situations that arise will often give him a good chance to further his skills and this can stand him in good stead for the more encouraging Rat year that follows.

Many Wood Snakes will decide to remain in their present place of work over the year. While not always satisfactory, this will often provide them with chances to add to their role. Throughout the year the Wood Snake would also do well to work closely with colleagues as well as take up any chances he has to meet others engaged in similar of types of work. Establishing good contacts and getting himself better known will enable him to draw on the support and advice that others are able to give. As with all Snakes, this is not a year for the Wood Snake to be too independent or reserved.

For those Wood Snakes seeking work, again the proverb 'Come prepared and succeed ...' is apt. When applying for positions, the better prepared the Wood Snake is, the better his chances. In some cases finding out more about the company and the duties involved can help to give his application more weight. Securing a new position will require patience and persistence, but any extra effort the Wood Snake makes can be to his benefit. Also, once in a new job, by mastering his duties and showing commitment, the Wood Snake will find that early good work can lead to further training and other possibilities. With the Wood Snake's prospects so promising in the following Rat year, the accomplishments of 2007 can prove important. March, May, June and September could see interesting work developments, but generally this is a year for the Wood Snake to concentrate on the challenges given him and build on his experience.

As with all Snakes, this is also a year when the Wood Snake will need to be careful in money matters. He would do well to keep track of his outgoings as well as budget in advance for forthcoming expenses. Keeping a set of accounts could help. The better he is able to manage his situation, the less likely problems are to arise. Similarly, when conducting important transactions or dealing with paperwork, he needs to check the details, implications and small print. Without increased vigilance, he could find himself having complex matters and correspondence to deal with. If difficulties do arise or the Wood Snake has any questions concerning a financial matter, he would do well to seek professional guidance. This is very much a year for care and control.

Throughout this sometimes tricky year the Wood Snake will be grateful of the support of family members, and whenever he is under pressure or facing decisions he should aim to share what is on his mind and pay careful heed to what others say. Also, when tired, he needs to be careful not to take any feelings of irritability out on others. This is a year for increased mindfulness. Wood Snakes, *do* take note.

The Pig year will, however, still see some domestic occasions that will mean a lot to the Wood Snake. For those who are parents, the achievements of their children will often be a source of pride and the Wood Snake's partner or a close relation could also enjoy some particularly good news. By playing his usual full part in family activities, as well as enjoying any celebrations that take place, the Wood Snake will find his domestic life will mean a great deal to him. Also, while travel may not figure prominently in

2007, he would still do well to take a holiday with those who are special to him. The break can do everyone good.

In view of the general busyness of the year the Wood Snake may decide to keep his social life relatively low key. However, it is important that he keeps in regular contact with close friends and doesn't deprive himself of the pleasure social occasions can bring. Going out can also be a good way for him to unwind and in this often demanding year it is important that he does give himself time to relax and enjoy the fruits he works so hard for. Wood Snakes who may feel alone or dispirited about their situation should also make the effort to go out more and become involved in new interests. Any positive steps they take can brighten their position considerably. April, May, July and December will see the best social opportunities.

Although this will be a demanding year for the Wood Snake, by being his careful self and setting about his plans and activities diligently, he can gain much from it. And what he accomplishes during the present year will prepare him for the success that awaits in the following one.

TIP FOR THE YEAR
'Come prepared and succeed; come unprepared and fail.' This *is* a year to be thorough and to set about your activities carefully. This is no time for rush or risk. Also, do consult others and seek advice on any troubling matters.

The Fire Snake
The Fire Snake has an ambitious nature and is always keen to make the most of himself and his abilities. However, he

is also a realist and when situations are not quite right then he is prepared to bide his time. In the Pig year, he will often feel that he can gain more by building on his experience and regarding what he does as an investment in his future. And with his prospects far more encouraging in the following Rat year, what he achieves in 2007 can be very much to his future benefit.

In his work the Fire Snake will often decide to remain in his present position and take advantage of any chances to add to his knowledge and skills. In some cases these could be through training opportunities, taking on greater responsibilities or becoming involved in new schemes and initiatives. By making the most of such chances *and* showing willingness, the Fire Snake will not only help his present position but also widen his scope for later.

In addition the Fire Snake should aim to work closely with his colleagues over the year and take up any chances he has to get to know others and build up contacts. Again, what he learns now can be to his long-term benefit.

For those Fire Snakes who are particularly keen to move on from their position or are seeking work, this can be an important year. However, they will need to give careful thought to what it is they now want to do as well as contact those who are able to offer guidance. If they are eligible for any training or refresher courses, they should take them up. The effort and initiative these Fire Snakes can put into the job-seeking process can often pay off. March, May, June and September could see the best opportunities.

As with all Snakes, however, the Fire Snake does need to be careful in money matters. With his existing and often considerable obligations, he does need to keep a close watch on his situation and control his spending. Without some discipline – and prudence – his outgoings could creep up and become greater than he anticipated. Also, if entering into a new agreement or dealing with important paper-work, he needs to check the small print. Rush or inatten-tion could lead to costly mistakes. This is very much a year for care.

Although the Fire Snake will often have many demands on his time, he would also do well to consider developing his personal interests or taking up a new one. If there is a skill it would be useful for him to learn or to become more proficient in, this could often add to the pleasure. The ways in which the Fire Snake can advance his knowledge can be a particularly valuable aspect of the year.

This year will also mark the start of a new decade in the Fire Snake's life and many will celebrate their 30th birthday in fine style. The year can also bring some other pleasing developments, with some Fire Snakes celebrating an addition to their family or the success of a loved one. In all the Fire Snake's undertakings, it is, however, important that he remains attentive to the views of others and avoids unnecessary haste. Should any disagreements arise, possibly as a result of tiredness or outside pressures, more time spent in discussion can be to the good of all. However, despite these more cautionary aspects, the Fire Snake's home life will often be special.

In view of the general activity of the year the Fire Snake will be selective in his socializing, but whenever he has invitations or there are events that appeal to him, he would do well to follow these up. Not only can they be enjoyable and a good way to meet others, but they can also help him to relax and unwind. And in the Pig year, it is important that he keeps his lifestyle in balance.

For the unattached Fire Snake the Pig year can also bring the prospect of an exciting new romance, but rather than act too hastily or build up high expectations in the early stages, the Fire Snake would do well to allow the relationship to grow in its own time. Again, this is a year favouring patience rather than haste. April, May, July and December will see the most social activity.

The Pig year may contain its mixed aspects, but by remaining careful and making the most of any chances to further his experience and knowledge, the Fire Snake can enjoy some achievements that will be of great future value. He will also appreciate the support and advice he is given, particularly from those who are dear to him.

TIP FOR THE YEAR
Be your careful and alert self. Avoid haste and take the time to think decisions through. Also, in complex matters, seek advice. This is a year for care, thoroughness and patience.

The Earth Snake
This is a year of interesting possibilities for the Earth Snake, although just how he fares depends a lot on his attitude. With discipline, focus and effort, he can make important progress, but should he waste chances or take a more laid-back approach, then his progress could be disappointing. In the Pig year the Earth Snake *will* need to be on his mettle.

For those Earth Snakes in education this will be a busy and important year, and with many sitting examinations which have a bearing on their future, it really would be worth them preparing well and putting in a special effort. Rather than leaving any revision and course work to the last moment (so putting themselves under increased pressure), they should aim to work steadily and consistently throughout the year. Again, attitude and approach can make an important difference.

During the year many of these Earth Snakes will give consideration to their future, deciding whether to remain in education, take a gap year or seek work. In making their decision, they would find it helpful to discuss their options with those who are able to give informed advice. While the Earth Snake may have his own views, he must not close his mind to what others may suggest. By listening *and* being open-minded, he could find new options opening up which he would do well to consider. To benefit, however, the Earth Snake does need to show a certain flexibility.

For those Earth Snakes who do seek work, the Pig year can be a challenging one. Often they will face much competition and some disappointments in their quest. Here again, attitude and approach will be important. If the Earth Snake remains persistent, seeks advice on application and interview techniques and learns from any feedback, his tenacity and willingness to learn will prevail. And although some Earth Snakes may regard any job they get as temporary, by proving their worth, they will be helping their reputation and future prospects.

For Earth Snakes currently in work this can be an important year. Again, by working hard and showing commitment, they will find their good work can lead to new opportunities or to good recommendations when they decide to move on. March, May, June and the period from September to mid-November could see the best work opportunities, but generally the Earth Snake should regard this as a year for adding to his qualifications and skills and building up his experience. With his prospects considerably brighter next year, what he learns now can often be far-reaching.

The Earth Snake will also need be careful in money matters. He should aim to save up for his plans and any larger purchases and be wary about succumbing to too many impulse buys or spending money unnecessarily. In the Pig year he does need to manage his money well, especially in view of all he wants to do. As with all Snakes, he should also be wary of taking risks and if he has any doubts or questions over any financial matter he would do well to seek advice.

The Earth Snake's social life will, though, be generally lively, with many Earth Snakes having great fun with their circle of friends and some enjoying romance too. Those who move for the purposes of work or education will have excellent chances to build up a new social circle. Friendships can also be made while travelling. However, while there will often be much for the Earth Snake to do and enjoy, during the course of the year certain friendships may sour or a romance may go through a difficult phase or come to an end. While this may hurt at the time, the lessons of the Pig year can ultimately leave the Earth Snake stronger and wiser.

As with all Snakes, the Earth Snake has a very independent side to his nature and often likes to keep his thoughts and feelings to himself. However, in this sometimes challenging year he would find it helpful to be more forthcoming, especially when thinking over his plans and options. Many around him are willing and keen to help, but he does need to be receptive to their words.

The Pig year will be a demanding one for the Earth Snake and to secure the results he desires he will need to remain disciplined and put in the effort. If he does so, however, what he achieves now can be of considerable help to his future prospects. The Pig year may not be an easy or smooth one for the Earth Snake, but it can be instructive and have long-term significance.

TIP FOR THE YEAR

Think decisions through. This is not a year for haste or impulsive action. The more careful and thorough you are, the better your decisions will be. Also, do be prepared to consult those with the knowledge and experience to guide you. Their support, advice *and encouragement* can be of great value.

FAMOUS SNAKES

Muhammad Ali, Tim Allen, Ann-Margret, Lord Baden-Powell, Kim Basinger, Björk, Tony Blair, Michael Bloomberg, Michael Bolton, Brahms, Pierce Brosnan, Casanova, Chubby Checker, Dick Cheney, Jackie Collins, Tom Conti, Jim Davidson, Cecil B. de Mille, Bob Dylan, Elgar, Sir Alex Ferguson, Sir Alexander Fleming, Andrew Flintoff, Mahatma Gandhi, Greta Garbo, Art Garfunkel,

J. Paul Getty, Dizzy Gillespie, W. E. Gladstone, Johann Wolfgang von Goethe, Princess Grace of Monaco, Stephen Hawking, Audrey Hepburn, Jack Higgins, Howard Hughes, Tom Hulce, Liz Hurley, James Joyce, Stacy Keach, Ronan Keating, Howard Keel, J. F. Kennedy, Carole King, Cyndi Lauper, Courtney Love, Mao Tse-tung, Chris Martin, Henri Matisse, Anthony Minghella, Robert Mitchum, Alfred Nobel, Mike Oldfield, Aristotle Onassis, Jacqueline Onassis, Pablo Picasso, Mary Pickford, Brad Pitt, Daniel Radcliffe, Franklin D. Roosevelt, Mickey Rourke, J. K. Rowling, Jean-Paul Sartre, Franz Schubert, Shakira, Charlie Sheen, Brooke Shields, Paul Simon, Delia Smith, Madame Tussaud, Shania Twain, Dionne Warwick, Charlie Watts, Ruby Wax, Oprah Winfrey, Victoria Wood, Virginia Woolf.

11 FEBRUARY 1918 ~ 31 JANUARY 1919	*Earth Horse*
30 JANUARY 1930 ~ 16 FEBRUARY 1931	*Metal Horse*
15 FEBRUARY 1942 ~ 4 FEBRUARY 1943	*Water Horse*
3 FEBRUARY 1954 ~ 23 JANUARY 1955	*Wood Horse*
21 JANUARY 1966 ~ 8 FEBRUARY 1967	*Fire Horse*
7 FEBRUARY 1978 ~ 27 JANUARY 1979	*Earth Horse*
27 JANUARY 1990 ~ 14 FEBRUARY 1991	*Metal Horse*
12 FEBRUARY 2002 ~ 31 JANUARY 2003	*Water Horse*

THE
HORSE

THE PERSONALITY OF THE HORSE

'Do what you can, with what you have, where you are.'
Theodore Roosevelt, a Horse

The Horse is born under the signs of elegance and ardour. He has a most engaging and charming manner and is usually very popular. He loves meeting people and likes attending parties and other large social gatherings.

The Horse is a lively character and enjoys being the centre of attention. He has considerable leadership qualities and is much admired for his honest and straightforward manner. He is an eloquent and persuasive speaker and has a great love of discussion and debate. He also has a particularly agile mind and can assimilate facts remarkably quickly.

He does, however, have a fiery temper and although his outbursts are usually short-lived, he can often say things which he will later regret. He is also not particularly good at keeping secrets.

The Horse has many interests and involves himself in a wide variety of activities. He can, however, get involved in so much that he can often waste his energies on projects which he never has time to complete. He also has a tendency to change his interests rather frequently and will often get caught up with the latest craze or 'in thing' until something better or more exciting turns up.

The Horse also likes to have a certain amount of freedom and independence. He hates being bound by petty rules and regulations and as far as possible likes to feel that he is answerable to no one but himself. But despite this spirit of freedom, he still likes to have the support and encouragement of others in his various enterprises.

Due to his many talents and likeable nature, the Horse will often go far in life. He enjoys challenges and is a methodical and tireless worker. However, should things go against him and he fail in any of his enterprises, it will take a long time for him to recover and pick up the pieces again. Success to the Horse means everything. To fail is a disaster and a humiliation.

The Horse likes to have variety in his life and he will try his hand at many different things before he settles down to one particular job. Even then, he will probably remain alert to see whether there are any better opportunities for him to take up. He has a restless nature and can easily get bored. He does, however, excel in any position which allows him sufficient freedom to act on his own initiative or which brings him into contact with a lot of people.

Although the Horse is not particularly bothered about accumulating great wealth, he handles his finances with care and will rarely experience any serious financial problems.

The Horse also enjoys travel and loves visiting new and faraway places. At some stage during his life he will be tempted to live abroad for a short period of time and due to his adaptable nature he will find that he will fit in well wherever he goes.

The Horse pays a great deal of attention to his appearance and usually likes to wear smart, colourful and rather distinctive clothes. He is very attractive to others and will often have many romances before he settles down. He is loyal and protective to his partner, but despite his family commitments he still likes to retain a certain measure of independence and have the freedom to carry on with his own interests and hobbies. He will find that he is especially well suited to those born under the signs of the Tiger, Goat, Rooster and Dog. He can also get on well with the Rabbit, Dragon, Snake, Pig and another Horse, but he will find the Ox too serious and intolerant for his liking. The Horse will also have difficulty in getting on with the Monkey and the Rat – the Monkey is very inquisitive and the Rat seeks security, and both will resent the Horse's rather independent ways.

The female Horse is usually most attractive and has a friendly, outgoing personality. She is highly intelligent, has many interests and is alert to everything that is going on around her. She particularly enjoys outdoor pursuits and often likes to take part in sport and keep-fit activities. She also enjoys travel, literature and the arts, and is a very good conversationalist.

Although the Horse can be stubborn and rather self-centred, he does have a considerate nature and is often willing to help others. He has a good sense of humour and will usually make a favourable impression wherever he goes. Provided he can curb his slightly restless nature and keep tight control over his temper, he will go through life making friends, taking part in a multitude of different activities and generally achieving many of his objectives. His life will rarely be dull.

THE FIVE DIFFERENT TYPES OF HORSE

In addition to the 12 signs of the Chinese zodiac there are five elements, and these have a strengthening or moderating influence on the sign. The effects of the five elements on the Horse are described below, together with the years in which the elements were exercising their influence. Therefore those Horses born in 1930 and 1990 are Metal Horses, those born in 1942 and 2002 are Water Horses, and so on.

Metal Horse: 1930, 1990

This Horse is bold, confident and forthright. He is ambitious and a great innovator. He loves challenges and takes great delight in sorting out complicated problems. He likes to have a certain amount of independence and resents any outside interference in his affairs. He has charm and a certain charisma, but he can also be very stubborn and rather impulsive. He usually has many friends and enjoys an active social life.

Water Horse: 1942, 2002

The Water Horse has a friendly nature and a good sense of humour and is able to talk intelligently on a wide range of topics. He is astute in business matters and quick to take advantage of any opportunities that arise. He does, however, have a tendency to get easily distracted and can change his interests – and indeed his mind – rather frequently, and this can often work to his detriment. He is nevertheless very talented and can often go far in life. He pays a great deal of attention to his appearance and is usually smart and well turned out. He loves to travel and also enjoys sport and other outdoor activities.

Wood Horse: 1954

The Wood Horse has a most agreeable and amiable nature. He communicates well with others and is able to talk intelligently on many different subjects. He is a hard and conscientious worker and is held in high esteem by his friends and colleagues. His opinions are often sought and, given his imaginative nature, he can often come up with some very original and practical ideas. He is usually widely read and likes to lead a busy social life. He can also be most generous and often holds high moral views.

Fire Horse: 1966

The element of Fire combined with the temperament of the Horse creates one of the most powerful forces in the Chinese zodiac. The Fire Horse is destined to lead an exciting and eventful life and to make his mark in his chosen profession. He has a forceful personality and his intelligence and resolute manner bring him the support and admiration of many. He loves action and excitement and his life will rarely be quiet. He can, however, be rather blunt and forthright in his views and does not take kindly to interference in his own affairs or to obeying orders. He is a flamboyant character, has a good sense of humour and will lead a very active social life.

Earth Horse: 1918, 1978

This Horse is considerate and caring. He is more cautious than some of the other types of Horse, but he is wise, perceptive and extremely capable. Although he can be rather indecisive at times, he has considerable business acumen and is very astute in financial matters. He has a quiet, friendly nature and is well thought of by his family and friends.

PROSPECTS FOR THE HORSE IN 2007

The Year of the Dog (29 January 2006 to 17 February 2007) is a generally encouraging one for the Horse, although in the closing months he would do well to watch his independent and self-willed nature. To make progress he will need to liaise with others and build up support for what he wants to do. A go-it-alone attitude could spell problems. The more the Horse acts in co-operation with others, the better this part of the year will go.

In his domestic life this will be a particularly busy time, sometimes made all the more so by the fact that some Horses will have moved during the Dog year and/or will be keen to set about ambitious home projects or make certain acquisitions. With so much practical activity, the Horse does need to remain well organized. However, while the closing months of the Dog year will be busy, the Horse will enjoy many of the family occasions that take place as well as the opportunities to spend time with relations he does not often see.

The Horse can also look forward to increased activity in his social life at this time and for those who are unattached or enjoying new-found romance, this can be an exciting time.

In his work the Horse will need to work closely with others. With a sometimes heavy workload or additional pressures to cope with, he will find that joint effort will lead to more being accomplished.

The Year of the Pig begins on 18 February and will be a mixed one for the Horse. In some matters he will enjoy considerable good fortune, but in others there could be pressures and delays. However, the Horse is blessed with a resourceful nature, and while some of the year may not go as smoothly as he may like, he can still emerge with gains to his credit.

One area which is encouragingly aspected is his financial situation. During the Pig year many Horses can look forward to a noticeable rise in their income and some could also receive money from another source, including a possible gift, bonus or the maturing of a savings policy. Those with a more enterprising nature could also supplement their earnings thanks to an idea or skill or some free-lance work. Financially, the Pig year can be a much-improved one.

In view of this upturn the Horse would do well to manage his resources carefully. By giving some thought to any more substantial purchases and plans, he will not only make more satisfying choices as a result but often obtain better value too. If he is able to make any savings or add to an existing plan or pension policy, what he is able to set aside now could grow into a useful asset in the future. With good planning and control, many Horses will be able to improve on their current situation and help their future too.

The Horse would also do well to consider taking a holiday over the year, and by giving careful thought to his destination, he will appreciate the places he gets to see as well as benefit from the rest and change his travels can bring. His personal interests can also benefit him over the year. Not only can these help to keep his lifestyle in balance but they can also give him the chance to get out of doors, meet others and take additional exercise. In this often busy year it is important that the Horse gives time to himself as well as appreciates *and benefits* from the rewards that his efforts bring.

In his domestic life the Horse will play his usual central role, helping and advising loved ones as well as doing a lot around the home. The practical activity so often seen in the Dog year is set to continue, although in this already busy year the Horse does need to be careful not to become involved in too much all at once. Also, if attempting any ambitious or strenuous projects himself, it is important that he follows the recommended procedures and the safety guidelines. This is not a year for risks. Similarly, if commissioning others to carry out repairs or work for him, it would be worth him getting several quotations as well as planning carefully what needs to be done. Practical activities do need careful consideration.

The Horse's social life is positively aspected and during the course of the year he will enjoy meeting up with friends as well as attending a variety of social events. Some of his interests and activities could lead to him adding to his social circle. On a personal level, the Pig year is an encouraging one. April and May could be quite active for social matters and see new friendships and possible romance, but the busiest and most exciting times socially will be in the second half of the year, particularly in the closing months, from October onwards.

As far as the Horse's work is concerned, this will be an important year. With his commitment and willingness to work hard, he could well secure promotion or move to a more responsible (and remunerative) position. However, while there will be opportunities to advance his career, the Horse's workload will often be heavy and sometimes made all the more demanding by delays, problems and pressures. Despite its opportunities, the Pig year can be an exacting one.

To deal with the demands of the year the Horse would find it helpful to show some flexibility in his approach. Being prepared to think around problems and difficult situations will lead to better progress being made. Rather than remain frustrated by what he cannot do, the Horse should concentrate on what he can. With an adaptable approach, he can, even in the face of sometimes difficult conditions, achieve some notable successes.

For those Horses seeking work the Pig year can bring some good opportunities, but to be successful these Horses will need to remain determined. There will be disappointments along the way, but by keeping faith with themselves and their skills, many will secure what will be an ideal position. Results *will* need be worked for and the Pig year can be a hard taskmaster, but the Horse, tenacious and hard-working, certainly has it in him to triumph over the challenges the year will present. March and May could bring some good openings, but generally the second half of the year will be better and more productive, with further opportunities arising from late September to mid-December.

The Year of the Pig will be a busy one for the Horse and there will be pressures and problems, but by being adaptable, drawing on the support of others and rising to the challenges, he will have the chance to show his true qualities. Also, despite the demanding nature of the year, there will be rewards for his efforts, with a noticeable improvement in his financial situation, the chance to travel and continued pleasure from his personal interests. The support of family and friends will also be of value. The second half of the Pig year will be better than the first, with the last quarter seeing the Horse reaping some well-deserved (and sometimes hard-won) success.

The Metal Horse

There is a Chinese proverb which the Metal Horse would do well to bear in mind this year: 'The gem cannot be polished without friction, nor man perfected without trials.' Some of the situations the Metal Horse will face in 2007 will certainly test him. However, he will emerge wiser, more confident and with some important personal achievements to his credit. Despite its pressures, the Pig year will leave a valuable legacy.

For those Metal Horses in education this is a year for focus and discipline. To do well and secure the results they want, these Metal Horses will need to put in the effort as well as have faith in their own abilities. Sometimes they could find certain subjects difficult or be disappointed with some of the feedback or marks they may receive, but by learning from this and any mistakes they may have made, they will be better prepared for next time. As the proverb states, trials help perfect man, and the situations and pressures of the Pig year can be instructive.

Also, as the Metal Horse sets about studying and preparing for examinations, he should remember that what he is doing now is for his long-term benefit and by making the effort he will not only be helping his present situation but also increasing his range of options for later.

For those Metal Horses who are in work or who seek work this year, the Pig year can again be a challenging one. For those already working, there will be times when they will feel bored and unfulfilled and perhaps consider that their work is unappreciated. However, while their situation may not always be satisfactory, the position they have is still an important foothold on the employment ladder and can lead to something better. If they contact those able to give advice and information, they could be given ideas worth pursuing. This particularly applies to those Metal Horses who feel they are not in the right line of work. Some of these Metal Horses may also decide to return to education or consider an apprenticeship. Doing something positive about their situation can prove helpful both now and in the future. March and May could see interesting developments, but the best chances will arise in the second half of the year, particularly from late September to mid-December.

For those Metal Horses seeking work again the Pig year can be difficult. In some cases, there may be few openings and fierce competition. Also, these Metal Horses could find themselves lacking the experience and skills that certain positions require, and there will be disappointments in their quest. By remaining determined, however, and seeking advice, these Metal Horses *will* find their perseverance being rewarded. And once on the employment ladder they will find that other possibilities can open up. The Pig year, for all its pressures and disappointments, can have considerable long-term value.

In addition to the experience, skills and qualifications the Metal Horse can gain over the year, he should also consider furthering his personal interests. In some cases learning new techniques or skills can lead to him achieving more, and if he sees any courses that appeal or has chances to add to what he does, he should follow them up. Those who are keen to develop a particular skill or interest with a view to turning it into a vocation may find what they learn to be of immense value. Metal Horses, do take note.

As with other Horses, the Metal Horse's financial prospects are generally positive this year. Those in work, or who obtain work during the year, will find their earnings will allow them to do more, while those in education will often find ways to supplement their position. In addition, some Metal Horses could benefit from an enterprising idea they have. Generally, the Metal Horse's efforts and willingness can lead to an improvement in his financial situation. However, to benefit, he would find it helpful to keep close watch on his spending as well as save towards any more expensive purchases and plans he may have in mind.

The Metal Horse's social prospects are also encouraging and he will find himself much in demand. As a result of his various activities, he will find his social circle widening quite considerably. The Pig year will certainly bring happy times, although a word of caution does need be sounded. Over-indulgence or a succession of late nights could start to have an effect and leave the Metal Horse tired, not at his best and prone to minor ailments. In the Pig year he does need to strike a balance in his lifestyle as well as be mindful of his well-being. However, on a social level, this will be a busy and often enjoyable year with April, May and the last quarter seeing the most activity.

With the pressures the Pig year will bring and some of the decisions the Metal Horse will need to take, whether educationally or concerning work choices, it is also important that he talks to others and listens carefully to their advice. Family members can be especially helpful. Knowing the Metal Horse as well as they do, their words, support and advice can serve him well.

The Pig year may not be the easiest of years for the Metal Horse and he will need to work hard to make progress. His achievements can, however, prove of great value, especially in the longer term. And despite the pressures, the year will also contain some enjoyable times, particularly socially and in the way the Metal Horse is able to further his personal interests.

Whenever facing problems or decisions, do seek the advice of others. Also remember that skills and qualifications acquired now can open up possibilities later on. It *is* worth making the effort.

The Water Horse

This will be an improved year for the Water Horse, and with commitment and good support, he will fare well.

For those Water Horses in work the year will bring considerable change, with some deciding to retire or to reduce their working hours. Not only will these Water Horses welcome the additional free time this now gives, but they will view the year as the start of a new chapter in their lives. However, to make most of their time and opportunities, these Water Horses should give careful thought to what they would like to do and then set their plans in motion. As the saying goes, 'There is no time like the present.'

With this being a year of change, many Water Horses will decide to set themselves a new personal challenge. For some this could be in the form of taking up a new interest or skill and perhaps enrolling on a suitable course or joining an activity group or society in their area. Any positive steps the Water Horse can take will be very much to his advantage.

The Water Horse is also blessed with an adventurous nature and travel will again appeal to him over the year. If there is a particular place he would like to visit or he sees a travel offer that interests him, he should follow it up. The Pig year is one for acting positively. In addition, many

Water Horses will receive invitations to visit family and friends living some distance away, and these too would be worth taking up. As the Water Horse will find, visiting others and discovering different areas can often be fun. And for the unattached Water Horse, travel could also have a pleasing social element.

With his often active lifestyle the Water Horse usually takes good care of himself, but over the Pig year he would do well to give consideration to his general well-being. If, for instance, he is reliant on convenience foods he could find switching to a more balanced diet will give him more energy. Similarly, if he lacks general exercise, some additional walking, swimming or other physical activity could help. However, before starting to make changes, the Water Horse should seek medical guidance on the most suitable way to proceed.

The Water Horse will value his domestic life over the year and will often be grateful for the advice and input of others. In some cases, encouraging others to join him in his interests can give what he does greater meaning and purpose.

With his practical nature the Water Horse will also spend time carrying out projects and improvements to his home. Those who may have moved in the previous Dog year or decide to move this year will often have ambitious ideas in mind. However, despite their eagerness, these Water Horses do need to allow plenty of time to carry through their plans. Problems, delays and last-minute snags can occur and the Water Horse will often find that his plans take longer to complete than he anticipated. Where accommodation matters are concerned, patience and some forbearance will be needed. Also, while this is a positive year for financial matters, the Water Horse does need to keep a watch on his accommodation and, if applicable, moving costs. He should also make sure insurance policies and premiums are kept up to date. To avoid problems and additional costs, he does need be vigilant when dealing with accommodation matters and important paperwork.

However, while there is a need for care, many Water Horses can look forward to some good fortune in money matters. This can include a bonus from their work, a gift, the fruition of a policy or the chance to earn something extra from an idea or skill they have. By using his money well and setting sums aside for accommodation plans, travel and, if he is able, for the future as well, the Water Horse will often be pleased with what he is able to do. This is a year when careful thought and planning will serve him well.

With his outgoing nature the Water Horse also attaches much importance to his social life and this too will see an upturn over the year. Those Water Horses who take up new interests or become involved in different activities will often come into contact with others. Those who would welcome more companionship, perhaps as a result of moving to a new area or other changes in their personal circumstances, will find that by going out more and possibly getting involved in community or charity work, they can enjoy a brighter social life. For social activities, mid-March to May and the last quarter of the year are especially favourable.

Overall this will be a pleasing year for the Water Horse and by using his time well, planning his various activities and acting upon his ideas, he will do a great deal. However, with the niggling aspects that can prevail in the Pig year (especially in the first half), he does need to show some patience as well as liaise closely with others.

TIP FOR THE YEAR
Try out something new, especially as far as your personal interests are concerned. These can open up some rewarding possibilities for you. Also, with practical activities, do allow plenty of time.

The Wood Horse

This will be a generally satisfying year for the Wood Horse, although throughout he will need to remain realistic in his activities and plans. This is not a year for embarking on major change or for taking substantial risks and, as with all Horses this year, the Wood Horse will need to show a good deal of patience.

In his work the Wood Horse will fare best by concentrating on the areas in which he has most experience rather than looking to switch to something different. For those who are relatively new to their current position or have seen recent changes in their place of work, this is an ideal year to focus their attention on their duties and get better established. Also, because of their experience and background, some Wood Horses could be given the chance to take on more specialist tasks or a supervisory role, and their new responsibilities will often bring them greater fulfilment.

Although many Wood Horses will remain with their present employer over the year, for those who are particularly keen to move on or are seeking work, the Pig year can bring some interesting developments. However, securing a new position will require considerable determination. Sometimes there could be a lack of suitable openings or considerable competition for certain positions, but by persisting, emphasizing their experience and stressing what they could bring to the role, many Wood Horses will be successful in their quest. To make progress in the Pig year *will* call for effort and patience, but fortunately the Wood Horse is blessed with much fortitude. The best work opportunities will occur in March, May and the period from late September to early December.

The Wood Horse will fare well in money matters over the year and could not only enjoy a rise in income but also benefit from a gift or a sum from another source. Some Wood Horses may also be able to supplement their earnings through additional work or an interest they have. Financially, the aspects are certainly encouraging. As a result, the Wood Horse could consider reducing any borrowings he may have as well as setting sums aside for his current plans and for the longer term. The better he can manage his finances, the more he will benefit from the improvement the year will bring.

Many Wood Horses will spend considerable sums on their home over the year, often making alterations as well as buying new fittings and furnishings. Some may even move. Accommodation matters will certainly feature prominently for many. Here again, the Wood Horse will need to be thorough, check any obligations he may be taking on and, in keeping with the general nature of the year, be prepared to show some patience. Despite his eagerness, his plans may take longer to complete than he envisaged.

In addition to spending on his home, the Wood Horse would also do well to make sure he takes a holiday over the year. Travel is favourably aspected and a break from his routine will do him a lot of good. In addition there could be chances for him to go away at short notice, perhaps for a weekend break or to visit someone, and this too can work out well.

It would also be beneficial for the Wood Horse to give some thought to his general well-being over the year. To keep himself on good form and do all he wants, he does need to look after himself. If, at any time, he thinks some modifications could help, or he is feeling below par, he should seek advice. The attention he can give to his well-being and his lifestyle can be to his benefit.

Domestically, this will be a busy year. In addition to their existing commitments, many Wood Horses will devote much time to their home and garden, as well as involving themselves in many other things besides. In view of the often high level of activity, it is important that the Wood Horse remains well organized and consults those around him. The better his planning, the more he can achieve. Also, he should ensure time is set aside for spending with others and enjoying the rewards that he (and everyone else) has worked so hard for. In this active year, quality time spent with loved ones should not be sacrificed. The Pig year can provide some meaningful occasions.

This also applies to the Wood Horse's social life. Although he will often have many demands on his time, he should make the most of his opportunities to go out. His social life can be a good way for him to unwind and enjoy himself and, with his outgoing nature and wide interests, he not only makes popular company but also enjoys meeting others. Late March to May and the last quarter of the year will be the most active times socially and for those Wood Horses who would welcome new friendships or perhaps even romance, the Pig year can see a considerable improvement in their situation.

The Pig year is a generally promising one for the Wood Horse, although to do well he will need to plan his activities carefully as well as liaise closely with others. He will also need to show some patience, particularly as some of his plans may take longer to realize than he anticipated.

TIP FOR THE YEAR
In view of all the activity of the year it is important that you keep your lifestyle in balance. Make sure quality time is spent with those who are special to you and do not drive yourself so hard that your social life and personal interests suffer. Strive for a sensible balance.

The Fire Horse

The Fire Horse possesses a determined nature and is always keen to make the most of his situation. However, in the Pig year he will need to tread carefully. As all Horses will find, plans can be subject to delay and alteration, and the Fire Horse could also find a lot being expected of him. However, while the year will bring its pressures, it will also have its positive aspects and will be of long-term value.

Work-wise this can be a demanding year, with the Fire Horse facing a heavy workload as well as sometimes challenging objectives. His situation may not be helped by niggling problems that crop up, the attitude of others or the workings of bureaucracy. However, while the year will contain its exasperating moments, by focusing his attention on his duties and doing his best, the Fire Horse will find his talents, industry and persistence leading to some worthy achievements.

Many Fire Horses will decide to remain in their current position during the year and to build on their experience, but for those who are keen to progress or are seeking work, the Pig year will bring some interesting opportunities. However, their best prospects will be in the areas in which they already have expertise rather than anything too different. In their quest, these Fire Horses would do well to draw on the support and information available to them. This could include contacting agencies, speaking to those able to offer advice and, if they are eligible, going on training or refresher courses. Progress in the Pig year will require determination and persistence, but by doing all they can to improve their chances, many Fire Horses will be successful in gaining a new position. March, May and the period from October to mid-December could see the best opportunities.

The Fire Horse can look forward to an improvement in his financial situation over the year and, as well as an increase in income, some Fire Horses may also be able to supplement their earnings through an interest or idea they can put to profitable use. The Pig year can see quite a financial upturn, but the Fire Horse does still need to manage his money well rather than proceed on too much of an ad hoc basis. This is a year for discipline, and as well as saving up for all his plans, the Fire Horse should consider setting something aside for the longer term. Even small amounts set aside regularly can grow into a useful asset in future years.

This will also be an active year as far as the Fire Horse's domestic life is concerned. In particular both younger and more senior relations will look to him for advice and support and there could be some important decisions to take. Although the Fire Horse may have his concerns about some of the plans and attitudes that others may have, by being willing to discuss various options, his input and judgement will prove of great value. Again, important decisions should not be rushed, and the more discussion and openness the better.

In addition to helping those close to him, the Fire Horse will also play an important role in keeping his household well-organized. Here his talents will be truly appreciated. However, he should also make sure that others do their fair share. At busy times – and there will be quite a few this year – it is important that he asks for (and obtains) support and assistance.

However, despite the often demanding nature of the Pig year, it will also contain some meaningful times for the Fire Horse. There may be family successes to celebrate and perhaps a memorable holiday. The year may be busy, but it will also have its pleasures.

The Fire Horse should also make sure his own personal interests and social life do not suffer due to the various activities and pressures of the year. Both can be excellent ways for him to relax and unwind. For some Fire Horses, their interests can also have a strong social element or enable them to take additional exercise. Whatever the Fire Horse does, in this busy year it is important that he spends some time on the activities he enjoys rather than continually drives himself hard.

Generally, while the year will bring pressures and the Fire Horse will need to show patience, his efforts, diligence and experience will serve him well. Financially, this can be an improved year and his home life will also be important and meaningful. However, with many demands on his time, he does need to strike a balance in his lifestyle as well as draw on the assistance available to him.

TIP FOR THE YEAR
Remain focused and disciplined. Concentrate on your priorities and use your time well. This is no year to become diverted from your aims or to spread your energies too widely. Also, to keep your lifestyle in balance, make sure you spend time with those who are special to you.

The Earth Horse
This will be a reasonable year for the Earth Horse and one which can also have important long-term value.

In his work the Earth Horse can look forward to making steady progress and many Earth Horses will take on new responsibilities over the year. Often this will be with their present employer and their experience and in-house knowledge will stand them in good stead. However, a lot will be expected of the Earth Horse and there could be much for him to learn. Some parts of the year will be challenging, but by focusing on what needs to be done, he will gain invaluable experience. Progress made in 2007 can be a stepping-stone to greater progress in the years ahead.

For those Earth Horses who feel there are limited opportunities where they are or who are keen to widen their experience in other areas, again the Pig year can bring significant opportunities. However, to benefit, these Earth Horses will need to show initiative. There will often be fierce competition for certain positions and they will need to stress their experience and qualities to prospective employers. Progress in the Pig year will require determination *and* persistence.

This also applies to those Earth Horses seeking work. Although some may have become disheartened with their situation, deep down the Earth Horse does know he has the talents and capabilities that can take him far, and with effort and persistence he may well be successful in getting back onto the employment ladder. The Pig year may not be an easy one, but it can pave the way to future success.

For all Earth Horses, interesting work developments can take place in March and May, but the second half of the year will be generally easier than the first, especially the months from late September to early December. Also, with the year's emphasis on personal development, if the Earth Horse has skills he is keen to develop or there is a qualification which could be useful to him, he should follow through his ideas. In this respect, too, what he does now will often be of future benefit.

The Pig year will also see an improvement in the Earth Horse's finances. In addition to an increase in income, he could also receive sums from other sources and an idea he has could bring a useful return. However, to reap the benefits, the Earth Horse should manage his money carefully. Good budgeting and planning will certainly allow him to do that much more.

As with last year, accommodation matters could feature prominently, with some Earth Horses moving and/or spending considerable sums on their home. Where large transactions are concerned, the Earth Horse needs to take careful note of all the implications and, if possible, budget for these in advance. Should he have any questions or uncertainties regarding a financial matter, it is important that he seeks advice before proceeding.

As far as the Earth Horse's domestic life is concerned, this can be a rewarding year. Although the Earth Horse and loved ones may face demands and pressures, especially in their work and daily commitments, by listening to and supporting each other, they can make this a special time. Admittedly, some of the year will be tiring, especially for those Earth Horses with young families, but there could also be good cause for celebration, whether through a house move, an addition to the family or a personal success.

With his often busy lifestyle the Earth Horse may be more selective in his socializing this year, but he should still aim to stay in contact with his friends and go out to events that appeal to him. His social life is, after all, an excellent way for him to unwind. For the unattached, the Pig year could also hold some exciting romantic possibilities, with a chance meeting leading to a wonderful new relationship. April, May and October to December will be the most active months socially and here again the second half of the Pig year will be better than the first.

While the Earth Horse will need to work hard to make progress in the Pig year, the experience he gains can prove significant in his future success and he will be encouraged by the support of those around him.

Although there will be many demands on your time, do spend time with those who are special to you. Also make the most of chances to further your knowledge and skills. What you do now will be an important investment in your future.

FAMOUS HORSES

Neil Armstrong, Rowan Atkinson, José Manuel Barroso, Samuel Beckett, Ingmar Bergman, Leonard Bernstein, Cherie Blair, Helena Bonham Carter, James Blunt, David Cameron, James Cameron, Jackie Chan, Ray Charles, Chopin, Sir Sean Connery, Billy Connolly, Catherine Cookson, Elvis Costello, Kevin Costner, Cindy Crawford, Michael Crichton, James Dean, Clint Eastwood, Thomas Alva Edison, Harrison Ford, Aretha Franklin, Bob Geldof, Samuel Goldwyn, Billy Graham, Gene Hackman, Rolf Harris, Rita Hayworth, Jimi Hendrix, Janet Jackson, Calvin Klein, Lemar, Lenin, Annie Lennox, Desmond Lynam, Sir Paul McCartney, Nelson Mandela, Angela Merkel, Michael Moore, Ben Murphy, Sir Isaac Newton, Louis Pasteur, Harold Pinter, Lou Reed, Rembrandt, Ruth Rendell, Jean Renoir, Condoleezza Rice, Theodore Roosevelt, Helena Rubenstein, David Schwimmer, Alexander Solzhenitsyn, Rachel Stevens, Barbra Streisand, Kiefer Sutherland, Patrick Swayze, John Travolta, Kathleen Turner, Vivaldi, Robert Wagner, Denzil Washington, Billy Wilder, Andy Williams, Brian Wilson, the Duke of Windsor, Will Young.

13 FEBRUARY 1907 ～ 1 FEBRUARY 1908		*Fire Goat*
1 FEBRUARY 1919 ～ 19 FEBRUARY 1920		*Earth Goat*
17 FEBRUARY 1931 ～ 5 FEBRUARY 1932		*Metal Goat*
5 FEBRUARY 1943 ～ 24 JANUARY 1944		*Water Goat*
24 JANUARY 1955 ～ 11 FEBRUARY 1956		*Wood Goat*
9 FEBRUARY 1967 ～ 29 JANUARY 1968		*Fire Goat*
28 JANUARY 1979 ～ 15 FEBRUARY 1980		*Earth Goat*
15 FEBRUARY 1991 ～ 3 FEBRUARY 1992		*Metal Goat*
1 FEBRUARY 2003 ～ 21 JANUARY 2004		*Water Goat*

THE
GOAT

THE PERSONALITY OF THE GOAT

'Follow your honest convictions and be strong.'
William Makepeace Thackeray, a Goat

The Goat is born under the sign of art. He is imaginative, creative and has a good appreciation of the finer things in life. He has an easy-going nature and prefers to live in a relaxed and pressure-free environment. He hates any sort of discord or unpleasantness and does not like to be bound by a strict routine or rigid timetable. He is not one to be hurried against his will, but despite his seemingly relaxed approach to life, he is something of a perfectionist and when he starts work on a project he is certain to give his best.

The Goat usually prefers to work in a team rather than on his own. He likes to have the support and encouragement of others and if left to deal with matters on his own he can get very worried and tend to view things rather pessimistically. Wherever possible he will leave major decision-making to others while he concentrates on his own pursuits. If, however, he feels particularly strongly about a certain matter or has to defend his position in any way, he will act with great fortitude and precision.

The Goat has a very persuasive nature and often uses his considerable charm to get his own way. He can, however, be rather hesitant about letting his true feelings be known and if he were prepared to be more forthright he would do much better as a result.

The Goat tends to have a quiet, somewhat reserved nature, but when he is in company he likes he can often become the centre of attention. He can be highly amusing, a marvellous host at parties and a superb entertainer. Whenever the spotlight falls on him, his adrenaline starts to flow and he can be assured of giving a sparkling performance, particularly if he is allowed to use his creative skills in any way.

Of all the signs in the Chinese zodiac, the Goat is probably the most gifted artistically. Whether it is in the theatre, literature, music or art, he is certain to make a lasting impression. He is a born creator and is rarely happier than when occupied in some artistic pursuit. But even in this the Goat does well to work with others rather than on his own. He needs inspiration and a guiding influence, but when he has found his true *métier*, he can often receive widespread acclaim and recognition.

In addition to his liking for the arts, the Goat is usually quite religious and often has a deep interest in nature, animals and the countryside. He is also fairly athletic and there are many Goats who have excelled in some form of sporting activity or who have a great interest in sport.

Although the Goat is not particularly materialistic or concerned about finance, he will find that he will usually be lucky in financial matters and will rarely be short of the necessary funds to tide himself over. He is, however, rather self-indulgent and tends to spend his money as soon as he receives it rather than make provision for the future.

The Goat usually leaves home when he is young but he will always maintain strong links with his parents and the other members of his family. He is also rather nostalgic and is well known for keeping mementoes of his childhood and souvenirs of places that he has visited. His home will not be particularly tidy, but he knows where everything is and it will also be scrupulously clean.

Affairs of the heart are particularly important to the Goat and he will often have many romances before he finally settles down. Although he is fairly adaptable, he prefers to live in a secure and stable environment and he will find that he is best suited to those born under the signs of the Tiger, Horse, Monkey, Pig and Rabbit. He can also establish a good relationship with the Dragon, Snake, Rooster and another Goat, but he may find the Ox and Dog a little too serious for his liking. Neither will he care particularly for the Rat's rather thrifty ways.

The female Goat devotes all her time and energy to the needs of her family. She has excellent taste in home furnishings and often uses her considerable artistic skills to good advantage. She takes great care over her appearance and can be most attractive to others. Although she is not the most organized of people, her engaging manner and delightful sense of humour create a favourable impression wherever she goes. She is also a good cook and usually derives much pleasure from gardening and outdoor pursuits.

The Goat can win friends easily and people generally feel relaxed in his company. He has a kind and understanding nature and although he can occasionally be stubborn, he can, with the right support and encouragement, live a happy and very satisfying life. And the more he can use his creative skills, the happier he will be.

THE FIVE DIFFERENT TYPES OF GOAT

In addition to the 12 signs of the Chinese zodiac there are five elements and these have a strengthening or moderating influence on the sign. The effects of the five elements on the Goat are described below, together with the years in which the elements were exercising their influence. Therefore those Goats born in 1931 and 1991 are Metal Goats, those born in 1943 and 2003 are Water Goats, and so on.

Metal Goat: 1931, 1991

This Goat is thorough and conscientious in all that he does and is capable of doing very well in his chosen profession. Despite his confident manner, he can be a great worrier and he would find it helpful to discuss his concerns with others rather than keep them to himself. He is loyal to his family and employers and will have a small group of particularly close friends. He has good taste and is usually highly skilled in some aspect of the arts. He is often a collector of antiques and his home will be very tastefully furnished.

Water Goat: 1943, 2003

The Water Goat is very popular and makes friends with remarkable ease. He is good at spotting opportunities but does not always have the necessary confidence to follow them through. He likes to have security both in his home life and work and does not take kindly to change. He is articulate, has a good sense of humour and is usually very good with children.

Wood Goat: 1955

This Goat is generous, kind-hearted and always eager to please. He usually has a large circle of friends and involves himself in a wide variety of activities. He has a very trusting nature but he can sometimes give in to the demands of others a little too easily and it would be in his interests if he were to stand his ground more often. He is usually lucky in financial matters and, like the Water Goat, is very good with children.

Fire Goat: 1907, 1967

This Goat usually knows what he wants in life and often uses his considerable charm and persuasive personality to achieve his aims. He can sometimes let his imagination run away with him and has a tendency to ignore matters which are not to his liking. He is rather extravagant in his spending and would do well to exercise a little more care when dealing with financial matters. He has a lively personality, many friends, and loves attending parties and social occasions.

Earth Goat: 1919, 1979

This Goat has a considerate and caring nature. He is particularly loyal to his family and friends and invariably creates a favourable impression wherever he goes. He is reliable and conscientious in his work but sometimes finds it difficult to save and never likes to deprive himself of any little luxury he might fancy. He has numerous interests and is often very well read. He usually derives much pleasure from following the activities of the various members of his family.

PROSPECTS FOR THE GOAT IN 2007

The Year of the Dog (29 January 2006 to 17 February 2007) will have been a mixed one for the Goat and not all his activities will have gone as smoothly as he would have liked. In the closing months, he should remain careful and alert.

In his work the Goat will need to remain focused on his responsibilities and concentrate on the areas he knows best. This is no time for him to get diverted from his main aims or distracted by petty or unhelpful matters. If he has the opportunity to widen his experience, undertake training or take on new duties, he should make the most of it. With his prospects showing a marked improvement in the approaching Pig year, positive action will prove helpful. October and November could see some interesting developments.

The Goat will also need to be careful in financial matters. This is no time for risks and with the closing months of the year being a traditionally more expensive time, if he can save towards his more substantial purchases, as well as spread some of them out, he could find this helpful.

With his amiable nature the Goat usually enjoys excellent relations with others, but with the aspects as they are, he does need to remain attentive in the closing months of the Dog year. Without care a *faux pas* or unguarded comment could cause problems or misunderstandings. However, while there is a need for care and mindfulness, there will still be some enjoyable and personally rewarding times, with September and December seeing much domestic and social activity.

The Year of the Pig, which begins on 18 February, will be a much-improved one for the Goat. Almost as soon as it starts he may sense the tide beginning to turn in his favour and feel determined to improve his situation. This is also a time to draw a line under any recent disappointments and *look to move forward*. With purpose, self-belief and the favourable aspects now emerging, the Goat may find many possibilities opening up for him.

One area which is especially well aspected is the Goat's work. The Pig year will now give him the chance to profit from his skills and often special talents. For those Goats who are currently unfulfilled in their present position, feel in a rut or are seeking work, the Pig year offers hope. Purposeful action can lead to a definite improvement over the year.

For those Goats who are keen to move their career forward, opportunities can arise quickly and sometimes in fortuitous ways. As senior colleagues move on, promotion opportunities can suddenly open up, and chance conversations can also alert the Goat to openings worth pursuing. Events will often work in his favour and even if certain applications do not go his way, there will often be a reason why and a better opportunity will soon appear.

Those Goats who are seeking work or who decide to change their career during the year can also find this an encouraging time. By actively following up vacancies that interest them, as well as drawing on the advice and support that is available, many will secure an opening which can give their career new impetus. By making the most of this and mastering their duties and responsibilities, these Goats will often feel more inspired and fulfilled than they have for some time. The Pig year can bring them the opportunity they have been wanting for so long and help set their career on a more satisfying track. From the beginning of the Pig year to early April and then September and October will see the best opportunities. For those Goats whose work involves presentation or allows them to draw on their creativity, this can be an especially encouraging year and fortune will certainly favour the committed and enterprising.

The Goat's financial prospects are also favourably aspected, and with the progress so many will make at work, their income can show a noticeable increase. Some Goats could also benefit from a gift, a maturing policy or some good fortune enjoyed by other members of their family. Overall, the Goat's financial prospects are certainly encouraging. However, he will still need to manage his money well and should be particularly wary of succumbing to too many temptations. While he will want to reap the rewards of his hard work and success, he would do well to think carefully about any more costly purchases and plans. Too much haste could involve him spending more than is necessary or regretting certain purchases. Control over the purse-strings would be wise.

Also, while much will go the Goat's way during the year, he must be careful not to push his luck too far. If he is tempted by anything speculative or risky, he does need to check all the implications involved as well as seek appropriate advice. This may be a year of financial good fortune, but he should not become careless. Goats, do take note.

This will be an exciting year as far as the Goat's home life is concerned. As always, he will play a pivotal role and will do much to encourage, advise and support those who are dear to him. In turn, when he has pressures of his own and would welcome assistance or even just a listening ear, he should let others know. To benefit, he does need to be forthcoming. There could be personal and family events to celebrate, however, and many Goats can look forward to some special occasions in their domestic life.

The Pig year can also mark an upturn in the Goat's social life, with an increasing number of invitations and opportunities to go out. Often his interests will have a good social element. For the unattached, the year holds excellent romantic possibilities, and someone the Goat meets during the year and finds has similar interests to his own could quickly become an important part of his life. For those Goats who may start 2007 at a low personal ebb, the Pig year holds encouraging prospects, although, to help matters, these Goats would do well to consider ways in which they can improve their present situation. Purposeful action on their part, whether by taking up new interests, joining local groups or just going out more, can mark the beginning of an important new chapter in their lives. The Pig year holds exciting prospects, with March, June to August and December being particularly active months for socializing and meeting others.

In almost all respects the aspects that prevail during the Pig year are encouraging for the Goat. However, to benefit, it does rest with the Goat to make the most of himself *and* his many strengths. With purpose and a willingness to put himself forward, he will find the Pig year holds much promise, and he will be helped by the supportive nature of others and the goodwill shown towards him.

The Metal Goat

This will be a year of considerable opportunity for the Metal Goat and by making the most of himself and his opportunities, he will not only achieve a great deal but also help his future prospects. To benefit, the Metal Goat does need to be willing to put himself forward, but with a positive outlook, he can make this a successful and pleasing year.

For those Metal Goats in education this will be an important year, especially as many will be preparing for exams as well as considering their future options. Although sometimes the Metal Goat may feel daunted by the amount he has to learn, by remaining organized, especially with revision and any course work he has to do, he can look forward to making good progress. Also, while he may have his stronger subject areas, he should not close his mind to those he may find more difficult. By giving his best, he could surprise himself. Some of the Pig year will ask a lot of the Metal Goat, but it is worth putting in the effort.

Throughout the year, if the Metal Goat has problems with certain subjects or what is being asked of him, he should tell others. As he will find, it is better to be open and ask for help rather than worrying, becoming despondent or struggling with work he does not understand.

The Metal Goat will also derive much satisfaction from his personal interests over the year and should make the most of chances to further these. If there is a school club or local interest group he could join, this would be well worth considering. With the encouraging aspects that prevail, this is very much a time when the Metal Goat should make the most of the opportunities available.

For those Metal Goats who decide to seek employment rather than remain in education, much will depend upon their attitude and approach. These Metal Goats will need to put themselves forward and be willing to make an effort, otherwise disappointment could loom. Once in a position, although the Metal Goat may initially find the work routine and sometimes boring, by being prepared to make the most of his situation he will soon find himself being rewarded with more interesting responsibilities. The Pig year is an encouraging one for the Metal Goat, but much depends on his attitude. The first three months of the year could see some encouraging developments and there could also be some good chances to make progress later in the year, notably in September and October 2007 and January 2008. Also, for those Metal Goats who remain in education, there could be opportunities to earn something extra, and by taking up such chances, they will not only be helping their financial situation but could also make new friends.

The Pig year is positively aspected as far as the Metal Goat's social life is concerned and throughout the year he will value the support of his close circle of friends. His interests and daily activities can also lead to new friendships. On a social level the Metal Goat will find himself in demand. For those Metal Goats who may be shy or not feel as much a part of the social scene as they would like, the Pig year can bring the gift of an important new friendship or the chance to pursue activities that will bring them into contact with those they will feel more comfortable with. The Pig year is a supportive one as far as the Metal Goat's social life is concerned.

The Metal Goat's home life will also go well and while he may sometimes desire a little more independence, he will often be grateful for the support and encouragement he is given. Whenever he has important decisions to make or concerns that may be bothering him, it is important that he is prepared to discuss these. This way those close to him will be better able to help and advise. Also, by being willing to play his part in the home, including helping with certain household tasks, he will be able to enhance the rapport and understanding he has with others. In this, as in so much else during the year, his effort, willingness and contribution can make an important difference.

In most respects the Pig year holds good prospects for Metal Goat but, as with all years, there are certain areas which do require greater care. When he is with others, especially when out socializing, the Metal Goat does need to be careful not to get carried away in the excitement of certain situations and say or do things which he could come to regret. In some situations he may need to hold his ground and make sure his views are known, especially at times when important decisions are being considered. If he is not open and frank, he may risk wrong or inappropriate choices being made. Metal Goats, do speak up *and be heard.*

Overall, though, by making most of the situations and opportunities that the year will bring, the Metal Goat will accomplish a great deal. And he can take heart too, because his efforts can be *very* much to his future benefit.

TIP FOR THE YEAR
Have faith in yourself and your abilities. Even though there may be pressures and some difficult moments, by doing your best and making the most of your situation, you will find your efforts bearing fruit.

The Water Goat

This will be a satisfying year for the Water Goat, although to make the most of the favourable aspects, he will need to stay well organized and be prepared to act upon his ideas, otherwise valuable chances could be lost. This is very much a year for seizing the initiative and being bold.

For those Water Goats in work this can be an important year. In view of the considerable experience they have built up there will often be opportunities to become involved in more specialist tasks and, in some cases, take on the promotion that they have long sought. Again, though, to benefit from the special opportunities that the year will bring, these Water Goats will need to put themselves forward and make their experience count.

Alternatively, some Water Goats who will choose to retire or reduce their working commitments this year. These Water Goats will welcome the chance to spend more time in the ways they want, and with careful planning can make this a personally rewarding year.

As far as financial matters are concerned, this will be an improved year. For some Water Goats this will be through an increase in income or a bonus payment, the fruition of a policy or a gift. However, to fully benefit, the Water Goat does need to manage his money well rather than be tempted to spend too readily. Here again, good planning will help, and if the Water Goat has any expensive purchases and plans he would like to carry out, it would be worth him costing these carefully as well as waiting for favourable buying opportunities. Patience and careful consideration will often lead to better purchases. The Water Goat will also find it helpful to give some attention to his financial position over the year and if he is able to reduce any borrowings or set something aside for the future, this would be worth considering. With this being a positive year for financial matters, his care and good management can reward him well.

The Water Goat is also blessed with a creative nature and over the year should make much of his talents and ideas. Those who enjoy craftwork or expressing themselves through writing, art, music, photography or some other art form should not be reticent about putting forward what they produce. They could enjoy some encouraging responses. Those Water Goats who now have more time available for interests and recreational pursuits should also consider furthering their skills and knowledge, perhaps through personal study, enrolling on a course or setting themselves new challenges. By giving themselves something purposeful to do, they can add a richness to the year.

The Pig year will also bring some good travel opportunities and the Water Goat should make the most of these. In particular, if he sees a travel opportunity that appeals or there is a place he is keen to visit, he should follow it up. Many Water Goats will also get the chance to go away for short breaks or to visit family and friends living some distance away. For those who would welcome new friendships and the chance to meet others, a well-chosen holiday could be a good way to lift their spirits.

With his amiable nature the Water Goat very much values his social life and in 2007 this will again not disappoint. There will often be opportunities for him to go out as well as to take part in activities and events in his local area. Any new interests the Water Goat becomes involved with can also be a good way for him to meet others. For those who would welcome a brighter and more fulfilling social life, action and involvement are the key. March, June to August and December will be the best and most active months socially.

As far as the Water Goat's domestic life is concerned, this can be a personally rewarding year with some surprises. In particular a younger relation could have some pleasing and unexpected news which will much delight the Water Goat. He will also be grateful for the support shown for his various activities, and when considering new interests or ideas, he would do well to talk these over with his loved ones. Others can help the Water Goat get so much more out of the year.

However, while so much can go well for him, one thing that the Water Goat will need to watch over the year is acting in haste, especially in hurrying through plans and purchases. The more care and time he can take, the better his decisions will be. In addition, when dealing with important paperwork or matters which could have financial implications, he will again need to be thorough rather than rush or overlook details. Water Goats, do take note.

In most respects this will be a positive and satisfying year for the Water Goat and by making the most of his ideas and strengths and the situations that arise, he can look forward to some fine achievements. The love, friendship and support of others can also help make this a rewarding and often special year.

TIP FOR THE YEAR

This is a year for action and resolve. With determination and support, backed by your own personal qualities, you really can accomplish a lot. Believe in yourself, set your plans in motion and go after what *you* want.

The Wood Goat

The Wood Goat will enjoy a marked improvement in his fortunes during the Pig year and for those who may start the year in low spirits, it holds much brighter prospects. However, to benefit, the Wood Goat will need to take action. This is very much a year for acting on his aims and ambitions as well as drawing a line under any recent setbacks. Indeed, some Wood Goats will find the Pig year representing the start of a new chapter in their lives.

In the Wood Goat's work the aspects are especially encouraging. For those who are well established in their career and keen to make progress, there will be excellent chances to take on greater responsibilities and secure promotion. In some cases, positions they have wanted in their present place of work will now become available; in others, they will see ideal openings with other employers. By keeping alert the Wood Goat can make significant headway and secure some often hard-earned and sometimes overdue success.

For those Wood Goats who may feel unfulfilled and consider there is a lack of opportunity where they are, this too is a year for decisive action. Little will change unless they do, and by seizing the initiative, making enquiries and considering what it is they really want to do, they can open up some interesting possibilities. While sometimes making a change will be daunting, these Wood Goats will often feel that their actions have given their career a new lease of life and will feel more motivated and inspired than they have felt for a long time.

This also applies to those Wood Goats seeking work. Although many will have experienced some recent disappointments, the Pig year can give rise to some exciting possibilities. To benefit, however, these Wood Goats will need to remain persistent, obtain information and guidance and take advantage of any retraining or refresher courses that may be available. Their efforts and initiative may well lead to them setting their career off on a new track. The period from the start of the Pig year to early April, then September and October and January 2008 could see some particularly good opportunities, but throughout the year the Wood Goat's prospects are encouraging and with determined action, he can make significant progress.

The year is also favourable for financial matters and in addition to enjoying an increase in income many Wood Goats could benefit from some financial good fortune, often in the form of a gift or bonus. In view of this, many will decide to go ahead with plans and purchases for their accommodation as well as for their interests and travel. However, as with all Goats, this is no time for the Wood Goat to be too hasty and he should take his time when making more sizeable purchases or conducting important transactions. In addition, if he is in a position to make savings or set something aside for the future, this would be well worth considering.

The Pig year is well aspected for travel and the Wood Goat should try to go away at some time. A break from his usual routine will do him a lot of good. Those with special interests, for instance in art, culture, history or sport, will find that by planning their itinerary carefully, they can make their holiday all the more special. In addition there could be opportunities for the Wood Goat to take short breaks over the year and by taking up invitations and seizing his chances, he will often enjoy his trips.

Being born under the sign of art, there are many Wood Goats who have a creative side to their nature and, for those who enjoy more expressive pursuits, this would be an excellent year to take their talents further. Any Wood Goats who have let their interests lapse recently would do well to set some time aside for recreational pursuits they enjoy. Positive action on their part can be to their benefit as well as sometimes open up other possibilities in the future.

Domestically, this will be a busy year and good organization and communication will be important. The Wood Goat does need to remain mindful of those close to him and take their views into account. If he fails to consult others or sets about his plans in too much of a rush, problems could arise. Here again, this is a year when patience and good planning are called for. There could, however, be some exciting family news for the Wood Goat to celebrate, especially concerning the success of a younger relation.

Socially, the Pig year holds good prospects and over the year there will again be many activities and events for the Wood Goat to enjoy. His interests (particularly new ones) and travels could have a pleasing social element and for those Wood Goats who would welcome more companionship or perhaps romance, the Pig year is splendidly aspected. A chance meeting could quickly transform their situation. March, June to August and December to mid-January will be the most active months socially.

The Pig year certainly holds excellent prospects for the Wood Goat, but to benefit he will need to be prepared to make the most of his situation. In the Pig year he is very much in the driving seat and with purpose, resolve and the support of others, he can achieve a great deal.

TIP FOR THE YEAR
Do not underestimate what you can accomplish. Use your ideas and talents and make the most of yourself. With self-belief, this can be a significant time and its effects can be far-reaching.

The Fire Goat

This year not only marks the start of a new decade in the Fire Goat's life but also holds particularly good prospects for him. Indeed, many Fire Goats will decide to take determined action to make more of their potential and their efforts will do much to help get their forties off to a bright and encouraging start.

As far as the Fire Goat's work is concerned, this will be a year of change. Those who feel disillusioned with their present position and consider themselves in a rut will find the Pig year bringing significant developments. However, to benefit, these Fire Goats will need to consider how they would like their career to develop. With careful thought and some advice from agencies, professional organizations and other contacts, they could learn of openings worth considering as well as possibilities they may not have been aware of. In some cases they could also find it helpful to consider training courses or evening classes to further their skills. Anything positive that they can do can widen their prospects.

For those Fire Goats established in their career the Pig year can bring some important opportunities. As they approach and enter their forties, many will regard this a suitable time to make progress, and their determination and faith in what they can offer can drive their career forward. As senior colleagues move on or other opportunities arise, the Fire Goat should be swift in putting himself forward. With resolve, enthusiasm and the desire to make more of himself, he can benefit from this auspicious year. For work developments, February to early April and mid-August to October are particularly favourable.

In addition to the encouraging aspects concerning his work, the Fire Goat can derive much satisfaction from his personal interests over the year, especially those that have a creative element. Those Fire Goats who, because of other commitments, have let their interests slide recently, should aim to set time aside for activities they enjoy. In the Pig year it is important that the Fire Goat keeps his lifestyle in balance.

Another area the Fire Goat would do well to consider is his well-being. With the Pig year being a time of change and opportunity, any positive steps he can take can be beneficial. If he seeks medical advice on what is best for him to do, he may well be able to make a real difference to how he feels.

In view of the progress the Fire Goat will make in his work he will often enjoy a rise in income, and with the aspects as they are, many Fire Goats could also receive a sum from another source. The Fire Goat's financial prospects are certainly promising, and by carefully planning his major purchases and setting sums aside for existing obligations, he will be pleased with the general improvement that takes place. Also, with this marking his 40th year, if he has thoughts of taking a special holiday, it would be worth him saving up for it in advance. Good planning can lead to him doing that much more.

The Fire Goat will value his domestic life over the year and while it will often be busy, there will be many special occasions for him to appreciate, including not only the possible marking of his own 40th birthday but also some key family events and successes. However, while so much will go well, as in all years, problems and tensions will sometimes raise their head. When pressures are great and tiredness sets in, patience may be thin, tempers may become frayed and minor problems may get out of proportion. At such times, the Fire Goat should speak of his concerns. By being open, he will enable those close to him to understand as well as to help. Domestically, this can be good year, but it is also one for openness and mindfulness.

Over the year the Fire Goat's social life can bring him much pleasure and while he may be selective in his socializing, he will often enjoy the times he does go out. Also, as a result of changes in his work as well as his interests and activities, he will often have the chance to extend his social circle. For those Fire Goats who would welcome the chance to meet others and perhaps find romance, the Pig year could have some important surprises in store. March, June to August, December and January 2008 will be the most active months socially.

The Pig year certainly holds much promise for the Fire Goat, but a lot does rest with him. To make the most of his opportunities, he will need to be bold and put himself forward. Also, some of the work changes that arise and the actions he takes will bring times of pressure, but these are inevitable on the path of progress, and by accepting this and rising to the challenge, the Fire Goat can look forward to making important headway. His 40th year can be an exciting, sometimes challenging time, but with determination and support, it can also be a time of positive change.

TIP FOR THE YEAR
Look to further your position. Positive, determined action on your part can lead to important *and* far-reaching developments.

The Earth Goat

In recent years the Earth Goat will have seen many events take place. Some will have gone in his favour, but there will also have been disappointments and regrets. For many Earth Goats, the Dog year will not have been the easiest. However, the Earth Goat can now take heart. The aspects are now moving very much in his favour.

In his work the aspects are especially encouraging and the Earth Goat will find himself being able to make more of his strengths and take on greater responsibilities. In some cases the reputation and knowledge he has built up in his present place of work can make him a strong candidate for promotion, while for those Earth Goats keen to move elsewhere, again their experience and sometimes contacts they have can serve them well. For those Earth Goats who are established on a career path this can be a successful *and* encouraging time.

For those who are unfulfilled in their current situation or seeking work, this can also be an important year. By giving some thought to the type of work that they would now like to do and making enquiries, many will find interesting and sometimes exciting possibilities opening up for them. The onus to take action does rest with the Earth Goat himself, but even tentative expressions of interest can set powerful wheels in motion. In addition, if the Earth Goat feels it would help to undertake some training or retraining, again he should make enquiries and see what is possible. Positive and willing action on his part can set him off on a new and often more suitable career path.

Workwise, the most interesting developments will take place from the beginning of the Pig year to early April and then again in September and October. Though there may be a few disappointments in store, the Earth Goat should not lose heart. With determination, faith in his abilities and positive action, he can find important doors opening for him. What he can achieve in 2007 can have long-term significance.

The progress the Earth Goat makes in his work will also lead to a welcome rise in income, and financially this can be an improved year. However, with his many commitments, the Earth Goat does need to manage his money well and should be wary of succumbing to too many spur of the moment purchases. Without some control, anything extra could quickly be spent, and not always in the most advantageous way. Also, with personal and possible family and accommodation expenses likely over the year, the Earth Goat would do well to save towards these rather than spend his money too quickly. This is a year requiring financial discipline. However, with the aspects as they are, the Earth Goat could enjoy some luck over the year and if he sees a competition which interests him he would do well to enter it. The Pig year can have some lucky moments!

The Earth Goat will derive much satisfaction from his personal interests over the year and those who enjoy keeping themselves active, whether by taking part in sport or by walking, cycling or in some other activity, will often benefit from what they do. In addition, the many Earth Goats who spend time on more creative pursuits will enjoy experimenting with their ideas. Those Earth Goats who are keen to make more of their creative talents, perhaps on a freelance or vocational basis, may find the year bringing some exciting developments. This is a time for the Earth Goat to put himself forward and to use his talents well.

As far as the Earth Goat's relations with others are concerned, this will be a pleasing time, and with the Pig year's emphasis on home and family there could also be cause for celebration, perhaps due to a marriage, an addition to the Earth Goat's family or a move to more suitable accommodation. The Earth Goat will particularly appreciate his home life and could also have good reason to value the assistance of more senior relations. If he finds himself under pressure at any time, or in a dilemma over certain decisions, he would do well to ask for advice. Several times over the year he will be particularly appreciative of the input and support of those who are close to him.

The aspects are also encouraging for those Earth Goats who may have had problems in their personal life over the last few years. The Pig year is a time for moving forward, and by taking action, becoming involved in new interests and getting to meet others, they can not only improve their general situation but also make some important new friendships and even enjoy a wonderful new romance. On a personal level this is a promising year, with March, June to August, December and January being good months for socializing and meeting others.

The Pig year is certainly an encouraging one for the Earth Goat, but it does rest with him to act positively on his ideas and opportunities. If he remains reticent then he risks missing out. He will, however, be well supported in most of his activities and many Earth Goats will be buoyed up by pleasing developments in their personal life. Overall, a promising year.

Be determined and *take action*. The longer you prevaricate, the greater the risk that good opportunities could be lost. This is very much a time to make the most of your chances.

FAMOUS GOATS

Pamela Anderson, W. H. Auden, Jane Austen, Daniel Bedingfield, Cilla Black, Lord Byron, Leslie Caron, Coco Chanel, Mary Higgins Clark, Nat 'King' Cole, Jamie Cullum, Robert de Niro, Catherine Deneuve, Charles Dickens, Ken Dodd, Sir Arthur Conan Doyle, Daphne du Maurier, Umberto Eco, Douglas Fairbanks, Dame Margot Fonteyn, Noel Gallagher, Bill Gates, Mel Gibson, Whoopi Goldberg, Mikhail Gorbachev, John Grisham, Larry Hagman, Oscar Hammerstein, George Harrison, Sir Edmund Hillary, John Humphrys, Billy Idol, Julio Iglesias, Sir Mick Jagger, Norah Jones, Ulrika Jonsson, Nicole Kidman, Sir Ben Kingsley, John le Carré, Doris Lessing, Franz Liszt, Sir John Major, Michelangelo, Joni Mitchell, Rupert Murdoch, Randy Newman, Des O'Connor, Sinead O'Connor, Michael Owen, Michael Palin, Eva Peron, Marcel Proust, Keith Richards, Julia Roberts, William Shatner, Gary Sinise, Jerry Springer, Lana Turner, Mark Twain, Rudolph Valentino, Vangelis, Barbara Walters, John Wayne, Fay Weldon, Bruce Willis.

2 FEBRUARY 1908 ⌢ 21 JANUARY 1909   *Earth Monkey*

20 FEBRUARY 1920 ⌢ 7 FEBRUARY 1921   *Metal Monkey*

6 FEBRUARY 1932 ⌢ 25 JANUARY 1933   *Water Monkey*

25 JANUARY 1944 ⌢ 12 FEBRUARY 1945   *Wood Monkey*

12 FEBRUARY 1956 ⌢ 30 JANUARY 1957   *Fire Monkey*

30 JANUARY 1968 ⌢ 16 FEBRUARY 1969   *Earth Monkey*

16 FEBRUARY 1980 ⌢ 4 FEBRUARY 1981   *Metal Monkey*

4 FEBRUARY 1992 ⌢ 22 JANUARY 1993   *Water Monkey*

22 JANUARY 2004 ⌢ 8 FEBRUARY 2005   *Wood Monkey*

THE
MONKEY

THE PERSONALITY OF THE MONKEY

'Men who are resolved to find a way for themselves will always find opportunities enough; and if they do not lie ready to hand, they will make them.'

Samuel Smiles, a Monkey

The Monkey is born under the sign of fantasy. He is imaginative, inquisitive and loves to keep an eye on everything that is going on around him. He is never backward in offering advice or trying to sort out the problems of others. He likes to be helpful and his advice is invariably sensible and reliable.

The Monkey is intelligent, well read and always eager to learn. He has an extremely good memory and there are many Monkeys who have made particularly good linguists. The Monkey is also a convincing talker and enjoys taking part in discussions and debates. His friendly, self-assured manner can be very persuasive and he usually has little trouble in winning people round to his way of thinking. It is for this reason that the Monkey often excels in politics and public speaking. He is also particularly adept in PR work, teaching and any job which involves selling.

The Monkey can, however, be crafty, cunning and occasionally dishonest, and he will seize on any opportunity to make a quick gain or outsmart his opponents. He has so much charm and guile that people often don't realize what he is up to until it is too late. But despite his resourceful nature, the Monkey does run the risk of outsmarting even himself. He has so much confidence in his abilities that he rarely listens to advice or is prepared to accept help from anyone. He likes to help others but prefers to rely on his own judgement when dealing with his own affairs.

Another characteristic of the Monkey is that he is extremely good at solving problems and has a happy knack of extricating himself (and others) from the most hopeless of positions. He is the master of self-preservation.

With so many diverse talents the Monkey is able to make considerable sums of money, but he does like to enjoy life and will think nothing of spending his money on some exotic holiday or luxury which he has had his eye on. He can, however, become very envious if someone else has what he wants.

The Monkey is an original thinker and despite his love of company, he cherishes his independence. He has to have the freedom to act as he wants and any Monkey who feels hemmed in or bound by too many restrictions can soon become unhappy. Likewise, if anything becomes too boring or monotonous, the Monkey soon loses interest and turns his attention to something else. He lacks persistence and this can often hamper his progress. He is also easily distracted, a tendency which all Monkeys should try to overcome. By concentrating on one thing at a time, the Monkey will almost certainly achieve more in the long run.

The Monkey is a good organizer and even though he may behave slightly erratically at times, he will invariably have some plan at the back of his mind. On the odd occasion when his plans do not work out, he is usually quite happy to shrug his shoulders and put it down to experience. He will rarely make the same mistake twice and throughout his life he will try his hand at many different things.

The Monkey likes to impress and is rarely without followers or admirers. Many are attracted by his good looks, his sense of humour, or simply because he instils so much confidence.

Monkeys usually marry young and for it to be a success their partner must allow them time to pursue their many interests and indulge their love of travel. The Monkey has to have variety in his life and is especially well suited to those born under the sociable and outgoing signs of the Rat, Dragon, Pig and Goat. The Ox, Rabbit, Snake and Dog will also be enchanted by the Monkey's resourceful and outgoing nature, but he is likely to exasperate the Rooster and Horse, and the Tiger will have little patience with his tricks. A relationship between two Monkeys will work well – they will understand each other and be able to assist each other in their various enterprises.

The female Monkey is intelligent, extremely obser-vant and a shrewd judge of character. Her opinions are often highly valued and, having such a persuasive nature, she invariably gets her own way. She has many interests and involves herself in a wide variety of activi-ties. She pays great attention to her appearance, is an elegant dresser and likes to take particular care over her hair. She can be a doting parent and will have many good and loyal friends.

Provided the Monkey can curb his desire to take part in everything that is going on around him and concentrate on one thing at a time, he can usually achieve what he wants in life. Should he suffer any disappointment, he is bound to bounce back. He is a survivor and his life is usually both colourful and eventful.

THE FIVE DIFFERENT TYPES OF MONKEY

In addition to the 12 signs of the Chinese zodiac there are five elements and these have a strengthening or moderating influence on the sign. The effects of the five elements on the Monkey are described below, together with the years in which the elements were exercising their influence. Therefore those Monkeys born in 1920 and 1980 are Metal Monkeys, those born in 1932 and 1992 are Water Monkeys, and so on.

Metal Monkey: 1920, 1980
The Metal Monkey is very strong-willed. He sets about everything he does with dogged determination and often prefers to work independently rather than with others. He is ambitious, wise and confident, and is certainly not afraid of hard work. He is very astute in financial matters and usually chooses his investments well. Despite his somewhat independent nature, he enjoys attending parties and social occasions and is particularly warm and caring towards his loved ones.

Water Monkey: 1932, 1992

The Water Monkey is versatile, determined and perceptive. He also has more discipline than some of the other Monkeys and is prepared to work towards a certain goal rather than be distracted by something else. He is not always open about his true intentions and when questioned can be particularly evasive. He can be sensitive to criticism but also very persuasive and usually has little trouble in getting others to fall in with his plans. He has a very good understanding of human nature and relates well to others.

Wood Monkey: 1944, 2004

This Monkey is efficient, methodical and extremely conscientious. He is also highly imaginative and is always trying to capitalize on new ideas or learn new skills. Occasionally his enthusiasm can get the better of him and he can get very agitated when things do not quite work out as he had hoped. He does, however, have a very adventurous streak and is not afraid of taking risks. He also loves travel. He is usually held in great esteem by his friends and colleagues.

Fire Monkey: 1956

The Fire Monkey is intelligent, full of vitality and has no trouble in commanding the respect of others. He is imaginative and has wide interests, although sometimes these can distract him from more useful and profitable work. He is very competitive and always likes to be involved in everything that is going on. He can be stubborn if he does not get his own way and he sometimes tries to indoctrinate those who are less strong-willed than himself. He is a lively character, attractive to others and most loyal to his partner.

Earth Monkey: 1908, 1968

The Earth Monkey tends to be studious and well read, and can become quite distinguished in his chosen line of work. He is less outgoing than some of the other types of Monkey and prefers quieter and more solid pursuits. He has high principles, a very caring nature and can be most generous to those less fortunate than himself. He is usually successful in handling financial matters and can become very wealthy in old age. He has a calming influence on those around him and is respected and well liked. He is, however, especially careful about whom he lets into his confidence.

PROSPECTS FOR THE MONKEY IN 2007

The Year of the Dog (29 January 2006 to 17 February 2007) will have been a fair one for the Monkey, although he will have needed his wits about him. As it draws to a close, he should still be careful about taking risks or acting without the support of others. If he retains too independent an attitude, problems could loom and misjudgements be made.

In the Monkey's work there could be some good opportunities to extend or change his role in some way. By being prepared to adapt, he can make good headway and may benefit from interesting developments in November. He would also do well to work closely with others rather than too much on his own. The more support and co-operation he enjoys, the better he will fare.

As far as money matters are concerned, the Dog year requires care and the Monkey should be wary of risks and hurried and ill thought out purchases. Financially, this is a time for caution and for the Monkey to be on his guard.

As far as his domestic and social life is concerned, the Monkey can look forward to some pleasing times, and for those Monkeys who are unattached or enjoying romance, the closing months of the Dog year can be a busy and exciting time. For socializing, late November to early January can be a particularly lively and pleasing time. However, with so much happening, it is important that the Monkey remains aware of the feelings of others and consults them over various plans and arrangements. To get the most from the closing months of the Dog year, the Monkey needs to talk, liaise and listen.

The Year of the Pig starts on 18 February and will be a variable one for the Monkey. Plans and activities may not always go as smoothly as he would like, and the year could also bring its pressures and problems. However, while the aspects may be mixed, the Monkey is blessed with a perceptive and resourceful nature, and by remaining alert and wary he can often avoid or minimize some of the trickier aspects of the year and emerge with some worthy gains to his credit.

In his work this will be an interesting year and although his progress may not always meet his expectations, by concentrating on his duties and objectives he will not only add to his experience but also pave the way for his future progress. Over the year many Monkeys will find themselves with a heavy workload and increased pressure and while this may sometimes be daunting, it can give the Monkey a good opportunity to develop his skills. As has so often been shown, challenges do bring out the best in people, and so it will be for the Monkey. The Pig year may not be plain sailing, but it can be an instructive time and a significant one, especially in view of the more favourable Rat year that follows.

Many Monkeys will decide to remain in their present position over the year and build on their experience, but for who are those keen to make a change, the Pig year can bring some important developments. Although obtaining a new position will not be easy, by putting in for vacancies that appeal to them and stressing to prospective employers what they can offer, many Monkeys will find their persistence rewarded. While taking on something different will sometimes involve a steep learning curve, by rising to the challenge these Monkeys will not only be advancing their career but also widening their scope for later. March, June, late September, October and January could contain the best opportunities.

However, whether the Monkey remains where he is or decides to move, throughout the Pig year he will need to remain thorough and careful in his work. This is no year for him to take risks or short cuts or be tempted to push his luck or resourcefulness too far. Progress *will* need to be worked for and the Pig year can provide some timely warnings for the careless, the risk-taker and the impatient. Monkeys, do take note and *be thorough*.

This advice also applies to financial matters. While the Monkey can generally fare well in the Pig year, this is still a time for caution. Without care, spending could creep up and the Monkey might not always put his money to its best use. He does need to be mindful of this and keep a sensible control over the purse-strings. He should also be wary of financial risks or committing himself to schemes without checking the details. Carelessness and undue haste could cost him dear. Monkeys, be warned.

Many Monkeys will, though, spend quite considerable sums on their home over the year, particularly in buying equipment and other items that will help make life easier and more comfortable. Again the Monkey should plan his purchases carefully and consult closely with others before making choices. If he can be patient he may well benefit from good buying opportunities too. Again, it is a case of waiting rather than proceeding in too much haste.

With his outgoing and genial nature, the Monkey attaches considerable importance to his relations with others and this year once again his personal life will generally go well. In his home life he will often do much to help and encourage loved ones, and whenever they are under pressure or have important decisions to take, his support will be particularly appreciated. In addition he will enjoy spending time with those close to him, and joint activities, particularly home improvement projects, will bring pleasure and satisfaction to all.

However, while a lot will go well, the Monkey will sometimes need to show a certain flexibility over plans and arrangements as well as remain mindful of the views of others. He may be keen for his own views to prevail, but in the Pig year consultation can help prevent misunderstandings and possible differences of opinion. Monkeys, do bear this in mind and listen to the views of those around you.

The Monkey will appreciate his social life over the year, and March, July to September and December will be particularly busy times. However, while the Monkey will often enjoy himself, yet again he does need to be mindful of the views of others. This is a year requiring tact and discretion. Provided the Monkey remains careful, though, his social life will often go well.

Generally, the Monkey can fare reasonably well in the Pig year, although he will need to be careful and thorough in his various undertakings. While the year will sometimes bring increased work pressures, and certain plans and activities may take longer to carry out than he would like, by being patient (not always a Monkey strong point!) and liaising well with others he can still accomplish a great deal. And the progress he makes now can be instrumental in the success he will enjoy in the more favourable Rat year that follows.

The Metal Monkey

There is a Chinese proverb which the Metal Monkey would do well to bear in mind this year: 'Slow and steady wins the race.' To make progress in the Pig year will require both patience and persistence. This is no year for haste or for the Metal Monkey to stretch his energies or attention too widely. Instead it calls for focus and discipline.

To get the best from the year, the Metal Monkey would do well to give careful thought to his aims and plans for the next 12 months. This will not only help him to channel his energies more effectively but will also give him something to work towards. Talking to those close to him about his aims and plans can be helpful and lead to him being given useful advice. In some cases, just mentioning certain ideas can help to set them in motion.

As far as his work is concerned, this can be a significant year, and if the Metal Monkey has particular ambitions he is keen to reach, he should look at ways in which he can achieve them. Again, seeking advice can help, and if the Metal Monkey feels it would be useful to undertake some extra training, obtain another qualification or acquire certain skills, he should look at ways of doing this. By taking positive steps he will be doing himself *and* his prospects considerable good.

Over the year many Metal Monkeys will be able to benefit from opportunities in their present place of work and whether this is through promotion or becoming involved in other responsibilities, by making the most of the openings that arise, they will not only learn more about different aspects of their work but also help their career development. Again, what the Metal Monkey accomplishes over the year (including sometimes meeting challenging objectives) will be to his long-term benefit.

Those Metal Monkeys who are dissatisfied with their present situation or are seeking work would also do well to consider what it is they now want to do. By making enquiries, obtaining information and putting themselves forward they will, in time, be offered the chance they are seeking. And once in a new position, by showing commitment and mastering their responsibilities, they will soon become established in a new and often more suitable line of work. With the Metal Monkey's prospects being so promising in the following Rat year, the experience he gains now can prove important. March, June, late September, October and January could see the best work opportunities.

The progress the Metal Monkey makes in his work will often lead to a rise in income and financial matters are generally positive over the year, although this is still a time for care. With all his commitments as well as some of his more expensive plans, the Metal Monkey will need to keep a close watch on his outgoings, otherwise money could be spent all too easily and not always in the best way. The Pig year calls for planning and control.

The Metal Monkey would also do well to give some thought to his general well-being over the year, especially if he does not tend to get much regular exercise. In some cases he could find walking more or taking up activities such as swimming, cycling or some other form of exercise will do him good. If he seeks medical guidance on the best way to proceed and then makes a few modifications to his general lifestyle, he will often be able to make a real difference to how he feels.

As far as the Metal Monkey's domestic life is concerned, this can be a special and often constructive year. Again, the more thought that the Metal Monkey can give to what he wants to do over the year, the more he can achieve. If there are any home improvements he would like to make, if he plans these out carefully and allows plenty of time for their completion, he will often be delighted with the results. He will also be grateful for the support and input of loved ones, although he does need to be open with his thoughts rather than keep them close to his chest, as some Metal Monkeys tend to do. More openness on his part will also help maintain the good rapport he has with those around him.

Also, for those Metal Monkeys with young families, or those who become parents in 2007, there will be times when they will feel tired or under pressure, and at such times it is important that these Metal Monkeys ask for help rather than try to do too much on their own. This is very much a year when it is in the Metal Monkey's interests to be more forthcoming.

While the Metal Monkey will often have many demands on his time over the year, it is also important that he keeps in regular contact with his friends. They can often be helpful and supportive. In addition, with possible changes in his work and the various interests he pursues, the Metal Monkey will often have the chance to get to know others and may make some close and important friends. March, late June to September and December will generally be the most active months socially.

Overall, the Metal Monkey can fare well in the Pig year, but he does need to give careful thought to his plans and objectives and set about his activities with care. This is not a year for rush or risk. However, he will be well supported and the experience he gains over the year will stand him in excellent stead for the more progressive and exciting Rat year that follows.

TIP FOR THE YEAR

While you may be eager to see your plans realized, this is a year for planning, preparation and patience. 'Slow and steady wins the race' and persistent, patient effort on your part will, over time, deliver the results you want.

The Water Monkey

With his keen, inquisitive nature and ability to get on well with so many, the Water Monkey has much in his favour, and a lot can go well for him over the year. However, to make the most of his opportunities, he will need to set about his activities with diligence and care.

For those Water Monkeys in education this will be a particularly important year and they will need to make an effort. This is no time to slack or waste opportunities. When the young Water Monkey has exams to prepare for or work to complete, the extra time and commitment he can give will often be reflected in the marks he obtains. Similarly, by working consistently and conscientiously throughout the year, rather than leaving a lot to the last moment, he will make better progress as well as take greater satisfaction in what he does. In addition, as he moves on to more advanced work, what he studies can provide him with a solid foundation on which to build in the future. Commitment now can have an important bearing on his future progress and it really is worth making the effort.

While most Water Monkeys will remember this and fare well during the year, for those who slack or believe there will be time left for them to catch up later, the Pig year can teach them some hard and sometimes necessary lessons. Those who waste their time and opportunities could come to regret it later. Fortunately these words only apply to a small minority of Water Monkeys, but all Water Monkeys should remember that the Pig year is very much one for effort and commitment.

The Water Monkey should also make good use of the facilities that are available to him. In particular, for those Water Monkeys who are keen and skilled in a certain area, whether art, music, sport, drama or another activity, taking advantage of chances to practise and develop what they do can not only bring real pleasure but also new skills.

Also, with the Water Monkey's wide interests and inquisitive nature, if there is a subject or activity that appeals to him and he wants to find out more, he should make enquiries. For some Water Monkeys, activities started in the Pig year can be a source of considerable pleasure both now and in following years. However, to benefit, it does rest with the Water Monkey to take action.

The Water Monkey will value the comradeship of his many good friends over the year and will often find himself in demand. With some of the new activities he gets involved with there will often be chances for him to meet others and form what can become long and loyal friendships. On a personal and social level, the Pig year is favourably aspected.

The Water Monkey will need to be careful in financial matters, however. With all his various activities and the plans and purchases he has in mind, he will need to be disciplined in his spending. This includes being wary of making too many impulse buys. Also, while he may be keen to improve on his situation, he should be careful if tempted to take risks or get involved in any 'too good to be true' offers or schemes. If he rushes into things without checking the actual situation and obtaining advice, he could find himself losing money. Financially, this is a year for vigilance and discipline. However, by being careful and making enquiries the Water Monkey could find a way of earning something extra. It is a feature of the Pig year that a willingness to make an effort will be recognized and rewarded.

The Water Monkey's home life will be important to him over the year and if he is willing to talk over his activities, hopes and thoughts, those around him will be able to encourage and advise. However, to profit from the assistance others can give, the Water Monkey will need be forthcoming rather than vague and evasive! Becoming involved in family activities as well as sometimes helping with tasks and household chores will be another good way for him to enhance the rapport he shares with those around him.

For those Water Monkeys who were born in 1932 this is also a year to be open and forthcoming. By involving others in their activities and being prepared to discuss their ideas and plans, as well as any concerns, they will find others are better able to assist them and more will be achieved as a result. The more senior Water Monkey should also take advantage of the opportunities that come his way over the year. Whether these are invitations to visit others or chances to pursue certain interests, if he takes action, he can find the Pig year bringing some happy times. Again, though, this is a year for seizing opportunities, otherwise they could be lost.

The Pig year does hold considerable promise for the Water Monkey, but just how much he benefits does rest with him. By making the most of his chances and his situation, he can make satisfying progress. But should he let chances slip, then the Pig year can bring disappointment and regret. This is not a year to waste.

TIP FOR THE YEAR
Consider ways in which you can develop your personal interests and skills. Positive action will not only benefit you now but can also open up possibilities for later.

The Wood Monkey

The Wood Monkey likes to keep himself active and during the Pig year there will be activity aplenty. This will be a busy and important year for him, and with care, good planning and the support of others, a lot can go in his favour.

As the Pig year starts the Wood Monkey would find it helpful to give some thought to what he wants to do over the next 12 months. Having some plans in mind will not only help him to direct his energies in a more purposeful way but also make him more alert to possibilities as they become available. 'Chance favours the prepared mind', as the saying goes, and if he prepares well, chance will indeed favour the Wood Monkey during the year.

For those Wood Monkeys in work this will be a year of important developments and if there are ambitions or objectives that the Wood Monkey is keen to realize, he should take action. In particular, if he wants to make more of his skills, there will be some good opportunities for him to do so. These could include transferring to more specialist duties or taking on greater responsibilities, but if he takes action the Wood Monkey will find his initiative and background can stand him in excellent stead.

Alternatively, some Wood Monkeys will be keen to retire or reduce their working commitments over the year. Here again, by considering what they want to do and thinking through the implications, these Wood Monkeys will often be able to seize the initiative and move towards what they want.

Another factor which will be of considerable value to the Wood Monkey over the year will be the support and goodwill of his colleagues and many good contacts. Whenever he is considering making a change, if he talks to those who are able to give informed advice, he will be helped in making a decision that is right for him. Also, as so often in the Pig year, he must not be rushed into taking action or making a decision until he feels he is ready. This is a year for proceeding carefully and steadily, not in haste.

As far as money matters are concerned, this is a year when good planning can make an important difference. By looking ahead and, when possible, setting money aside for forthcoming purchases and activities, the Wood Monkey will not only be able to do that much more but also help his overall situation. Proceeding in a careful and measured way will also enable him to benefit from some favourable buying opportunities. In addition, some Wood Monkeys could find a skill, idea or interest they have helping to bring them something extra. The Pig year certainly rewards effort and enterprise.

In addition to managing his resources well, the Wood Monkey also needs to be thorough with any financial forms and paperwork he receives. To delay or pay insufficient attention to what could be important matters could be to his detriment and cost. Wood Monkeys, do take note, and if there is anything that is not clear, do obtain advice. If not dealt with promptly or properly, financial or bureaucratic matters can give rise to problems. Wood Monkeys, be warned!

Although travel does not tend to figure prominently for the Monkey in the Pig year, the Wood Monkey would still do well to consider going away for a holiday as well as taking up any invitations to visit others. Not only will he benefit from the rest and change of scene this will bring, but by planning his trips carefully, he can look forward to seeing some inspiring sights and attending some interesting events.

Another area the Wood Monkey would do well to consider over the year is his own well-being. While he does tend to keep himself active, he should make sure he takes sufficient exercise as well as has a healthy and balanced diet. The attention and care he can give to himself can make a real difference. However, before making any changes, he should seek medical guidance. Similarly, if he is troubled by any ailment over the year, he should get it checked out.

As far as the Wood Monkey's home life is concerned, this will be an active year. During 2007 many Wood Monkeys will decide to make some improvements to their home. However, practical activities and purchases should not be rushed, and the more time and thought spent costing options and undertaking practical work, the more satisfying the results will be. Those Wood Monkeys who decide to move should also make careful plans and allow themselves ample time to look for new accommodation. Important decisions should not be rushed.

In addition to the considerable practical activity likely to be seen over the year, there will also be some special family events for the Wood Monkey to enjoy. These can include good news concerning a younger relation as well as a family occasion or success to celebrate. Those close to the Wood Monkey will often seek out his advice and assistance on various matters, and his input will be valued. Yet again he will play a full and central role in family life.

In view of the Wood Monkey's various interests and contacts, his social life can also bring him much pleasure over the year. In some cases new activities and interests or changes in his work situation can lead to him widening his social circle. He will, though, often be grateful for the support and camaraderie of his friends. Any Wood Monkeys who would welcome a more fulfilling social life will find that a greater willingness on their part to go out and to get to know others can add something extra to their year. As with so much during 2007, positive action can bring results.

The Pig year certainly holds much promise for the Wood Monkey, but central to this is *good planning*. By carefully thinking through his objectives and working steadily toward them, the Wood Monkey can achieve so much more. Also, throughout the year, he will benefit from the support and goodwill of those around him.

TIP FOR THE YEAR
Do not be over-hasty. Allow time for your thoughts and plans to take shape. Also, tiresome though it may seem, deal with paperwork, forms and financial matters very carefully. This is a year to be thorough and diligent, especially when there are important implications involved.

The Fire Monkey

This will be an interesting year for the Fire Monkey, although to make the most of it he will need to remain determined and persistent. This is no year for rushing or expecting fast results.

Many Fire Monkeys will have seen considerable change in their work over the last few years and some will have changed the nature of what they do. Those who have experienced recent change or still may be relatively new in their present position will find this a good time to concentrate on their duties and learn more about the different aspects of their work. This way they will not only derive greater satisfaction from what they do but also become more settled in their new role. Establishing a good reputation now can also be useful for when they decide to move on. Good opportunities may well arise in the more favourably aspected Rat year that follows. For many Fire Monkeys, this can be a constructive year workwise and one which can have importance for the future.

For Fire Monkeys who are dissatisfied with their present position or seeking work, this can also be a significant time. By giving careful thought to what they would like to do, making enquiries *and persisting* in their quest, many will be successful in gaining an interesting new position which can lead on to other possibilities. March, June, late September to early November and January could see the best opportunities.

The Fire Monkey could also consider developing some of his personal interests over the year, perhaps through enrolling on a course or setting time aside for practice or background study. If there is a new interest that appeals to him, he should take positive action and follow it up. His personal interests can also have a pleasing social element.

As with all Monkeys over the year, the Fire Monkey should ensure he takes sufficient exercise as well as eating a healthy and balanced diet. If not, he could find himself becoming prone to minor ailments or lacking his usual zest and energy. Fire Monkeys, do take note, and if feeling below par or considering starting a new exercise regime, do seek proper medical advice.

In money matters the Fire Monkey can fare well this year and there could be chances to supplement his earnings with some extra work or by putting an idea or skill to good use. However, to benefit from any increase in income, the Fire Monkey needs to manage his situation well and keep a close watch on his spending, and when dealing with financial forms and paperwork, he needs to be thorough and vigilant. Carelessness or delay could be to his detriment.

As far as the Fire Monkey's domestic life is concerned, this will be an active year and it will also contain some particularly enjoyable occasions. Good communication will help and can lead to better rapport and understanding. Both younger and more senior relations will often look to the Fire Monkey for advice and support, and the Fire Monkey's thoughtfulness, input and time can make an appreciable difference.

In many ways this can be a useful and constructive year for the Fire Monkey and by setting about his activities with care and making the most of his chances he will not only be satisfied with his progress but also add considerably to his experience and standing. The Pig year will prepare the way for the exciting times he is soon to enjoy.

TIP FOR THE YEAR
Make the most of any opportunities to add to your experience and skills. What you do this year can be instrumental in your later success. Also spend time on your personal interests, as these can provide a balance to your lifestyle.

The Earth Monkey
This will be a generally positive year for the Earth Monkey, although he will need to be realistic in both his undertakings and expectations. This is not a year to set his sights too high or expect sweeping success. With effort, a good approach and the support of others, he can, however, look forward to making reasonable progress as well as enjoying much that this interesting year will offer.

In his work the Earth Monkey will need to remain disciplined and focused. For those Earth Monkeys who are established in a particular career, this is very much a time when they should use their knowledge and talents well and add to their experience. By taking advantage of any training opportunities and chances to meet others as well as becoming more familiar with other aspects of their work, they can help both their current situation and future prospects.

Many of these Earth Monkeys will remain with their present employer during the Pig year, but for those who would welcome a change, the Pig year can be an important one. By carefully considering their next step, many of these Earth Monkeys will secure a position which will help them to broaden their experience. This is not a year for the Earth Monkey to expect major breakthroughs, but it can be a time of steady progress.

For those Earth Monkeys seeking work the Pig year will be an important one, and by carefully considering their options and seeking advice, many will learn of possibilities worth considering. Once they are given an opportunity, it will provide the foothold they need as well as the chance to gain what will be invaluable experience. March, June, late September to early November and the first weeks of 2008 could bring the best developments.

The need for discipline and focus this year also applies to money matters. With all his existing commitments as well as some of the plans he has in mind, especially for his accommodation, the Earth Monkey will need to watch his outgoings and be wary of impulse purchases. In addition, when considering buying anything costly, it could be to his advantage to shop around and compare terms and offers. The Earth Monkey should also take time and care over paperwork, otherwise there is a risk that delayed payments or lapsed policies could incur additional cost, or that important documents, including receipts and guarantees, could be mislaid. The Earth Monkey does need to remain his efficient and organized self if he is to avoid becoming involved in some time-consuming correspondence.

The Earth Monkey should also make sure he takes regular exercise and, at more demanding times, has sufficient rest. And while travel does not tend to figure prominently for Monkeys in the Pig year, the Earth Monkey should also make sure that he takes a break at some time during the year. The rest, change of scene and chance to visit new areas can do him a lot of good.

In his home life this will be a busy year, with many calls on his time. For those Earth Monkeys who are parents there will be successes and achievements to celebrate, but there could also be times when they will despair over the attitude and activities of younger family members. However, by showing that they care and taking the time to both talk *and* listen, these Earth Monkeys can do much to guide and encourage. With good communication and understanding, home life will generally go well for the Earth Monkey and he can look forward to some fine occasions. He will also derive much satisfaction from some of the home improvement projects he tackles over the year, although here again he will need to allow plenty of time and avoid rush and impatience.

The Earth Monkey should not neglect his social life, and keeping in regular contact with friends and taking up invitations to social events that appeal to him can add another enjoyable and beneficial element to the year. Any Earth Monkey who has had some recent problems in his personal life should make the effort to go out more and become involved in new interests. If he acts positively, the Pig year can bring a marked improvement in his situation. For socializing, March, the period from July to September, December and January could be the best times.

In most respects this is a positive year for the Earth Monkey and although progress may not be easy, swift or substantial, his achievements can help prepare the way for the success he can look forward to in following years.

TIP FOR THE YEAR
Avoid acting on impulse. Think through your actions and take advice from those you trust. This is a year for proceeding carefully and being realistic in your aims and undertakings. Also, make the most of any chances to add to your skills, as this will help towards your future success.

FAMOUS MONKEYS

Gillian Anderson, Jennifer Aniston, Francesca Annis, Christina Aguilera, J. M. Barrie, Johnny Cash, Jacques Chirac, Patricia Cornwell, Joan Crawford, Leonardo da Vinci, Bette Davis, Danny De Vito, Celine Dion, Michael Douglas, Mia Farrow, F. Scott Fitzgerald, Ian Fleming, Dick Francis, Paul Gauguin, Jerry Hall, Tom Hanks, Harry Houdini, P. D. James, Pope John Paul II, Julius Caesar, Buster Keaton, Alicia Keys, Bob Marley, Walter Matthau, Kylie Minogue, V. S. Naipaul, Peter O'Toole, Anne Robinson, Mary Robinson, Mickey Rooney, Diana Ross, Donald Rumsfeld, Gerhard Schröder, Michael Schumacher, Tom Selleck, Omar Sharif, Wilbur Smith, Rod Stewart, Jacques Tati, Elizabeth Taylor, Dame Kiri Te Kanawa, Justin Timberlake, Venus Williams.

22 JANUARY 1909 ⁓ 9 FEBRUARY 1910   *Earth Rooster*

8 FEBRUARY 1921 ⁓ 27 JANUARY 1922   *Metal Rooster*

26 JANUARY 1933 ⁓ 13 FEBRUARY 1934   *Water Rooster*

13 FEBRUARY 1945 ⁓ 1 FEBRUARY 1946   *Wood Rooster*

31 JANUARY 1957 ⁓ 17 FEBRUARY 1958   *Fire Rooster*

17 FEBRUARY 1969 ⁓ 5 FEBRUARY 1970   *Earth Rooster*

5 FEBRUARY 1981 ⁓ 24 JANUARY 1982   *Metal Rooster*

23 JANUARY 1993 ⁓ 9 FEBRUARY 1994   *Water Rooster*

9 FEBRUARY 2005 ⁓ 28 JANUARY 2006   *Wood Rooster*

THE
ROOSTER

THE PERSONALITY OF THE ROOSTER

'A wise man will make more opportunities than he finds.'
Francis Bacon, a Rooster

The Rooster is born under the sign of candour. He has a flamboyant and colourful personality and is meticulous in all that he does. He is an excellent organizer and wherever possible likes to plan his various activities well in advance.

The Rooster is highly intelligent and usually very well read. He has a good sense of humour and is an effective and persuasive speaker. He loves discussion and enjoys taking part in any sort of debate. He has no hesitation in speaking his mind and is forthright in his views. He does, however, lack tact and can easily damage his reputation or cause offence by some thoughtless remark or action. He has a very volatile nature and should always try to avoid acting on the spur of the moment.

The Rooster is usually very dignified in his manner and conducts himself with an air of confidence and authority. He is adept at handling financial matters and organizes his financial affairs with considerable skill. He chooses his investments well and is capable of achieving great wealth. Most Roosters save or use their money wisely, but there are a few who are the reverse and are notorious spend-thrifts. Fortunately, the Rooster has great earning capacity and is rarely without sufficient funds to tide himself over.

Another characteristic of the Rooster is that he invariably carries a notebook or scraps of paper around with him. He is constantly writing himself reminders or noting down important facts lest he forgets – the Rooster cannot abide inefficiency and conducts all his activities in an orderly, precise and methodical manner.

The Rooster is usually very ambitious, but can be unrealistic in some of what he hopes to achieve. He occasionally lets his imagination run away with him and while he does not like any interference from others, it would be in his own interests to listen to their views a little more often. He also does not like criticism, and if he feels anybody is doubting his judgement or prying too closely into his affairs, he is certain to let his feelings be known. He can also be rather self-centred and stubborn over relatively trivial matters, but to compensate for this he is reliable, honest and trustworthy, and this is appreciated by all who come into contact with him.

Roosters born between the hours of five and seven, both at dawn and sundown, tend to be the most extrovert of their sign, but all Roosters like to lead an active social life and enjoy attending parties and big functions. The Rooster usually has a wide circle of friends and is able to build up influential contacts with remarkable ease. He often belongs to several clubs and societies and involves himself in a variety of different activities. He is particularly interested in the environment, humanitarian affairs and anything affecting the welfare of others. He has a very caring nature and will do much to help those less fortunate than himself.

He also gets much pleasure from gardening and while he may not spend as much time in the garden as he would like, his garden is invariably well kept and productive.

The Rooster is generally very distinguished in his appearance and if his job permits he will wear an official uniform with great pride and dignity. He is not averse to publicity and takes great delight in being the centre of attention. He often does well at PR work or any job which brings him into contact with the media. He also makes a very good teacher.

The female Rooster leads a varied and interesting life. She involves herself in many different activities and there are some who wonder how she can achieve so much. She often holds very strong views and, like her male counterpart, has no hesitation in speaking her mind or telling others how she thinks things should be done. She is supremely efficient and well organized and her home is usually very neat and tidy. She has good taste in clothes and usually wears smart but very practical outfits.

The Rooster usually has a large family and takes a particularly active interest in the education of his children. He is very loyal to his partner and will find that he is especially well suited to those born under the signs of the Snake, Horse, Ox and Dragon. Provided they do not interfere too much in the Rooster's various activities, the Rat, Tiger, Goat and Pig can also establish a good relationship with him, but two Roosters together are likely to squabble and irritate each other. The rather sensitive Rabbit will find the Rooster a bit too blunt for his liking, and the Rooster will quickly become exasperated by the ever-inquisitive and artful Monkey. He will also find it difficult to get on with the anxious Dog.

If the Rooster can overcome his volatile nature and exercise tact, he will go far in life. He is capable and talented and will make a lasting – and usually favourable – impression almost everywhere he goes.

THE FIVE DIFFERENT TYPES
OF ROOSTER

In addition to the 12 signs of the Chinese zodiac there are five elements and these have a strengthening or moderating influence on the sign. The effects of the five elements on the Rooster are described below, together with the years in which the elements were exercising their influence. Therefore those Roosters born in 1921 and 1981 are Metal Roosters, those born in 1933 and 1993 are Water Roosters, and so on.

Metal Rooster: 1921, 1981

The Metal Rooster is a hard and conscientious worker. He knows exactly what he wants in life and sets about everything in a positive and determined manner. He can at times appear abrasive and he would almost certainly do better if he were more willing to reach a compromise with others rather than hold so rigidly to his beliefs. He is very articulate and most astute when dealing with financial matters. He is loyal to his friends and often devotes much energy to working for the common good.

Water Rooster: 1933, 1993

This Rooster has a very persuasive manner and can easily gain the co-operation of others. He is intelligent, well read and enjoys taking part in discussions and debates. He has a seemingly inexhaustible amount of energy and is prepared to work long hours in order to secure what he wants. He can, however, waste a lot of valuable time worrying over minor and inconsequential details. He is approachable, has a good sense of humour and is highly regarded by others.

Wood Rooster: 1945, 2005
The Wood Rooster is honest, reliable and often sets himself high standards. He is ambitious, but he is also more prepared to work in a team than some of the other types of Rooster. He usually succeeds in life but does have a tendency to get caught up in bureaucratic matters and attempt too many things at the same time. He has wide interests, likes to travel and is very caring and considerate towards his family and friends.

Fire Rooster: 1957
This Rooster is extremely strong-willed. He has many leadership qualities, is an excellent organizer and is most efficient in his work. Through sheer force of character he often secures his objectives, but he does have a tendency to be very forthright and not always consider the feelings of others. If he can learn to be more tactful he can often succeed beyond his wildest dreams.

Earth Rooster: 1909, 1969
This Rooster has a deep and penetrating mind. He is efficient, perceptive and particularly astute in business and financial matters. He is also persistent and once he has set

himself an objective, he will rarely allow himself to be deflected from achieving his aim. He works hard and is held in great esteem by his friends and colleagues. He usually enjoys the arts and takes a keen interest in the activities of the various members of his family.

PROSPECTS FOR THE ROOSTER IN 2007

The Rooster is a keen planner and likes to set about his activities in a careful and organized manner. However, in the Dog year (29 January 2006 to 17 February 2007) this will not always have been possible and problems and pressures will sometimes have disrupted his plans. The Dog year will certainly have brought its vexations and in the closing months the Rooster will need to remain careful.

In his work he would do well to concentrate on his own duties and on the areas in which he can best use his talents. Even though the pressure may sometimes be great, good work now can do much to help his prospects in the forthcoming Pig year. Also, whether in work or seeking it, any additional experience the Rooster can gain can help his situation. In this respect the closing months of the Dog year can be a constructive time.

This is not a time for financial risks, however, and the Rooster will need to be prudent in money matters. With the closing months of the year being a generally expensive time, he would be helped by budgeting in advance for any increased outlay, as well as spreading out his purchases.

More positively, the Rooster's social life is set to become busier at this time and there will be quite a few occasions for him to enjoy. However, while most will go well, there will be times when the Rooster would do well to watch his sometimes candid tongue. A careless comment could cause problems and he does need to remain on his guard.

Domestically, the closing Dog months will see a lot happening, and by liaising well with others and spreading out his various commitments, the Rooster will enjoy many of the activities and events that take place. In addition, there could be some excellent chances to travel as the year draws to a close.

The Year of the Pig starts on 18 February and will herald an improvement in the Rooster's fortunes. This is a year for moving forward and for setting about plans with renewed determination.

The Rooster's work prospects are especially encouraging and he will have chances to use his skills in a more satisfying way. This is very much a year for action, particularly for those Roosters who are disillusioned with their present position or lack of recent progress. The onus to take that action does rest with them, but, as many will find, once they start to look around and make applications, the wheels of change can very quickly begin to turn their way. This also applies to those Roosters seeking work. While again many will have become disillusioned with their situation, by remaining persistent and preparing well for any interview as well as taking advantage of any retraining schemes for which they are eligible, they can find their extra initiative opening some important doors for them.

The prospects are also favourable for those Roosters who are well established in their career. By putting themselves forward and looking to build on their position, many will be able to make important headway, either through promotion or through new opportunities elsewhere. The period from March to early May and September could see some encouraging work developments.

The progress the Rooster makes in his work can also bring an improvement in his income. However, to benefit, the Rooster does need to remain careful in money matters and keep a watchful eye on his spending. Some Roosters do tend to be spendthrifts and without care, anything extra the Rooster earns could quickly come to be spent. Ideally, he should spread out his more substantial purchases for the year and watch his outgoings. Also, should he be tempted by anything of a more speculative nature, he needs to be vigilant and check the implications. This is not a year for risks or being lax in anything which could have repercussions. Roosters, do take note. While earnings can improve, spending does need careful control.

As far as the Rooster's home life is concerned, this promises to be a full and interesting year. As always the Rooster will have plans he is keen to carry through – especially improvements to his home and garden – but he does need to consult others and listen to their views. In domestic matters, dialogue and good communication will make a considerable difference over the year, as well as help maintain the good understanding the Rooster shares with others. Being prepared to tackle projects together can also add to the quality of domestic life.

In addition to the practical activity seen over the year there will also be many memorable occasions for the Rooster to enjoy. Whether going out or entertaining visitors at home (the Rooster makes an attentive host) or taking breaks and holidays, he can take a great deal of pleasure in his domestic life.

The Rooster's social life also holds interesting prospects and he will often have invitations and other chances to go out. Over the year he will get to meet many new faces and for the unattached this can be a year of exciting romantic prospects. Such are the aspects that quite a few unattached Roosters will become engaged, marry or settle down with a partner. For affairs of the heart, this can certainly be a significant time. May, June, August and December will see the most social activity and could also contain some exciting personal developments.

In view of the active nature of the year it is also important that the Rooster allows himself time to relax and unwind and enjoy the rewards of his hard work. He will often benefit from his interests and recreational pursuits, including sometimes spending more time out of doors or meeting up with others. Many Roosters could also be attracted by a new interest over the year and will welcome the challenge this brings. The Rooster's personal interests can also help to keep his lifestyle in balance and in this fine and busy year it is important that he sets aside time for himself and the activities he enjoys.

Overall, the Pig year is an encouraging one for the Rooster, particularly workwise, and there will be excellent chances for him to make more effective use of his strengths. Financially, too, the year can bring an improvement, although the Rooster will need to keep a close watch on his outgoings. Where his relations with others are concerned, the support, help and goodwill of those around him can make an important difference. However, throughout the year the Rooster does need to act in co-operation with others rather than too much on his own. For some, affairs of the heart can also make this a special time.

The Metal Rooster

This is a year of considerable potential for the Metal Rooster and by acting upon his aims and aspirations and using his chances well, he will accomplish a great deal.

In his work this is a year of important developments and with the experience he has behind him and his desire to make more of himself (the Metal Rooster does have a keen and ambitious nature), he is set to do very well over the next 12 months. Many Metal Roosters, with the knowledge and the reputation they have built up, are likely to be given the opportunity to take on greater responsibilities and will be strong candidates for promotion. By making the most of the chances offered them and putting in for the vacancies that become available, these Metal Roosters will often be successful in furthering their career. Also, with the aspects as they are, one step forward can be a prelude to others. Career-wise, what the Metal Rooster achieves in 2007 can have considerable long-term value.

The prospects are also encouraging for those Metal Roosters who are seeking work or feeling unfulfilled and hoping for a change. Again, by making enquiries and following up suitable openings, many will secure what will be an interesting position and, importantly, one which has the potential for future development. Even if certain applications do not go their way, these Metal Roosters will be learning from the experience and in some cases feedback and other suggestions could alert them to other possibilities to consider.

For work developments, March to early May, September and early October are particularly favourable times, but such are the aspects that whenever chances present themselves, the Metal Rooster should act swiftly. This is a year of potential *and* progress.

The Metal Rooster will also benefit from the good working relations he enjoys with so many of his colleagues and should take up any opportunities he has to become better known. This way he will not only be helping his present situation, but also paving the way for success in the future. In addition, if the Metal Rooster feels he needs greater experience in a certain area or that an additional qualification would help, he should consider ways in which he can obtain this, even if it involves studying in his own time. Positive effort and commitment on his part can be to his present *and future* benefit.

The success the Metal Rooster enjoys over the year will lead to an often noticeable rise in income and some Metal Rooster could also benefit from money from another source. This will be an improved year financially, although to benefit the Metal Rooster will need to remain disciplined. With his existing commitments and the plans he has in mind, especially for his accommodation, he does need to watch his spending and, whenever possible, save towards more expensive purchases. He should also be wary of succumbing to too many temptations or impulse purchases. Some control and patience would be beneficial, particularly in view of some of the more favourable buying opportunities that will arise over the year. In addition, if the Metal Rooster takes on any major obligation or is tempted to enter into anything of a more speculative nature, it is important that he checks the details as well as gets sound advice. While his earnings may increase in the Pig year, this is no time for risks or complacency. Metal Roosters, do take note.

As far as the Metal Rooster's personal life is concerned, this will be an interesting and potentially exciting year. Those Metal Roosters with a partner will often have many plans they will be keen to carry out, especially on their home. In addition many couples could have some good personal news to celebrate, including a possible addition to the family. Domestically, the Pig year can certainly give rise to some special times. However, during the year the Metal Rooster does need to make sure he listens closely to his loved ones. Although he may be eager to proceed with certain plans, at times it would be prudent for him to show greater consideration. Also, those Metal Roosters who are newly married, have just set up home together or who start a family will need to make adjustments to their lifestyle and here again the Metal Rooster will need to be accommodating. However, with an awareness of this need for flexibility, the Pig year can go well and contain some truly memorable moments.

This will also be an active year as far as the Metal Rooster's social life is concerned, with many chances to go out and a good variety of events to attend. There will also be opportunities to get to know others and extend his social circle. On a personal level the Metal Rooster will find himself much in demand, with late April to June, August and December seeing the most social activity.

For the unattached Metal Rooster this is a well-aspected year and someone he meets during it, often in a fortuitous way, can quickly become special. Affairs of the heart can be important as well as bring much happiness.

The Metal Rooster will also enjoy any breaks and holidays he takes over the year, especially as they will give him the chance to spend more time with those who are close to him. His travels can also be a good way for him to have a break from his usual routine and to relax and unwind. In this often full and active year, this can do him a lot of good.

Generally, this is a highly promising year for the Metal Rooster and one which will give him the opportunity to advance his career and to make more effective use of his skills and strengths. In addition, what he learns now can prove very helpful to his future prospects. Many Metal Roosters can also look forward to some pleasing developments in their personal life, with affairs of the heart often helping to make this a special time.

TIP FOR THE YEAR
This is a year for acting on your hopes and ambitions and using your strengths and skills. Look to make the most of your opportunities, and your determination – combined with the experience you already have behind you – will stand you in excellent stead.

The Water Rooster

This will be a pleasing year for the Water Rooster and by setting about his activities in his usual earnest way he can look forward to accomplishing a great deal.

For those Water Roosters born in 1993 this will be an important year in their education, especially as they now move on to more advanced work. Although there will often be many subjects to cover as well as sometimes project work to carry out, with a readiness to learn, these young Water Roosters will often enjoy many aspects of their schoolwork and will be encouraged by the progress they feel themselves to be making. Many could also discover a particular aptitude for certain subjects and this in turn can have an encouraging effect on other areas. This is very much a year for the young Water Rooster to put in the effort and *show his true capabilities.*

The Water Rooster will also enjoy developing other skills, and if he has a fondness for sport, music, dance or some other area, he should make the most of his chances to take this further. By practising and developing his skills, perhaps through after-school or local clubs, he will find his enthusiasm and willingness to learn leading on to other possibilities. Some Water Roosters could also be attracted to new interests over the year and whenever they see something that appeals to them, they would do well to find out more. This is very much a year for looking to develop their interests and talents.

The young Water Rooster will value the company of his close group of friends over the year and will also get to meet others, often as a result of his new interests, and make new friends. Any Water Rooster who may be shy or not as involved in the social scene as he would like may also find an important new friendship being made over the year, and this can make a real difference to how he feels. The Pig year is very supportive of the Water Rooster.

As far as the young Water Rooster's home life is concerned, he does need to be open and forthcoming. That way those close to him will be better able to understand, help and encourage him. Although there could be differing views and the young Water Rooster may welcome greater independence, with good communication and a willingness to show some flexibility, he can find his home life generally going well. Joining in with various family activities and plans can also lead to much enjoyment.

For those Water Roosters born in 1933 this will also be an interesting year, and by setting about their activities in their usual enthusiastic and good-hearted way, they can enjoy some good results.

For many of these Water Roosters their home and, if they have one, garden will bring them considerable pleasure and they will often have plans for improvements. However, while, in their usual eager way, they will be keen to see their plans realized, they do need to be wary of acting in haste. The more time they can spend in considering what they want to achieve as well as in choosing and costing their options the better.

The Water Rooster will, as always, take a special interest in the activities of those close to him, and if younger relations find themselves under pressure or with important decisions to take, the Water Rooster's readiness to help and advise will be especially valued. Similarly, if he himself has any concerns or would welcome assistance with certain tasks, he should ask. In the Pig year the willingness of family members and close friends to help each other will be important.

The more senior Water Rooster will also take pleasure in pursuing his various hobbies and interests over the year and if he decides to contact other enthusiasts or is involved in a local group, he will often welcome the chance to talk with others as well as to share his knowledge and insights. Again, the Water Rooster's talents and approachable nature will serve him well.

The generally positive aspects of the year also extend to money matters and many Water Roosters will benefit from a gift, a maturing policy or some other source of income. However, while this will be welcome, the Water Rooster does need to manage his finances carefully. When making large purchases or entering into important agreements, he would do well to check the terms and implications and ensure that what he is considering fully satisfies his requirements. Important purchases and agreements should not be rushed. Similarly, when completing financial paper-work, the Water Rooster needs to be thorough. If he should have any questions or doubts, he would do well to seek advice. Without care, problems could result. Water Roosters, take note.

Overall, though, for both younger and more senior Water Roosters, the Pig year holds encouraging prospects and by making most of their situation, ideas and opportunities, they will be pleased with what they are able to accomplish. The help and support they receive will also be an important and encouraging feature of the year.

TIP FOR THE YEAR

Make the most of the opportunities available to you and do draw on the readiness of others to support and advise. With their help, backed by your own keen nature, you can make this a successful and personally rewarding year.

The Wood Rooster

This is a promising year for the Wood Rooster, although to make the most of it he will need to remain disciplined and focused on what he wants to do. If not, there is a risk that he could spread his energies too widely and not achieve as much as he otherwise might.

For those Wood Roosters in work this can be an important year and while a lot may be expected of them, by remaining disciplined and using their skills, they will often be satisfied with what they are able to do. Many will also benefit from opportunities that become available in their present place of work, perhaps moving on to a more specialist role or becoming involved in an interesting new project. The Pig year can often allow the Wood Rooster to use his talents in a more fulfilling and purposeful way.

For those Wood Roosters who are seeking work or looking for a way to supplement their income, perhaps on a part-time or casual basis, again the Pig year can bring some interesting opportunities. However, in order to secure a position, these Wood Roosters will need to persevere as well as to stress to prospective employers their experience and the contribution they feel they could make. Their extra input can be an important factor in their success. Late March to early May and September could see some encouraging developments as far as the Wood Roster's work prospects are concerned.

The Wood Rooster's efforts at work can also make a difference to him financially, although he will need to remain his careful self when dealing with money matters. In particular, he does need to deal promptly and thoroughly with any financial paperwork he receives and should he have any problems or uncertainties, he would do well to seek advice. Also, he could find it helpful to save up for some of the more expensive plans he has in mind. Good budgeting and control will not only help his overall situation but also lead to him being able to do that much more. In general, the Pig year does require a disciplined approach.

One area which will be especially satisfying, however, will be the Wood Rooster's personal interests and he will thoroughly enjoy spending time on these. If he can meet other enthusiasts, perhaps at a local group, he will find this can add much to his pleasure and knowledge. Also, if he sees a new subject that appeals to him, he should find out more. With his enquiring mind, he can find new pursuits and activities developing in an encouraging manner. As many Wood Roosters will discover, their interests can also have a strong social element.

The Wood Rooster should also make the most of his chances to go out over the year and if there are local activities or events that appeal to him, he should follow these up. Similarly, if there are particular places he would like to visit or he sees an attractive travel offer, he should make enquiries and see what can be arranged. The Pig year can contain some interesting and pleasing occasions.

In his domestic life the Wood Rooster will particularly value the support and encouragement of those close to him, and whenever he has plans in mind, he should be willing to discuss them. The involvement and support of others can lead to so much more being achieved. During the course of the year he will also do much to assist and encourage family members and his care and judgement can often make a great difference. Many Wood Roosters could also have cause for some celebration over the year, especially concerning the news of a younger relation. Domestically, this will be a pleasing year and the better the liaison and co-operation, between the Wood Rooster and his loved ones, the richer his home life will be.

The Pig year certainly holds positive aspects for the Wood Rooster and will encourage him to make good use of his talents, strengths and personal interests. By concentrating his attention on what he has to do rather than spreading his energies too widely, he will often be satisfied with his achievements as well as enjoy many of his activities. Overall, a pleasing and often personally rewarding year.

TIP FOR THE YEAR
Consider furthering your personal interests in some way. By spending time in ways you enjoy, you will not only be doing yourself some good but also adding something extra to your lifestyle and to the year.

The Fire Rooster

Diligent, hard working and resourceful, the Fire Rooster has many fine qualities, and as he enters his fifties, he may well consider this a good time to take further steps towards some of his key aims. With determination, he will find that much can happen in the Pig year.

However, to make the most of this encouraging year, as it starts the Fire Rooster would do well to give careful thought to what he wants to accomplish over the next 12 months. By involving those close to him and running through ideas and possibilities, he could soon have something to work towards and to look forward to.

In his work the Fire Rooster will find his extensive experience serving him well, and as more senior colleagues move on or other openings occur, he will often be well placed and qualified to put in for promotion. In some cases this could be what he has been working towards for some time. This is very much a year for reaping the rewards of his recent commitment and good work. March to mid-May and September could see some particularly good opportunities, but with the aspects as they are, chances could arise throughout the year and the Fire Rooster would do well to act quickly.

This will also be an important year for those Fire Roosters who are keen to make a change in their career, perhaps feeling that they have done all they can in their present position or that they are in something of in a rut. By giving careful thought to what they now want to do and considering various possibilities, they can find some interesting doors opening for them, often in fortuitous ways. Positive and purposeful action can certainly lead to significant developments.

This also applies to those Fire Roosters who are seeking work. Again, by following up openings that interest them and making a special effort with their application, their initiative and determination will often give them the chance they need and give their career an important new impetus.

The progress the Fire Rooster makes in his work will lead to an increase in income, but with often expensive plans and ideas lined up, he will need to manage his money well. Whenever possible, saving up for forthcoming expenses can be helpful. Similarly, if he is in a position to reduce any borrowings as well as add to savings or pension policies, this could be worth considering. If he is able to put his money to good use, he can enjoy a much-improved financial position.

There will also be some good travel opportunities in 2007 and some Fire Roosters will choose to mark their fiftieth year with a special holiday or a trip to a favourite destination. Again, by carefully planning and budgeting in advance, the Fire Rooster will be able to enjoy himself and do a great deal. Luck could also play its part, with many Fire Roosters benefiting from advantageous travel offers.

As far as the Fire Rooster's domestic life is concerned, this will be a busy but pleasing year. In addition to the possible marking of his own birthday, there could also be some other memorable moments to celebrate, perhaps a wedding, the birth of a grandchild or some family success. The Fire Rooster will follow the progress of younger relations with much fondness and some advice he gives will prove especially helpful. His judgement and empathy will be particularly appreciated.

The Fire Rooster will also enjoy some of the practical projects he and his loved ones tackle over the year, including improvements to his home and/or garden. This is a year which favours joint effort and by discussing options and then setting about plans together, the Fire Rooster and his loved ones will delight in their achievements. However, while he may be keen to get tasks done, the Fire Rooster does need to be wary of taking on too many activities all at once. Good planning will be helpful. Also, at busy times, he should not hesitate to ask others for greater assistance, including with household chores. Fire Roosters, do take note. You do so much for others and should draw on their assistance when you need it.

Though the Fire Rooster will often have many demands on his time, it is also important that he does not let his personal interests or social life suffer over the year. Both can provide an important and necessary balance to his lifestyle. And by setting regular time aside for activities he enjoys as well as going to social occasions and local events that interest him, he will find the Pig year containing some particularly pleasing times. For those Fire Roosters who would welcome new friendships, romance or a fuller social life, the Pig year can bring a considerable improvement in their situation. In this respect, too, the Fire Rooster's fiftieth year can indeed be memorable, with the period from late April to June, August, December and January seeing the most social activity.

Overall, this will be a significant year for the Fire Rooster and, by going after what he wants and using his strengths and opportunities to advantage, he will accomplish a great deal. This is a year for action and progress.

TIP FOR THE YEAR

Be forthcoming about your aims and hopes and do draw on
the advice and assistance of those around you. The input of
others can help you to get so much more from this often
special year.

The Earth Rooster

The Earth Rooster has a very determined nature and
although his more recent progress may not always have
matched his expectations, especially in the sometimes challenging Dog year, he knows that he possesses some great
strengths and is capable of some fine achievements. He also
recognizes that with patience and determination, much is
possible. In 2007 he will be proved right and will be able to
make this both an important and successful year.

The aspects are particularly encouraging as far as the
Earth Rooster's work prospects are concerned and he can
look forward to making significant progress. This is very
much a year for him to build on his position and move his
career forward. The onus to act does rest with him, but by
actively following up vacancies and making enquiries, he
will soon find his efforts bearing fruit. Such are the aspects
that some interesting possibilities or ideas could occur just
as the Pig year starts and the early months of the year (to
mid-May) and September and early October could see
some favourable developments.

For those Earth Roosters seeking work this can be a
year of new starts and many will be successful in securing
a position which can set their career on a potentially
rewarding new track. For many, the Pig year can mark a

significant stage (or new start) in their career development.

The Earth Rooster's personal interests are also favourably aspected and over the year he should aim to take these further including, if appropriate, promoting what he does. Those Earth Roosters who enjoy more creative and expressive activities could enjoy an encouraging response and a few may be able to benefit financially from what they do. The Pig year rewards enterprise and talent.

Also, should the Earth Rooster see a particular activity or recreational pursuit that appeals to him, this would be a good time to find out more. In some cases activities or interests he takes up over the year can come to be significant as well as allow him to discover strengths he did not realize he had. Any time that the Earth Rooster can give to pursuing and developing his personal interests can be a source of much satisfaction over the year.

The Earth Rooster will also appreciate the travel opportunities that come his way, and whether he is visiting friends and relations, going away on holiday or taking spur of the moment outings or breaks, he will often enjoy what he does as well as some of the interesting places he visits. For many Earth Roosters their travels can also have a pleasing social element.

As far as money matters are concerned this will be an improved year, with many Earth Roosters enjoying a rise in income and some also being able to supplement this with overtime or a skill or idea they have. With effort and commitment, and by budgeting carefully for his various commitments and plans, the Earth Rooster will be pleased with how he fares. If he is patient when making some of his purchases and is prepared to look around, he could also save himself considerable outlay and acquire some excellent bargains. However, while he can fare well in financial matters, he does need to pay particular attention to any important paperwork he has to complete or any transactions concerning his accommodation. These do need to be handled carefully and thoroughly, and if appropriate, the Earth Rooster should seek professional advice.

As far as the Earth Rooster's home life is concerned, this will be a busy year and his ability to keep tabs on so many activities will certainly be appreciated. However, it is important that the Earth Rooster does not take on too much single-handed and makes sure that everyone does their fair share. There will also be some memorable times enjoying shared interests and any home and garden projects. Those Earth Roosters who are parents will enjoy watching the progress of their children and the Earth Rooster's ability to address any problems and encourage dialogue can do much to ease any tensions.

In view of the many activities the Earth Rooster is involved with he will often be fairly selective in his socializing this year. However, it is important that he does not allow this to undermine some of his friendships and he would do well to keep in contact with his friends as well as go to any social events that appeal to him. Also, as a result of interests he pursues or changes in his work, there may be opportunities for him to make new friends. For those Earth Roosters seeking new friendships and perhaps romance, someone met during the course of the year, often as a result of a new interest, can quickly become important.

For social opportunities May, June, August and December are the most promising months.

The Pig year holds good prospects for the Earth Rooster and there will be opportunities for him to make important progress in his work and more effective use of his talents and skills. To benefit, he does need to be prepared to put himself forward, but with self-belief and determination he can make this an important and personally rewarding year.

TIP FOR THE YEAR

Seize the initiative and go after what you want. Positive and enthusiastic action will be well rewarded. Also look to further your personal interests. These can benefit you in many ways and allow you to discover new talents.

FAMOUS ROOSTERS

Mohamed al Fayed, Fernando Alonso, Beyoncé, Cate Blanchett, Sir Michael Caine, Enrico Caruso, Eric Clapton, Joan Collins, Craig David, Daniel Day Lewis, Minnie Driver, Ms Dynamite, the Duke of Edinburgh, Gloria Estefan, Roger Federer, Errol Flynn, Dawn French, Stephen Fry, Melanie Griffith, Katharine Hepburn, Lleyton Hewitt, Catherine Zeta Jones, Diane Keaton, Søren Kierkegaard, D. H. Lawrence, David Livingstone, Ken Livingstone, Steve Martin, W. Somerset Maugham, Paul Merton, Bette Midler, Van Morrison, Yoko Ono, Dolly Parton, Michelle Pfeiffer, Mary Quant, Joan Rivers, Jenny Seagrove, Carly Simon, Britney Spears, Johann Strauss, Verdi, Richard Wagner, Serena Williams, Neil Young, Renée Zellweger.

10 FEBRUARY 1910 〜 29 JANUARY 1911   *Metal Dog*

28 JANUARY 1922 〜 15 FEBRUARY 1923   *Water Dog*

14 FEBRUARY 1934 〜 3 FEBRUARY 1935   *Wood Dog*

2 FEBRUARY 1946 〜 21 JANUARY 1947   *Fire Dog*

18 FEBRUARY 1958 〜 7 FEBRUARY 1959   *Earth Dog*

6 FEBRUARY 1970 〜 26 JANUARY 1971   *Metal Dog*

25 JANUARY 1982 〜 12 FEBRUARY 1983   *Water Dog*

10 FEBRUARY 1994 〜 30 JANUARY 1995   *Wood Dog*

29 JANUARY 2006 〜 17 FEBRUARY 2007   *Fire Dog*

THE
DOG

THE PERSONALITY OF THE DOG

'To be what we are, and to become what we are capable of becoming, is the only end of life.'

Robert Louis Stevenson, a Dog

The Dog is born under the signs of loyalty and anxiety. He usually holds very firm views and beliefs and is the champion of good causes. He hates any sort of injustice or unfair treatment and will do all in his power to help those less fortunate than himself. He has a strong sense of fair play and will be honourable and open in all his dealings.

The Dog is very direct and straightforward. He is never one to skirt round issues and speaks frankly and to the point. He can be stubborn, but he is prepared to listen to the views of others and will try to be as fair as possible in coming to his decisions. He will readily give advice where it is needed and will be the first to offer assistance when things go wrong.

The Dog instils confidence wherever he goes and there are many who admire him for his integrity and resolute manner. He is a very good judge of character and can often form an accurate impression of someone very shortly after meeting them. He is also very intuitive and can frequently sense how things are going to work out long in advance.

Despite his friendly and amiable manner, the Dog is not a big socializer. He dislikes having to attend large functions or parties and much prefers a quiet meal with friends or a chat by the fire. He is an excellent conversationalist and is often a marvellous raconteur of amusing stories and anecdotes.

The Dog is also quick-witted and his mind is always alert. He can keep calm in a crisis and although he does have a temper, his outbursts tend to be short-lived. He is loyal and trustworthy, but if he ever feels badly let down or rejected by someone, he will rarely forgive or forget.

The Dog usually has very set interests. He prefers to specialize and become an expert in a chosen area rather than dabble in a variety of different activities. He usually does well in jobs where he feels that he is being of service to others and is often suited to careers in the social services, the medical and legal professions and teaching. He does, however, need to feel motivated in his work. He has to have a sense of purpose and if ever this is lacking he can quite often drift through life without ever achieving very much. Once he has the motivation, however, very little can prevent him from securing his objective.

Another characteristic of the Dog is his tendency to worry and to view things rather pessimistically. Quite often his worries are totally unnecessary and are of his own making. Although it may be difficult, worrying is a habit which all Dogs should try to overcome.

The Dog is not materialistic or particularly bothered about accumulating great wealth. As long as he has the money necessary to support his family and to spend on the occasional luxury, he is more than happy. However, when he does have any spare money he tends to be rather a spendthrift and does not always put his money to its best use. He is also not a very good speculator and would be advised to get professional advice before entering into any major long-term investment.

The Dog will rarely be short of admirers, but he is not an easy person to live with. His moods are changeable and his standards high, but he will be loyal and protective to his partner and will do all in his power to provide a good and comfortable home. He can get on extremely well with those born under the signs of the Horse, Pig, Tiger and Monkey, and can also establish a sound and stable relationship with the Rat, Ox, Rabbit, Snake and another Dog, but will find the Dragon a bit too flamboyant for his liking. He will also find it difficult to understand the imaginative Goat and is likely to be highly irritated by the candid Rooster.

The female Dog is renowned for her beauty. She has a warm and caring nature, although until she knows someone well she can be both secretive and very guarded. She is highly intelligent and despite her calm and tranquil appearance she can be extremely ambitious. She enjoys sport and other outdoor activities and has a happy knack of finding bargains in the most unlikely of places. She can also get rather impatient when things do not work out as she would like.

The Dog usually has a very good way with children and can be a doting parent. He will rarely be happier than when he is helping someone or doing something that will benefit others. Providing he can cure himself of his tendency to worry, he will lead a very full and active life – and in that life he will make many friends and do a tremendous amount of good.

THE FIVE DIFFERENT TYPES OF DOG

In addition to the 12 signs of the Chinese zodiac there are five elements and these have a strengthening or moderating influence on the sign. The effects of the five elements on the Dog are described below, together with the years in which the elements were exercising their influence. Therefore those Dogs born in 1910 and 1970 are Metal Dogs, those born in 1922 and 1982 are Water Dogs, and so on.

Metal Dog: 1910, 1970

The Metal Dog is bold, confident and forthright and sets about everything he does in a resolute and determined manner. He has a great belief in his abilities and has no hesitation about speaking his mind or devoting himself to some just cause. He can be rather serious at times and can become anxious and irritable when things are not going according to plan. He tends to have very specific interests and it would certainly help him if he were to broaden his outlook and become more involved in group activities. He is extremely loyal and faithful to his friends.

Water Dog: 1922, 1982

The Water Dog has a very direct and outgoing personality. He is an excellent communicator and has little trouble in persuading others to fall in with his plans. He does, however, have a somewhat carefree nature and is not as disciplined or as thorough as he should be in certain matters. Neither does he keep as much control over his finances as he should, but he can be most generous to his family and friends and will make sure that they want for nothing. The Water Dog is usually very good with children and has a wide circle of friends.

Wood Dog: 1934, 1994

This Dog is a hard and conscientious worker and will usually make a favourable impression wherever he goes. He is less independent than some of the other types of Dog and prefers to work in a group rather than on his own. He is popular, has a good sense of humour and takes a keen interest in the activities of the various members of his family. He is often attracted to the finer things in life and can obtain much pleasure from collecting stamps, coins, pictures or antiques. He prefers to live in the country rather than the town.

Fire Dog: 1946, 2006

This Dog has a lively, outgoing personality and is able to establish friendships with remarkable ease. He is an honest and conscientious worker and likes to take an active part in all that is going on around him. He also likes to explore new ideas and providing he can get the necessary support and advice, he can often succeed where others have failed. He does, however, have a tendency to be stubborn. Providing he can overcome this, he can often achieve considerable fame and fortune.

Earth Dog: 1958

The Earth Dog is very talented and astute. He is methodical and efficient and is capable of going far in his chosen profession. He tends to be rather quiet and reserved but has a very persuasive manner and usually secures his objectives without too much opposition. He is generous and kind and is always ready to lend a helping hand when it is needed. He is also held in very high esteem by his friends and colleagues and is usually most dignified in his appearance.

PROSPECTS FOR THE DOG IN 2007

The Dog can do well in his own year (29 January 2006 to 17 February 2007) and in the closing months he should bear in mind the words of Virgil: 'Fortune favours the bold.' With determination and a willingness to go after his aims, he will be able to reap some fine rewards.

The Dog's relations with others are particularly well aspected and he will find himself in demand. In his home life there will often be various activities to plan and visits to arrange as well as tasks around the home to get underway. With discussion and co-operation, a lot can get done and the Dog will appreciate the events that take place.

Socially, too, the year will get busier in the closing months and the Dog will have quite a few invitations and other chances to go out. As a result, many Dogs will find themselves meeting new people, some of whom can turn into good friends and helpful contacts in the months ahead.

As far as work is concerned, many Dogs will face an increased workload at this time. However, this will give the

Dog a good chance to draw on his skills and for those who are keen to advance their career or who are looking for work, there could be some fine opportunities, especially from September to early December.

The Dog can also enjoy some financial good fortune in the closing months of his own year and could benefit from a bonus or sometimes generous gift. However, with his many outgoings and the purchases he is keen to make, he would do well to watch his spending and think carefully over what and when to buy. Some good planning could help.

Generally, the Dog year is a fine and constructive one for the Dog and he will be able to build on his progress in the next Chinese year.

The Year of the Pig starts on 18 February and will be a satisfying one for the Dog. Unlike some years, when the Dog may feel buffeted by events or not as in control of his situation as he would like, the general pace and nature of the Pig year will be to his liking. As a result, many Dogs will be able to make good headway over the year and enjoy some well-deserved success.

In his work the Dog will have an excellent chance to build on his present position and develop his strengths. Also, the qualities for which the Dog is so well known – including his loyalty, conscientiousness and ability to work well with many people – will stand him in excellent stead and when chances arise to take on additional responsibilities or someone is needed for particular duties, the Dog will often be well placed to benefit.

Many Dogs will decide to remain with their present employer over the year and will benefit from the in-house opportunities that arise. However, for those Dogs who are keen for a change or are seeking work, this can be a year of important developments. By deciding on the type of work they want and following up suitable openings, many will be successful in securing what can be an important position with potential for the future. With purpose and something definite in mind, these Dogs will often be able to move their career in the direction they want, as the year is supportive of their determination and resolve. March, April, July and October could see the best opportunities, but generally this is a year which offers encouraging prospects for the Dog and gives him the chance to use his qualities and talents to advantage.

The Pig year is also well aspected for money matters and many Dogs will enjoy a rise in income. Some may also be able to supplement this with some extra work or an enterprising idea. For many, their efforts and hard work will lead to an improvement in their situation. However, to benefit, the Dog should manage his finances with care and budget for any large purchases or forthcoming expenses. Discipline and careful control will be much better than proceeding on too much of an ad hoc basis. Also, if he is able, he would do well to consider reducing any borrowings he may have as well as saving for the longer term. Money invested sensibly now could grow into a useful asset that the Dog will be grateful of in the future.

The Dog will also benefit from his personal interests, and despite his generally busy and demanding lifestyle it is important that he allows himself time for recreational pursuits he enjoys and appreciates the rewards he works so hard for. In addition to his existing interests, he could be tempted to take up something new over the year. Whether creative, cultural, a new skill or something more physical, he will enjoy any new challenge as well as gain personally from what he does.

The Dog should also aim to go away at some time over the year and will appreciate the rest and change of scene this brings. However, he does need to check the travel arrangements as well as make sure *all* the documentation is in order. A mistake or error could cause inconvenience and possible delay. While holidays and breaks can go well and do him good, his actual travel arrangements do need close and thorough attention. Dogs, do take note.

With his caring nature the Dog always sets much store by his relations with others and both his domestic and social life will mean a great deal to him over the year. In his home life, the Dog's input and thoughtfulness will not only be appreciated but also lead to more being done. Some home projects and improvements can turn out particularly well and there could also be some family successes and news that will please everyone.

However, while the Dog's domestic life will be both active and satisfying, as with any year, differences of opinion will sometimes arise and views clash. When this occurs, a willingness on the part of everyone to talk and, where necessary, compromise will often lead to a speedier resolution as well as prevent tensions from overshadowing an otherwise agreeable year. With care and an open and forthcoming approach, the Dog can help to ease any tensions, and his ability to relate so effectively to others will prove a real asset.

The Dog will value his social life in the Pig year, especially some of the more informal gatherings where he can

talk to a select few – at larger events the Dog can sometimes feel ill at ease. There will be opportunities to go out
and events to attend, usually as a result of his interests,
and for the unattached, the Pig year holds excellent
romantic possibilities. March, June to August and
November could all see much social activity and for affairs
of the heart this can be an often exciting and memorable
year.

The Dog's prospects are certainly encouraging during
the Pig year and by acting upon his aims and ideas and
making the most of his chances, he can look forward to
accomplishing a great deal. Both his work and personal
interests can develop well over the year and his relations
with others can be positive and encouraging. For some,
there will be excellent prospects for romance as well. The
Dog will have good opportunity to use his talents and
personal qualities to advantage and can make this a satisfying and personally rewarding year.

The Metal Dog

This will be a constructive year for the Metal Dog, with
many of his activities and plans going well.

In his work the Metal Dog's experience and qualities
will serve him well. Although many Metal Dogs will
decide to remain where they are over the year, especially if
they are relatively new to their present position, by setting
about their duties in their usual conscientious way and
making the most of opportunities to add to their skills,
they will not only find their work more fulfilling but will
also be preparing themselves for when they next look to

move on. In this respect, what these Metal Dogs learn over the year can be of significant long-term value.

For those Metal Dogs who are eager to make a change or are seeking work, this can be a year of opportunity. To benefit, though, these Metal Dogs will need to give careful thought to the direction they would like their career to take. This is no year to seek change for change's sake. By focusing their efforts on the sort of work they now want, many will be successful in their quest and gain an opening which not only suits their talents but also has possibilities for the future. The longer-term implications of what the Metal Dog achieves during the Pig year should not be under-estimated. March to early May, July and October could see some positive career developments.

Finances are also encouragingly aspected this year and many Metal Dogs will enjoy an increase in income. Some may also be able to supplement this through an interest or idea they have. For the enterprising, the Pig year could mark the start of a potentially rewarding venture. However to make the most of his situation, the Metal Dog does need to keep careful control over his outgoings and budget for any expensive plans. With good management and some prudence he can improve on his financial situation considerably over the year. Also, if he is able to reduce any borrowings or make savings with a view to the longer term, this can be to both his present and future benefit.

Another beneficial area concerns the Metal Dog's personal interests, and while he will often have a lot to keep him occupied, it is important that he allows time for recreational pursuits he enjoys. Not only can these do him good but sometimes they can give him the chance to get additional exercise and also have an enjoyable social element. Those Metal Dogs who may have let their interests lapse recently should aim to rectify this over the year. By doing so, they will give their lifestyle – and the year – greater balance. Also, if the Metal Dog is sedentary for much of the day and gets little exercise at other times, he should look at ways in which he can correct this and take medical advice on what is best for him to do. The time and attention he can give to both his interests and his well-being can be very much to his advantage.

As far as the Metal Dog's home life is concerned, this will be a busy year and during it he will do much to help both younger and more senior relations. If his loved ones are facing problems or are in need of advice, his judgement and straight-talking ways will be particularly appreciated. However, while he will be so willing to assist, if at any time matters arise which he feels he does not have the knowledge or experience to deal with, he should not forget there are others he can turn to. In the Pig year it is important that the Metal Dog does not take on too much by himself and remembers that help is available should he need it. However, while, as with any year, problems will sometimes raise their head, generally the Metal Dog's home life will be a source of much pleasure.

This will also be a pleasing year socially, with the Metal Dog appreciating the events he decides to attend and the times he meets up with his friends. Many Metal Dogs will also enjoy the social element their interests can bring, and for those who are keen to make new friends and build up their social circle, spending time on interests and recreational pursuits in their area can be an excellent way to do this.

This is also an auspicious year for affairs of the heart and for those Metal Dogs who are alone and/or have experienced recent problems in their personal life, the Pig year can see quite a transformation in their situation. For many, the Pig year can mark the opening of a brighter chapter in their lives, with the chance to meet someone who will become very special.

The Pig year certainly holds good prospects for the Metal Dog, and by using his strengths well and spending time with his loved ones and in pursuits he enjoys, he will find much going in his favour. Pleasingly, his accomplishments, including the skills and knowledge he acquires over the year, can also be important factors in the progress he is set to make in following years.

TIP FOR THE YEAR
Two tips! Make the most of any chances you have to build on your skills. Also, do spend time with others and involve your loved ones in your hopes, activities and interests. Their support and encouragement will not only mean a lot to you, but will also help you to enjoy much more over the year.

The Water Dog

This is a year of considerable potential for the Water Dog, with a lot for him to look forward to. However, to benefit, the Water Dog does need to use his time wisely as well as keep his lifestyle in balance. To devote too much attention to one area could cause problems in another, and in this full year the Water Dog would do well to plan his various activities carefully.

On a personal level this will be an often memorable year and many Water Dogs will have good cause for celebration, perhaps through a marriage, an addition to their family or the realization of a long-held ambition. The Pig year can certainly bring some very special success, which in many cases the Water Dog will have worked towards for some time.

For those Water Dogs with a partner much time will be spent enjoying interests together and furthering ideas and plans. Many of these Water Dogs will also spend time on their accommodation, with some deciding to move. They will often delight in stamping their personality on their home and will take much pleasure in seeing their ideas take shape. This can be a special and happy time.

For Water Dogs who are currently unattached this can also be a year of often significant developments. In some cases someone they may have known for some time will become more special or a chance invitation may lead to a meeting with someone they have a natural affinity with. Romance will certainly be in the air and can bring quite a transformation to the Water Dog's life. For socializing and meeting others March, June to August, late October and November are the most promising months.

The Water Dog's personal interests are also excellently aspected and although he will often have many demands on his time, he should still make sure he allows time for activities he enjoys. Also, if he is able to add to his skills or set himself a new challenge, he will find this can add to the pleasure. Water Dogs who are keen to meet others and build up their social life will find their interests can be a good way to do this.

As far as the Water Dog's work is concerned, this will be an important year which will give many Water Dogs the chance to move on to greater responsibilities as well as to further their knowledge and skills. By making the most of the opportunities that arise, including any training that becomes available, the Water Dog will find the additional experience he gains serving him well both now and in the future. Workwise, this can be a significant *and* constructive time.

Many Water Dogs will decide to remain with their present employer over the year and become more established in their role, but those who feel there are better prospects elsewhere or would welcome a change should remain alert for possibilities. Many will be able to make important headway and secure a position which takes their career in the direction they want. As far as the Water Dog's prospects are concerned, this is an encouraging year. It is also one in which the Water Dog's skills and tenacity will be well rewarded. For work opportunities, March, April, July and October to mid-November are favourable times.

The progress the Water Dog makes in his work will lead to a welcome rise in income and some Water Dogs may also benefit from a gift or some unexpected assistance they receive over the year. However, with often considerable accommodation expenses, personal plans and various acquisitions in mind, the Water Dog will need to remain disciplined in his spending and budget carefully. This is very much a year for keeping sensible control over the purse-strings and saving towards more substantial expenses rather than proceeding on too much of an ad hoc basis.

The Water Dog also needs to be careful with any important paperwork he may have to deal with and should check the terms and implications thoroughly. Money matters, forms and transactions do need to be handled with care, and if the Water Dog has any uncertainties or questions, he should address these before proceeding. Similarly, if he is intending to travel, he should check his travel documentation before leaving. The extra attention and scrutiny that he can give to paperwork and financial matters over the year will be well worth his while.

The Pig year certainly holds encouraging prospects for the Water Dog, although he does need to balance his commitments. In some cases work pressures will take up much of his time and he does need to be careful that work does not continually encroach on his home life and other activities. He may be conscientious and committed, but in the Pig year he does need to strike a sensible balance. Similarly, those Water Dogs enjoying an especially active personal and social life need to be careful that a succession of late nights does not begin to take its toll. In the Pig year striking that balance is just so important. If the Water Dog does so, however, this can be a successful and rewarding year.

TIP FOR THE YEAR

This can be a special year for you but it will also be a busy one and you do need to organize your time, activities and commitments well. Amid all the activity, do make sure you set time aside for recreational pursuits. The main thing is to keep your commitments under control and your lifestyle in balance.

The Wood Dog

This will be a satisfying year for the Wood Dog and by making the most of the opportunities that arise and using his talents well, he will be pleased with what he achieves.

For those Wood Dogs born in 1994 this will be an encouraging year, and by working hard and showing commitment, many will not only make good progress in their schoolwork but also grow in their general confidence and outlook. These Wood Dogs will also welcome the chance to make more use of the facilities and equipment available to them as well as be able to put their new knowledge and skills to fuller use. Particularly for those who enjoy more creative or physical subjects (including sport), this can be a successful and personally rewarding time.

Friends who have similar interests will often encourage the Wood Dog, and by joining others, including in after-school clubs or local groups, he will not only enjoy himself but also sometimes get the chance to learn or practise new skills. The Pig year is a very encouraging one as far as the Wood Dog's development is concerned and he really will gain a lot by making the most of the chances given him.

However, while this is a positive time, as with any year, problems and pressures will sometimes arise. Whenever the Wood Dog has concerns, whether over subjects he is studying, problems at school or what is being asked or expected of him, it is important that he is forthcoming. 'A worry shared is a worry halved', as the saying goes, and the young Wood Dog will find this very true over the year. Whenever he has difficulties it is important that he remembers that there *are* people around who can help.

Also, during the year the young Wood Dog could be involved in some fairly active pursuits, and while he will often revel in the activity, he does need to remain careful and follow instructions, especially in sport. Without care, there is a risk that he could strain or hurt himself. The Pig year is not a time for unnecessary recklessness! Wood Dogs, do take note.

For the more senior Wood Dog, this can be a rewarding year. In his domestic life he will often be grateful for the support and encouragement of those dear to him and whenever he is considering ideas or would welcome assistance, it is important that he draws on the willingness of others to help. In addition to any home or garden projects he may busy himself with, his interests can be a source of much pleasure and over the year he will enjoy the time he spends pursuing these. Creative pursuits are particularly well aspected, with activities such as photography, art, writing and craftwork being both satisfying and therapeutic. Also, should the Wood Dog see a competition related to an interest of his, he would do well to consider entering it. Similarly, if he has the chance to put forward any work he has produced, he should do so. In many cases he will be encouraged by the feedback he is given and some Wood Dogs could even have good news to celebrate! This is a year for the Wood Dog to both use and enjoy his talents and ideas.

The Wood Dog is usually careful in handling money matters, but in the Pig year he must not let his vigilance slip. When dealing with financial forms, especially any concerning pensions, taxes or benefits, he does need to check the details carefully and seek advice if uncertain over any matter. Where his financial interests are involved, he needs to be both thorough and alert. In addition, if undertaking any travel, he should make sure all the documentation is in order before he leaves and that he has taken careful note of times and connections. His travels over the year can go well, but where paperwork is concerned, the Wood Dog does need to be vigilant. Wood Dogs, do take note.

Overall, this will be a pleasing year for the Wood Dog, and whether born in 1934 or 1994, by putting energy into his plans, interests and commitments and drawing on the support and advice of others, he will often take much satisfaction in his achievements.

TIP FOR THE YEAR
Use your strengths and talents well and make the most of your ideas. With a willing and keen approach you can take pleasure in many activities over the year.

The Fire Dog

This will be an important year for the Fire Dog, although to benefit from its encouraging aspects he would do well to give some thought to his plans for the next 12 months. This way he will not only have something purposeful to work towards, but can also accomplish that much more.

The Fire Dog's planning could concern almost any aspect of his life, but central to so much will be his family and domestic life. Whenever he has any thoughts about domestic arrangements or family activities, it is important that he puts them forward. These ideas could include improvements to the home (the Pig year favours practical activities), travel plans and recreational pursuits that can be shared and enjoyed, but over the year many of them will be taken up and will bring a good deal of satisfaction to everyone concerned.

The Fire Dog will also do much to assist both younger and more senior relations during the Pig year. Whether this involves giving his time, advising others about decisions they have to take or helping with certain tasks, again his input will be important and often of greater value than he may realize.

Another positively aspected area is the Fire Dog's personal interests and over the Pig year he should look to further these. This could be by setting himself a new project or challenge, improving a skill or technique, enrolling on a course or deciding to take up something new, but whatever he chooses to do it can again be a satisfying and often fulfilling use of his time. Those Fire Dogs who have recently retired will find that giving more time to an interest, whether an existing one or something different, can add another beneficial element to the year.

The Fire Dog would also do well to give consideration to his well-being over the year and if he does not tend to get much regular exercise or eat a sufficiently balanced diet, it would be worth him obtaining medical advice on how he can best correct this. Any modifications he can make, even if at first difficult, can make a difference. With this being an encouraging year, the thought, time and attention he gives to his own well-being can be to his benefit.

The Fire Dog will value his social life over the year and in addition to keeping in regular contact with his friends, if he gets involved with an interest group or enrols on a course he will find this can lead to some pleasing social occasions. In addition, if there are any local events or activities that appeal to him and he is able to go to them with family and friends, he will often thoroughly enjoy himself. His social life can certainly be rewarding in the Pig year. For socializing, March, June to August, November and December can be the best and busiest months and for some currently unattached Fire Dogs, romance can beckon and add a sparkle to the year.

For those Fire Dogs in work this will be a generally satisfying year and they will often have the opportunity to make more effective use of their knowledge and skills. Also, as a result of their experience, colleagues will look to them for guidance and advice, and once more the Fire Dog will play an important and valued role.

For those Fire Dogs who are seeking work or, alternatively, want to reduce their working commitments, the Pig year can again offer some interesting opportunities. By keeping alert for suitable openings and emphasizing their experience and skills (this is no year to undersell themselves), many will be successful in obtaining the change they have been wanting. Effort, determination and initiative can be well rewarded over the year.

As far as money matters are concerned, this will be a reasonable year for the Fire Dog, but good planning and budgeting would be wise. The Fire Dog would do well to make early provision for any large purchases or outgoings as well as keep a close watch on his general level of spending. Too many impulse purchases could mean he has to delay some of his plans later in the year. This is a time for care and control, especially in view of all the Fire Dog wants to do. Also, and as with all Dogs this year, the Fire Dog needs to be thorough when completing any financially-related forms, especially any concerning tax, pension or benefits. A delay, mistake or error could be to his detriment. Similarly, if intending to travel, he needs to check his travel documents and arrangements. Fire Dogs, do take note. The extra attention you can give to important paperwork will be well worth your while.

Overall, the Pig year holds considerable promise for the Fire Dog and by using his time well and working towards his objectives, he will achieve a great deal. In most aspects of his life this will be a pleasing and satisfying year.

TIP FOR THE YEAR
Be open with your thoughts and ideas and do involve others. With their input and assistance so much more can become possible.

The Earth Dog
One of the chief characteristics of the Earth Dog is his steadfastness. Once he has decided on a course of action, he pursues it with considerable determination and, in the Pig year, his efforts and persistence will be well rewarded.

In his work the aspects are especially encouraging and will enable the Earth Dog to make good headway as well as more effective – and fulfilling – use of his talents. By keeping alert for opportunities, whether in his present place of work or elsewhere, he may well be successful in progressing to greater responsibilities. The Earth Dog's determined nature will also be to his advantage and over the year he will impress many. For work opportunities, March, April, July and October are particularly favourable months, but once the Earth Dog has decided to advance his career, he could find all sorts of possibilities opening up very quickly.

The aspects are also encouraging for those Earth Dogs seeking work. Although some will have grown disillusioned with their situation, the Pig year offers real hope. It is the more difficult and testing times that often give rise to new possibilities, and the Pig year will offer many of these Earth Dogs the chance to set their career on a new path.

The progress the Earth Dog makes in his work can bring a rise in income and some Earth Dogs could also earn something extra by putting a skill or personal interest to profitable use. However, while his earnings and income can increase, the Earth Dog could have quite a few family and other expenses to meet and whenever possible he should budget for these in advance. He would also do well to keep watch on his outgoings and, if possible, consider reducing any borrowings as well as making some savings with a view to the longer term. With good management and financial housekeeping, he will be better able to enjoy the rewards of his good work as well as sometimes help his future position.

The Earth Dog's domestic life will see much activity over the year and there may be good cause for celebration, including a possible wedding, the birth of a grandchild or good news concerning the progress of a younger relation. The Pig year can contain some pleasing and memorable occasions. The Earth Dog will also value time spent with his loved ones on mutual interests and domestic projects as well as any outings, breaks or holidays. With his many ideas and general input, his home life will often go well and mean a lot to him. However, if at any time he feels under pressure or is tired and lacking in patience, it is important that he lets others know as well as asks for help. With all that he does for others, he should make sure that they have the chance to help him in return. Also, as he has so often found, good communication and dialogue can make a real difference.

The Earth Dog will value his close circle of friends over the year and will again appreciate their support and the interest they show in his various activities as well as the advice they can offer. Although, in view of all his other activities and commitments, he may be quite selective in his socializing, he will often thoroughly enjoy what he does and will appreciate the chance to relax and unwind. Those Earth Dogs who are particularly keen to build up their social life (especially if they have recently moved) will find new interests and activities excellent ways to meet others. For socializing, March, the months from late May to August and November will be promising.

Another valuable aspect of the year is the Earth Dog's own personal development and whether he is learning a new subject, obtaining an additional qualification or starting a new fitness discipline, he will often derive much satisfaction from what he does. This is very much a year for moving forward, and by setting himself something purposeful to do he will be adding another positive dimension to the year.

Generally, this is an encouraging year for the Earth Dog and will give him the chance to benefit from his talents and fine personal qualities. By making the most of his opportunities, he can look forward to accomplishing a great deal.

TIP FOR THE YEAR

Decide on your objectives and then take action. As Goethe wrote, 'Boldness has genius, power and magic in it.' This is a year to discover the magic and reap the benefits that boldness can bring.

FAMOUS DOGS

André Agassi, King Albert II of Belgium, Brigitte Bardot, Candice Bergen, Mary J. Blige, David Bowie, George W. Bush, Kate Bush, Laura Bush, Naomi Campbell, Mariah Carey, King Carl XVI Gustaf of Sweden, José Carreras, Paul Cézanne, Cher, Sir Winston Churchill, Bill Clinton, Leonard Cohen, Jamie Lee Curtis, Matt Damon, Charles Dance, Claude Debussy, Dame Judi Dench, Sally Field, Joseph Fiennes, Robert Frost, Ava Gardner, Judy Garland, George Gershwin, Lenny Henry, O. Henry, Victor Hugo, Barry Humphries, Holly Hunter, Michael Jackson, Al Jolson, Felicity Kendal, Jennifer Lopez, Sophia Loren, Joanna Lumley, Shirley MacLaine, Madonna, Norman Mailer, Barry Manilow, Freddie Mercury, Liza Minnelli, David Niven, Billie Piper, Sydney Pollack, Elvis Presley, Tim Robbins, Paul Robeson, Andy Roddick, Linda Ronstadt, Susan Sarandon, Jennifer Saunders, Claudia

Schiffer, Dr Albert Schweitzer, Sylvester Stallone, Robert Louis Stevenson, Sharon Stone, Jack Straw, David Suchet, Donald Sutherland, Chris Tarrant, Mother Teresa, Uma Thurman, Donald Trump, Voltaire, Prince William, Shelley Winters.

30 JANUARY 1911 ⌣ 17 FEBRUARY 1912	*Metal Pig*
16 FEBRUARY 1923 ⌣ 4 FEBRUARY 1924	*Water Pig*
4 FEBRUARY 1935 ⌣ 23 JANUARY 1936	*Wood Pig*
22 JANUARY 1947 ⌣ 9 FEBRUARY 1948	*Fire Pig*
8 FEBRUARY 1959 ⌣ 27 JANUARY 1960	*Earth Pig*
27 JANUARY 1971 ⌣ 14 FEBRUARY 1972	*Metal Pig*
13 FEBRUARY 1983 ⌣ 1 FEBRUARY 1984	*Water Pig*
31 JANUARY 1995 ⌣ 18 FEBRUARY 1996	*Wood Pig*
18 FEBRUARY 2007 ⌣ 6 FEBRUARY 2008	*Fire Pig*

THE
PIG

THE PERSONALITY OF THE PIG

'Be an opener of doors ...'

Ralph Waldo Emerson, a Pig

The Pig is born under the sign of honesty. He has a kind and understanding nature and is well known for his abilities as a peacemaker. He hates any sort of discord or unpleasantness and will do everything in his power to sort out differences of opinion or bring opposing factions together.

He is also an excellent conversationalist and speaks truthfully and to the point. He dislikes any form of falsehood or hypocrisy and is a firm believer in justice and the maintenance of law and order. In spite of these beliefs, however, the Pig is reasonably tolerant and often prepared to forgive others for their wrongdoings. He rarely harbours grudges and is never vindictive.

The Pig is usually very popular. He enjoys other people's company and likes to be involved in joint or group activities. He will be a loyal member of any club or society and can be relied upon to lend a helping hand at functions. He is also an excellent fundraiser for charities and is often a great supporter of humanitarian causes.

The Pig is a hard and conscientious worker and is particularly respected for his reliability and integrity. In his early years he will try his hand at several different jobs, but he is usually happiest where he feels that he is being of service to others. He will unselfishly give up his time for the common good and is highly valued by his colleagues and employers.

The Pig has a good sense of humour and invariably has a smile, joke or some whimsical remark at the ready. He loves to entertain and to please others, and there are many Pigs who have been attracted to careers in show business or who enjoy following the careers of famous stars and personalities.

There are, unfortunately, some who take advantage of the Pig's good nature and impose upon his generosity. The Pig has great difficulty in saying 'no' and, although he may dislike being firm, it would be in his own interests to say occasionally, 'Enough is enough.' The Pig can also be rather naïve and gullible; however, if at any stage in his life he feels that he has been badly let down, he will try to become self-reliant. There are many Pigs who have become entrepreneurs or forged a successful career on their own after some early disappointment in life. Although the Pig tends to spend his money quite freely, he is usually very astute in financial matters and there are many Pigs who have become wealthy.

Another characteristic of the Pig is his ability to recover from setbacks reasonably quickly. His faith and his strength of character keep him going. If he thinks that there is a job he can do or he has something that he wants to achieve, he will pursue it with a dogged determination. He can also be stubborn and, no matter how many may plead with him, once he has made his mind up he will rarely change his views.

Although the Pig may work hard, he also knows how to enjoy himself. He is a great pleasure-seeker and will quite happily spend his hard-earned money on a lavish holiday or an expensive meal – for the Pig is a connoisseur of good food and wine – or a variety of recreational activities. He also enjoys small social gatherings and if he is in company he likes he can very easily become the life and soul of the party. He does, however, tend to become rather withdrawn at larger functions or when among strangers.

The Pig is a creature of comfort and his home will usually be fitted with all the latest in luxury appliances. Where possible, he will prefer to live in the country rather than the town and will opt to have a big garden, for the Pig is usually a keen and successful gardener.

The Pig is very popular with others and will often have numerous romances before he settles down. Once settled, however, he will be loyal to his partner and he will find that he is especially well suited to those born under the signs of the Goat, Rabbit, Dog and Tiger and also to another Pig. Due to his affable and easygoing nature he can also establish a satisfactory relationship with all the remaining signs of the Chinese zodiac, with the exception of the Snake. The Snake tends to be wily, secretive and very guarded, and this can be intensely irritating to the honest and open-hearted Pig.

The female Pig will devote all her energies to the needs of her children and her partner. She tries to ensure that they want for nothing and their pleasure is very much her pleasure. She can be a caring and conscientious parent and has very good taste in clothes. Her home will either be very clean and orderly or hopelessly untidy. Strangely, there seems to be no in between with Pigs – they either love housework or detest it! The female Pig does, however, have considerable talents as an organizer and this, combined with her friendly and open manner, enables her to secure many of her objectives.

The Pig is usually lucky in life and will rarely want for anything. Provided he does not let others take advantage of his good nature and is not afraid of asserting himself, he will go through life making friends, helping others and winning the admiration of many.

THE FIVE DIFFERENT TYPES OF PIG

In addition to the 12 signs of the Chinese zodiac there are five elements and these have a strengthening or moderating influence on the sign. The effects of the five elements on the Pig are described below, together with the years in which the elements were exercising their influence. Therefore those Pigs born in 1911 and 1971 are Metal Pigs, those born in 1923 and 1983 are Water Pigs, and so on.

Metal Pig: 1911, 1971

The Metal Pig is more ambitious and determined than some of the other types of Pig. He is strong, energetic and likes to be involved in a wide variety of different activities. He is very open and forthright in his views, although he can be a little too trusting at times and has a tendency to accept things at face value. He has a good sense of humour and loves to attend parties and other social gatherings. He has a warm, outgoing nature and usually has a large circle of friends.

Water Pig: 1923, 1983

The Water Pig has a heart of gold. He is generous and loyal and tries to remain on good terms with everyone. He will do his utmost to help others, but sadly there are some who will take advantage of his kind nature and he should, in his own interests, be a little more discriminating and be prepared to stand firm against anything that he does not like. Although he prefers the quieter things in life, he has a wide range of interests. He particularly enjoys outdoor pursuits and attending parties and social occasions. He is a hard and conscientious worker and invariably does well in his chosen profession. He is also gifted in the art of communication.

Wood Pig: 1935, 1995

This Pig has a friendly, persuasive manner and is easily able to gain the confidence of others. He likes to be involved in all that is going on around him but can sometimes take on more responsibility than he can properly handle. He is loyal to his family and friends and derives much pleasure from helping those less fortunate than himself. He is usually an optimist and leads a very full, enjoyable and satisfying life. He also has a good sense of humour.

Fire Pig: 1947, 2007

The Fire Pig is both energetic and adventurous and he sets about everything he does in a confident and resolute manner. He is very forthright in his views and does not mind taking risks in order to achieve his objectives. He can, however, get carried away by the excitement of the moment and ought to exercise more caution in some of the enterprises in which he gets involved. He is usually lucky in money matters and is well known for his generosity. He is also very caring towards the members of his family.

Earth Pig: 1959

This Pig has a kindly nature. He is sensible and realistic and will go to great lengths in order to please his employers and to secure his aims and ambitions. He is an excellent organizer and is particularly astute in business and financial matters. He has a good sense of humour and a wide circle of friends. He also likes to lead an active social life, although he does sometimes have a tendency to eat and drink more than is good for him.

PROSPECTS FOR THE PIG IN 2007

The Year of the Dog (29 January 2006 to 17 February 2007) will have been an interesting one for the Pig, and with his prospects about to enjoy a considerable improvement in his own year, what he can achieve in the closing months can prove very helpful.

In his work the Pig should make the most of any chances to further his career. Whether these are training opportunities or the chance to take on new duties, anything positive he can do can be to his future benefit. The period from October to early December could see some interesting developments.

The Pig will have a growing number of expenses as the Dog year draws to a close and while he possesses a generous streak as well as the capacity to enjoy himself, he would be wise to keep watch on his spending as well as spread out some of his more seasonal outgoings. Without care, his spending in the final Dog months could be far greater than he anticipated. Pigs, do take note.

On a personal level the Pig will be much in demand and, with his genial and outgoing nature, will often enjoy himself. He will particularly welcome the chance to meet up with those he does not often get to see. However, with so much to arrange and think about it is important that the Pig draws on the help of others rather than tries to do too much by himself. He may be keen and willing, but at busy times he does need to make sure everyone in his household does their fair share.

Overall, the closing months of the year will be both a pleasing and constructive time for the Pig and his actions will help to prepare the way for the exciting times that await in his own year.

The Year of the Pig starts on 18 February, and as it does, or even just before, many Pigs will sense that the tide is once more beginning to turn their way. With the encouraging aspects and his own resourceful nature, the Pig is set to do well and enjoy many of the positive developments his own year will bring.

In his personal life this can be an especially rewarding time. Affairs of the heart are particularly well aspected and many Pigs who are currently unattached will find love over the year. For those already enjoying the early stages of romance the Pig year can also be an exciting time and many will settle down together or marry. For those Pigs with a partner, the year promises some special and often memorable moments. For some this could be an addition to their family, the realization of an ambition or a move to more suitable accommodation.

For those Pigs who have experienced problems in their personal life in recent years, this is a year to draw a line under what has happened and look to move forward. With this being an encouraging and supportive year, these Pigs may well find new friendships and love transforming their situation and marking the beginning of a much brighter phase in their life. For meeting others and socializing, March, April, August and September are especially favourable months.

Throughout the year the Pig will be encouraged by the support he is given by his loved ones and while he may like to set about his activities in his own way, by sharing his hopes and discussing his plans, as well as any concerns, he can be given useful advice as well as sometimes unforeseen help. Much goodwill can flow his way, but to benefit from this he does need to be forthcoming and receptive.

Also, while this is a favourable year, the Pig should be careful not to allow his over-eager nature to get the better of him. In particular if he decides to tackle some home improvement projects or is involved in a house move, he should concentrate his attention on what needs to be done rather than busy himself with lots of different activities all at once. Without care, he could over-commit himself and not make very effective use of his time and energy. Pigs, do take careful note and do plan your time wisely, especially where more practical undertakings are concerned.

As far as the Pig's work is concerned, the aspects are favourable, and thanks to their recent experience many Pigs will find themselves excellently placed to make progress. This could be through promotion in their present place of work or by furthering their experience elsewhere, but this is certainly a year for moving their career forward.

Those Pigs who consider themselves in a rut, are disillusioned with their recent progress or are seeking work will find their own year offering important prospects. If they actively pursue opportunities that appeal to them, their determination and talents will bring many the chance they have been hoping for. Fortune will favour the tenacious. March to mid-May, September and November could see some encouraging work developments.

Another factor which will be to the Pig's advantage over the year is the good working relationship he has with so many colleagues. During the year, he will not only benefit from their support but also from their willingness to help him, whether through advice, recommendations on his behalf or suggestions worth considering. By working well with others as well as getting himself better known, the Pig will enhance both his reputation and prospects. In this auspicious year, luck and good fortune will come to those prepared to put in the effort. As Gary Player once observed, 'The harder I work, the luckier I get.'

The Pig's financial prospects are also encouraging and his progress at work will often lead to a noticeable increase in income. Those Pigs who have a more enterprising nature may also profit from an idea they have or some additional work they can do. The Pig's earning abilities will certainly be on good form in his own year. To benefit, though, the Pig does need to manage his money carefully and would do well to budget for more major outgoings, including accommodation (and possibly moving) expenses. Also, when involved in any large transaction, he should take his time, consider his choices carefully and, if appropriate, obtain quotations and breakdowns of costs. Here the Pig's astute nature will serve him well and lead to better decisions as well as sometimes save unnecessary outlay. Financially, this is an improved year and with good management the Pig will be pleased with how he fares.

The Pig is very much in the driving seat in his own year and his energy and enthusiasm will often lead to some heartening results. He will be encouraged by the support he receives and his relations with others will often help to make the year all the more successful. For the Pig, his own year is one of the best.

The Metal Pig

The Metal Pig is both ambitious and determined and he knows he has the qualities and strengths to achieve a great deal. And while recent years will have seen much activity, there will be many Metal Pigs who will feel they have not yet realized their true potential. With this being the Pig's own year, many Metal Pigs will regard it as a time for action. As the saying reminds us, 'There is no time like the present' – and the present year *is* a time for the Metal Pig to act.

The Metal Pig's plans could concern several different areas of his life, but accommodation matters could feature strongly. Those Metal Pigs who would like to move to a more convenient or pleasant location should aim to make enquiries early on in the year. As they start the moving preparations, including clearing out unwanted items, they will find their actions will help to set the process in motion. Although the actual move will involve much effort, once settled in their new home these Metal Pigs will quickly appreciate the benefits and advantages as well as sometimes the extra space their new accommodation offers.

The Metal Pig's practical nature will be very evident over the year and while those who move will be heavily occupied with the process, those who remain where they are will often be busy with home and garden projects. Once the Metal Pig has plans in mind, he should waste little time in getting them under way, as he will soon delight in seeing his ideas take shape.

One word of warning that does need be sounded, though, is that the Metal Pig should not take any risks with his personal safety. In moving heavy weights, cumbersome objects or anything else that is particularly hazardous he does need to take special care or employ a professional. He may be keen, but he should not let this lead him into taking risks with his well-being. Metal Pigs, do take note.

The Metal Pig will be grateful for the support he receives over the year and will find that more can be accomplished by pooling ideas and strengths. Not only will he be helped by the input and encouragement of others, but he will often do much to assist those who are special to him. In particular, those Metal Pigs who are parents will find that the time they can give in helping, assisting and encouraging their children will often have far greater meaning than they may realize. Similarly, for those with more senior relations, the advice, time and support they can give will make a difference to those concerned. As far as the Metal Pig's home life is concerned, this will be a busy year but it can be especially rewarding.

In view of all the activity of the Pig year, many Metal Pigs will be selective in their socializing, but for those who would welcome new friends – and perhaps romance – the Pig year again holds promising prospects. These Metal Pigs will have good opportunities to meet others, either through their work or through their interests, and some will find the love they have been seeking for some time. For meeting others and social activities, the start of the Pig year to April and then August and September are especially favourable times.

The positive aspects of the year also apply to the Metal Pig's work and many will be successful in securing promotion and moving on to greater responsibilities. Similarly, those Metal Pigs who are seeking work or who would welcome the chance to take their career in a different direction should make enquiries, act on advice given and follow up openings that interest them. Their efforts will lead many to what will be an interesting new opportunity. The Pig year holds considerable potential for the Metal Pig, and by making the most of his abilities and opportunities, he can make important headway. Even if certain applications do not go his way, by persisting and having faith in his abilities, in many cases he will secure a position which will make good use of his talents. The period from March to mid-May, September, late October and November could see the best chances.

The progress the Metal Pig makes in his work will also lead to an increase in income and some Metal Pigs could also benefit from an additional sum of money they receive or earn from another source. However, with moving expenses for some, as well as current obligations, the Metal Pig would do well to keep a close watch on his financial position. Without care, his spending could sometimes be greater than he anticipated – or budgeted for. In view of his many plans and commitments, good control over his purse-strings would be wise.

Overall, the Pig year holds considerable potential for the Metal Pig and if he follows through his ideas, he can achieve a lot. This is a year of exciting possibilities.

TIP FOR THE YEAR
Do not let hopes, ideas or chances slip by – take determined action. As you will so often find, once you take the first step, many more can open up for you.

The Water Pig

There is a Chinese proverb which reminds us 'Every moment is precious' and for the Water Pig this year will be precious. This is a time of considerable opportunity for him.

His personal life is especially well aspected and many Water Pigs will enjoy significant developments this year.

For some this could be getting engaged, marrying, celebrating an addition to their family or moving to a new
home. On a personal level the Pig year promises considerable excitement as well as the realization of some of the
Water Pig's dreams!

For those Water Pigs who are currently unattached,
affairs of the heart are favourably aspected. Over the year
many of these Water Pigs will get to meet someone who
will quickly become special. For Water Pigs who have had
disappointments in a previous relationship and are perhaps
feeling disillusioned, the Pig year will offer the chance to
make a new start and move ahead wiser and with hope. By
looking forward as well as becoming involved in new activities, social groups and even, for some, moving to a new
area, these Water Pigs can see an exciting transformation
in their situation. The Pig year will help those who help
themselves. For socializing and meeting others March,
April, August and September are particularly favourable
months.

Another positive aspect of the year will be the way the
Water Pig is helped by family members and close friends,
and if he is ever in a dilemma over some matter or would
welcome advice, he should remember that there are many
who are willing to help.

As far as the Water Pig's work prospects are concerned,
this is a year of considerable opportunity. Many of those
Water Pigs who are already established in their chosen
career will have the chance to build on their experience and
take on greater responsibilities. In view of their ambitions
for the future, whenever an opportunity arises to move
their career forward, whether through covering for absent

colleagues, undertaking training or applying for a suitable vacancy, they should put themselves forward. By showing initiative and commitment, they can do much to help their situation. The headway the Water Pig makes and the experience he gains can also be instrumental in his later progress.

For those Water Pigs who are seeking work or feeling unfulfilled in what they are currently doing, this is also an important time. By considering carefully what they now want to do and where their real strengths and interests lie, many will be successful in gaining a position that they can build on in the future. Their quest will demand effort and perseverance, but the Pig year will give many the chance – and sometimes the fresh start – that they have been seeking.

For work opportunities, the period from March to mid-May, September and November are especially favourable. Throughout the Pig year, however, the Water Pig should remember that even if initial applications do not go his way, with determination and belief in what he can offer, he *will* prevail.

Financial matters are encouragingly aspected over the year and although the Water Pig will often have many expenses, he could also enjoy some good fortune over the year. This could be through a gift, a bonus, a maturing policy or even a competition win. However it comes about, many Water Pigs will benefit from receiving an extra sum over the year. In addition, an idea or special talent that the Water Pig has could help supplement his income. The Pig year does hold good opportunities and earning potential for the willing and keen Water Pig.

However, while the Water Pig's efforts can lead to an improvement in his income, he will still need to manage his financial situation carefully. With existing and new commitments he will need to budget for his outgoings, and with the more expensive plans he has for the year, he will do well to save up in advance. Also, rather than proceeding too hurriedly, by waiting for sales and other favourable buying opportunities, he could save himself a considerable amount. During his own year it would reward him to be both patient and alert.

In so many respects this will be a positive and encouraging year for the Water Pig. In his personal life, the love and support of another will often give special meaning to this time and many Water Pigs will also have good news to celebrate. At work, too, there will be chances to move forward and to make more satisfying use of skills and talents. This is a year of opportunity and one the Water Pig will enjoy.

TIP FOR THE YEAR

An action-oriented year, but with important decisions you do need to draw on the advice and experience of others. Remember more senior relations are often keen to assist and there are also experts, contacts and friends who can advise and help. In this important year, the assistance and goodwill of others can be of real value.

The Wood Pig

This will be a year of change and opportunity for the Wood Pig, and with good support from those around him, much will go his way.

For Wood Pigs born in 1935 this will be a year for forging ahead with plans, and important developments will result. As with many Pigs, accommodation matters will feature prominently for the Wood Pig and over the year quite a few will decide to move to accommodation that better suits their requirements. Although such a move will often be a wrench, especially if they have been living in the same place or area for some time, these Wood Pigs will quickly appreciate the advantages that their new home offers. Also, while the moving process will take up much time, by drawing on the readiness of others to assist and advise, these Wood Pigs will find some of the pressures and anxieties can be considerably eased.

For those Wood Pigs who remain where they are, again accommodation matters will feature prominently, as many will consider installing new equipment or making changes which will add to their comfort as well as improving their home. By carefully considering and costing their ideas, these Wood Pigs will often be delighted with the choices made. This is very much a year for setting plans and ideas in motion.

The Wood Pig has a creative side to his nature and over the year many Wood Pigs will take much satisfaction in the projects they set themselves. Some of these will again be related to their home, including designing, making or altering a variety of items. In addition if there is an interest or a technique they feel it could be helpful to learn, these Wood Pigs would do well to set some time aside for this and perhaps enrol on a suitable course. By doing something positive they will find their interests a source of much pleasure over the year.

The Wood Pig should also make the most of any travel opportunities that arise and if he sees an offer that appeals to him or there are places he is keen to visit, he should follow up his ideas. Some visits and outings, perhaps arranged at short notice, can also lead to some enjoyable occasions. With the aspects as they are, whenever the Wood Pig has travel ideas or opportunities, he would do well to act smartly upon them.

This can also be a fortunate year financially and many Wood Pigs will benefit from an extra sum of money, perhaps as a bonus payment or gift. With the year's luckier elements, some could also enjoy good fortune in a competition or contest they enter. However, while the aspects are positive, the Wood Pig does need to be careful when entering into important agreements and, particularly if moving, be aware of the costs and implications of his decisions. Should he have any uncertainties, it is important that he seeks advice and gets these addressed before proceeding. Financially, this can be a generally favourable year, but the Wood Pig does need to be vigilant and thorough.

Throughout the year the Wood Pig will be grateful for the support of his family and friends and will be helped and encouraged a great deal. However, should any of his loved ones express reservations about anything he may be considering, he would do well to listen carefully and think over what has been said. In some cases words of caution can prevent mistakes being made or lead the Wood Pig to coming up with a better approach. The Pig year, despite its positive aspects, is not a time for the Wood Pig to proceed regardless, and by listening closely to others and obtaining help and advice, he can achieve so much more.

The Wood Pig will appreciate the social occasions the year will bring and whether meeting up with friends or going to events that appeal to him, he will enjoy much of his socializing. Those Wood Pigs who would welcome a more active and fulfilling social life will find that by joining in with local activities and groups in their area they will often get to meet those with similar outlooks and, in some cases, make what will be a very special friendship. Socially, the Pig year is a very encouraging and supportive one.

For the Wood Pig born in 1995 this can be an eventful year. Some of these Wood Pigs will change their school and also start a new range of subjects. While this may sometimes be daunting, by doing his best and adapting well to change, the young Wood Pig will not only learn a lot over the year but also grow both in character and confidence.

Also, with the aspects being so encouraging, the young Wood Pig will delight in developing his personal interests as well as enjoy many good times with his friends. By making the most of the opportunities available to him and drawing on the support of those around him, he will enjoy a lot of what he does. Whenever any problems or difficulties raise their head, as they will in any year, he would do well to be open and prepared to talk to others. This way worries can be put into perspective and problems dealt with. Wood Pigs, do remember that help is available.

Overall, the Pig year will be an encouraging and often eventful one for the Wood Pig. For those born in 1935 there could be a possible change in accommodation and the year could also see them busy with various ideas, projects and interests. For the younger Wood Pig the year can bring a change of school or introduce them to new subjects, and by making most of their situation, these Wood Pigs can make satisfying progress as well as enjoy much of what opens up to them over the year. For both younger and more senior Wood Pigs, this can be a full but personally satisfying year.

TIP FOR THE YEAR

Spend time developing your interests. With your talents, ideas and creativity, you will find them not only a source of considerable pleasure but often bringing other benefits too.

The Fire Pig

This is the Fire Pig's own year and, as such, it will be a special one. Not only does it mark a new decade in the Fire Pig's life but is a time of often far-reaching developments. However, as the year starts, the Fire Pig would do well to give careful thought to what he wants to achieve over the next 12 months. With some plans and ideas in mind he will be better able to direct his energies as well as to benefit from the opportunities that will come his way.

With accommodation matters featuring prominently over the year, some Fire Pigs will decide to move, and in some cases quite some distance from where they presently live. Those who do move will often feel that a new home in a new location will represent a new chapter in their lives.

Those Fire Pigs who remain where they are will also often be keen to make changes to their accommodation. By discussing these with others and making careful plans, the Fire Pig will delight in the improvements made. However, whether moving, making purchases for his home or carrying out alterations, the Fire Pig should avoid unnecessary haste. Also, by keeping alert, especially during sale times, the Fire Pig could be fortunate in acquiring bargains not only for his home but also for himself.

The Fire Pig will also appreciate the domestic events that take place during the year. These will not only include the possible marking of his own sixtieth birthday but also other pleasing family events, perhaps a wedding, a graduation or the birth of a grandchild or great-grandchild.

An area that the Fire Pig will often spend time on during the year is his personal interests, and if there is something that has been intriguing him, or a technique or skill he wants to learn or improve on, by following up his ideas, perhaps by enrolling on a course or joining a society or group, his purposeful action will often reward him well.

The Fire Pig will enjoy the travelling he undertakes over the year and some will mark their sixtieth birthday with a special holiday, perhaps in a place that has long appealed to them. In addition the Fire Pig could receive invitations to visit family and friends living some distance away.

For those Fire Pigs in work this will be a satisfying year, particularly as it will give them greater opportunity to put their specialist skills and knowledge to effective use. As the year progresses, these Fire Pigs will often have the chance to become involved in new projects and initiatives or in training and mentoring others. The beginning of the Pig year to mid-May, September and November could bring some interesting work developments.

There will, however, be some Fire Pigs who will decide to retire or reduce their working commitments during the year. If these Fire Pigs give themselves something purposeful to do in the extra time they have, they will be pleased with how their decisions work out.

With this being the Fire Pig's own year, it will also have a lucky quality to it and many Fire Pigs will benefit from a financial gift or a bonus. In addition, some could discover a way to put an interest or skill to profitable use and thereby supplement their income. However, while the aspects may be encouraging, the Fire Pig will still need be careful in his financial dealings. Whenever he is involved in important transactions, especially any related to his accommodation, he should take his time and satisfy himself that everything is in order. Any extra care and attention that he can give his financial dealings will be well worth his while.

Overall, this is a year of considerable promise for the Fire Pig and by acting upon his ideas and making good use of opportunities, he will achieve a great deal.

TIP FOR THE YEAR
You may be keen and eager, but be wary of too much haste. The more time you can give to planning and preparation, the better you will fare. Also do draw on the readiness of others to help, support and advise.

The Earth Pig
This is an encouraging year for the Earth Pig and by setting about his objectives in his usual enthusiastic manner, he can look forward to accomplishing a great deal.

In his work, with his often extensive experience, the Earth Pig will be well placed to take advantage of the opportunities that will arise. Often these will be in his present place of work and here the Earth Pig's reputation, in-house experience and knowledge will make him a strong candidate for promotion. For those Earth Pigs who feel opportunities are limited where they are or would like to take their career in another direction, this is a time when they should take positive action. Employment agencies and professional organizations could suggest interesting possibilities, and by persisting in their quest, many Earth Pigs can look forward to making the change they want over the year.

The prospects are also encouraging for those Earth Pigs seeking work and by broadening the range of what they are prepared to consider as well as actively following up any vacancies they see, many will be given what can be an interesting opportunity. Late February to mid-May, September and November could see some positive work developments.

In view of the progress the Earth Pig will make in his work, he could enjoy a rise in income over the year and some Earth Pigs could also discover a way to supplement their earnings through an idea or an interest they have. However, while money may flow into the Earth Pig's account, without care it can flow out just as easily. The Earth Pig does need to manage his financial situation carefully, regulating his outgoings and budgeting in advance for his more expensive plans and purchases.

Another area which the Earth Pig would do well to give consideration to is his own well-being. If he is sedentary for large parts of the day or reliant on convenience food, he should give some thought to ways in which he could get additional exercise or modify his diet.

As far as relations with others are concerned, the aspects are particularly favourable. The Earth Pig possesses a warm and amiable nature and his ability to enjoy positive relations with many people will serve him well during the year. In his work the often good understanding he has with colleagues will do much to help his position and prospects. In his interests, too, meeting other enthusiasts, whether at a local society, on a course or at social events, can again be helpful. This is very much a year for him to be active and to use his personal skills well. As far as his social life is concerned, March, April, August and September could be the best and busiest times.

The aspects are also encouraging for those Earth Pigs who start the year disillusioned with their situation. By taking the decision to go out more and possibly become involved in a new range of activities and interests, they can build up a new social circle, and for some, significant romance can beckon.

As far as the Earth Pig's domestic life is concerned this will be a busy and often eventful year. The Earth Pig will do much to help both younger and more senior relations and here his ability to relate so effectively with others will be appreciated, as will his honest and constructive advice. There could also be some key family events taking place over the year, and the Earth Pig's attentiveness and organizational skills will again be a real asset. While he and his loved ones may lead busy and demanding lives, if the Earth Pig sets aside time for joint interests and activities, including a holiday or some short breaks, he will find his domestic life meaning a great deal to him as well as giving rise to some special times.

The Pig year holds encouraging prospects for the Earth Pig, but it does rest with him to act upon his hopes, ideas and opportunities. This is a year for moving forward.

TIP FOR THE YEAR

You have great personal gifts, including your ability to relate well to people. In this great year, make sure you use your talents well. Make new contacts and friends and consider joining groups that can help you to further your interests as well as professional organizations that can help with your career. That way more possibilities will open up for you.

FAMOUS PIGS

Bryan Adams, Woody Allen, Julie Andrews, Marie Antoinette, David Arquette, Fred Astaire, Humphrey Bogart, James Cagney, Maria Callas, Hillary Clinton, Duchess of Cornwall, Noël Coward, Oliver Cromwell, the Dalai Lama, Dido, Ben Elton, Ralph Waldo Emerson, Henry Ford, Stephen Harper, Ernest Hemingway, Henry VIII, Alfred Hitchcock, Sir Elton John, Tommy Lee Jones, Carl Gustav Jung, Boris Karloff, Stephen King, Hugh Laurie, Nigella Lawson, Meat Loaf, Ewan McGregor, Marcel Marceau, Ricky Martin, Johnny Mathis, Mozart, Michael Parkinson, Luciano Pavarotti, Iggy Pop, Maurice Ravel, Ronald Reagan, Ginger Rogers, Françoise Sagan, Carlos Santana, Arnold Schwarzenegger, Kevin Spacey, Steven Spielberg, Sir Alan Sugar, Emma Thompson, Jules Verne, Rachel Weisz, Michael Winner, the Duchess of York.

APPENDIX

———◆———

The relationships between the 12 animal signs, both on a personal level and business level, are an important aspect of Chinese horoscopes and in this appendix the compatibility between the signs is shown in the two tables that follow.

Also included are the names of the signs ruling the hours of the day and from this it is possible to find your ascendant and discover yet another aspect of your personality.

Finally, to supplement the earlier chapters on the personality and horoscope of the signs, I have included a guide on how you can get the best out of your sign and the year.

RELATIONSHIPS BETWEEN THE SIGNS

Personal Relationships

KEY

1 Excellent. Great rapport.
2 A successful relationship. Many interests in common.
3 Mutual respect and understanding. A good relationship.
4 Fair. Needs care and some willingness to compromise in order for the relationship to work.
5 Awkward. Possible difficulties in communication with few interests in common.
6 A clash of personalities. Very difficult.

	Rat	Ox	Tiger	Rabbit	Dragon	Snake	Horse	Goat	Monkey	Rooster	Dog	Pig
Rat	1											
Ox	1	3										
Tiger	4	6	5									
Rabbit	5	2	3	2								
Dragon	1	5	4	3	2							
Snake	3	1	6	2	1	5						
Horse	6	5	1	5	3	4	2					
Goat	5	5	3	1	4	3	2	2				
Monkey	1	3	6	3	1	3	5	3	1			
Rooster	5	1	5	6	2	1	2	5	5	5		
Dog	3	4	1	2	6	3	1	5	3	5	2	
Pig	2	3	2	2	2	6	3	2	2	3	1	2

Business Relationships

KEY

1 Excellent. Marvellous understanding and rapport.
2 Very good. Complement each other well.
3 A good working relationship and understanding can be developed.
4 Fair, but compromise and a common objective are often needed to make this relationship work.
5 Awkward. Unlikely to work, either through lack of trust, understanding or the competitiveness of the signs.
6 Mistrust. Difficult. To be avoided.

	Rat	Ox	Tiger	Rabbit	Dragon	Snake	Horse	Goat	Monkey	Rooster	Dog	Pig
Rat	2											
Ox	1	3										
Tiger	3	6	5									
Rabbit	4	3	3	3								
Dragon	1	4	3	3	3							
Snake	3	2	6	4	1	5						
Horse	6	5	1	5	3	4	4					
Goat	5	5	3	1	4	3	3	2				
Monkey	2	3	4	5	1	5	4	4	3			
Rooster	5	1	5	5	2	1	2	5	5	6		
Dog	4	5	2	3	6	4	2	5	3	5	4	
Pig	3	3	3	2	3	5	4	2	3	4	3	1

YOUR ASCENDANT

The ascendant has a very strong influence on your personality and, together with the information already given about your sign and the effects of the element on your sign, it will help you gain an even greater insight into your true personality according to Chinese horoscopes.

The hours of the day are named after the 12 animal signs and the sign governing the time you were born is your ascendant. To find your ascendant, look up the time of your birth in the table below, bearing in mind any local time differences in the place you were born.

11 p.m.	to	1 a.m.	The hours of the Rat
1 a.m.	to	3 a.m.	The hours of the Ox
3 a.m.	to	5 a.m.	The hours of the Tiger
5 a.m.	to	7 a.m.	The hours of the Rabbit
7 a.m.	to	9 a.m.	The hours of the Dragon
9 a.m.	to	11 a.m.	The hours of the Snake
11 a.m.	to	1 p.m.	The hours of the Horse
1 p.m.	to	3 p.m.	The hours of the Goat
3 p.m.	to	5 p.m.	The hours of the Monkey
5 p.m.	to	7 p.m.	The hours of the Rooster
7 p.m.	to	9 p.m.	The hours of the Dog
9 p.m.	to	11 p.m.	The hours of the Pig

RAT

The Rat ascendant is likely to make the sign more outgoing, sociable and careful with money. A particularly beneficial influence for those born under the signs of the Rabbit, Horse, Monkey and Pig.

OX

The Ox ascendant has a restraining, cautionary and steadying influence which many signs will benefit from. This ascendant also promotes self-confidence and willpower and is especially good for those born under the signs of the Tiger, Rabbit and Goat.

TIGER

The Tiger ascendant is a dynamic and stirring influence which makes the sign more outgoing, action-orientated and impulsive. A generally favourable ascendant for the Ox, Tiger, Snake and Horse.

RABBIT

The Rabbit ascendant has a moderating influence, making the sign more reflective, serene and discreet. A particularly beneficial influence for the Rat, Dragon, Monkey and Rooster.

DRAGON

The Dragon ascendant gives strength, determination and ambition to the sign. A favourable influence for those born under the signs of the Rabbit, Goat, Monkey and Dog.

SNAKE

The Snake ascendant can make the sign more reflective, intuitive and self-reliant. A good influence for the Tiger, Goat and Pig.

HORSE

The Horse ascendant will make the sign more adventurous, daring and on some occasions fickle. Generally a beneficial influence for the Rabbit, Snake, Dog and Pig.

GOAT

The Goat ascendant will make the sign more tolerant, easygoing and receptive. It could also impart some creative and artistic qualities. An especially good influence for the Ox, Dragon, Snake and Rooster.

MONKEY

The Monkey ascendant is likely to impart a delicious sense of humour and fun to the sign. It will make the sign more enterprising and outgoing – a particularly good influence for the Rat, Ox, Snake and Goat.

ROOSTER

The Rooster ascendant helps to give the sign a lively, outgoing and very methodical manner. Its influence will increase efficiency and is good for the Ox, Tiger, Rabbit and Horse.

DOG

The Dog ascendant makes the sign more reasonable and fair-minded as well as giving an added sense of loyalty. A very good ascendant for the Tiger, Dragon and Goat.

PIG

The Pig ascendant can make the sign more sociable and self-indulgent. It is also a caring influence and one which can make the sign want to help others. A good ascendant for the Dragon and Monkey.

HOW TO GET THE BEST FROM YOUR CHINESE SIGN AND THE YEAR

Each of the 12 Chinese signs possesses its own unique strengths and by identifying them you can use them to your advantage. Similarly, by becoming aware of possible weaknesses you can do much to rectify them and in this respect I hope the following sections will be useful. Also included are some tips on how you can get the best from the Year of the Pig.

The Rat

The Rat is blessed with many fine talents, but his undoubted strength lies in his ability to get on with others. He is sociable, charming and a good judge of character. He also possesses a shrewd mind and is good at spotting opportunities.

However, to make the most of himself and his abilities, the Rat does need to impose some discipline upon himself. He should resist the (sometimes very great) temptation of getting involved in too many activities all at the same time and should decide upon his priorities and objectives. By concentrating his energies on specific matters he will fare much better as a result. Also, given his personable manner, he should seek out positions where he can use his personal relations skills to good effect. For a career, sales and marketing could prove ideal.

The Rat is also astute in dealing with finance, but while often thrifty, he can sometimes give way to moments of indulgence. Although he deserves to enjoy the money he has so carefully earned, it may sometimes be in his interests to exercise restraint when tempted to satisfy too many expensive whims!

The Rat's family and friends are important to him and while he is loyal and protective towards them, he does tend to keep his worries and concerns to himself and would be helped if he were more willing to discuss his anxieties. Others think highly of him and are prepared to do much to help him, but for them to do so the Rat does need to be less secretive and guarded.

With his sharp mind, keen imagination and sociable manner, the Rat does, however, have much in his favour. When he has commitment, he can be irrepressible and, given his considerable charm, often irresistible as well! Provided he channels his energies wisely, he can make much of his life.

Advice for the Rat's Year Ahead

GENERAL PROSPECTS
A year of important developments and considerable change. However, to make the most of this the Rat will

need to show commitment and be adaptable. With flexibility and good support, much can be achieved.

CAREER PROSPECTS

This is a year for moving forward and for building on skills and experience. Progress will require effort, hard work and a willingness for the Rat to put himself forward, but by making the most of his strengths, he can look forward to making good headway.

FINANCE

A year to be thorough and careful and avoid risks. Important agreements and transactions will need particular attention. With some heavy expenses likely (including a possible move), any provision the Rat can make in advance can help.

RELATIONS WITH OTHERS

A promising year, with the Rat benefiting from the support and goodwill of many. His social life will become busier, with the prospect of new friendships and, for some, exciting new romance. The sociable Rat will be on good form and will very much enjoy the year.

The Ox

Strong-willed, determined and resolute, the Ox certainly has a mind of his own! He is persistent and sets about achieving his objectives with dogged determination. In addition he is reliable and tenacious and is often a source of inspiration to others. He is an achiever, and he often achieves a great deal. However, to really excel, he would do well to try and correct some of his weaknesses.

Being so resolute and having such a strong sense of purpose, the Ox can be inflexible and narrow-minded. He can be resistant to change and prefers to set about his activities in his own way rather than be dependent on others. His dislike of change can sometimes be to his detriment and if he were prepared to be more adaptable and adventurous he would find his progress easier.

The Ox would also be helped if he were to broaden his range of interests and become more relaxed in his approach. At times he can be so preoccupied with his own activities that he is not always as mindful of others as he should be, and his demeanour can sometimes be studious and serious. There are times when he would benefit from a lighter touch.

However, the Ox is true to his word and loyal to his family and friends. He is admired and respected by others and his tremendous willpower usually enables him to achieve a great deal in life.

Advice for the Ox's Year Ahead

GENERAL PROSPECTS

A positive year with good opportunities for the Ox to make more effective use of his strengths. However, he does need to put himself forward and draw on the support of others rather than be too independent in approach. With the backing of others, plus his own commitment, he can go far.

CAREER PROSPECTS
The Ox's strengths and often considerable experience will serve him well and good progress is possible. Positive action can lead to some interesting new opportunities. With this also being a fine year for personal development, new skills and qualifications can help the Ox's present *and* future prospects.

FINANCE
A reasonable year, but the Ox will need to remain his thorough self, especially when checking the terms of any new agreements or major transactions. He should also take his time and not be rushed. Care and good budgeting will help.

RELATIONS WITH OTHERS
This is a year when the support, goodwill and advice of others can make considerable difference, so the Ox should watch his sometimes go-it-alone nature. For the unattached, this can be an exciting year. Although the Ox will be busy, he should set time aside for his interests, loved ones and social life. It is very important that he keeps his life in balance.

The Tiger

Lively, innovative and enterprising, the Tiger enjoys an active lifestyle. He has a wide range of interests, an alert mind and a genuine liking of others. He likes to live life to the full. However, despite his enthusiastic and well-meaning ways, he does not always make the most of his considerable potential.

By being so versatile, the Tiger does have a tendency to jump from one activity to another or dissipate his energies by trying to do too much at the same time. To make the most of himself he should try to exercise a certain amount of self-discipline. Ideally, he should decide how best he can use his abilities, give himself some objectives and then stick to them. If he can overcome his restless tendencies, he will find he will accomplish much more as a result.

Also, in spite of his sociable manner, the Tiger likes to retain a certain independence in his actions, and while few begrudge him this, he would sometimes find life easier if he were more prepared to work in conjunction with others. His reliance upon his own judgement does sometimes mean that he excludes the views and advice of those around him, and this can be to his detriment. The Tiger may possess an independent spirit, but he must not let it go too far!

The Tiger does, however, have much in his favour. He is bold, original and quick-witted. If he can keep his restless nature in check, he can enjoy considerable success. In addition, with his engaging personality, he is well liked and much admired.

Advice for the Tiger's Year Ahead

GENERAL PROSPECTS

A year of interesting opportunity. However, the Pig year does warn against complacency, risks or paying insufficient attention to others. The Tiger can do well, but he does need to tread carefully!

CAREER PROSPECTS

Workwise, this is a particularly encouraging year and by making the most of his strengths and opportunities, the Tiger can make important progress. This is a time for action. However, it is not a year when the Tiger can let standards slip or push his luck too far. The Pig year does require him to be on his mettle.

FINANCE

While income will often increase, spending will need to be watched. Paperwork also needs to be handled carefully and promptly, otherwise there is a risk that the Tiger could be disadvantaged. This is a year to be thorough and vigilant.

RELATIONS WITH OTHERS

The Tiger will benefit greatly from the support he receives over the year and his contacts can be especially helpful in his work. However, in his home life the Tiger will need to be attentive, open and communicative. Travel and personal interests can lead to some good social opportunities.

The Rabbit

The Rabbit is certainly one who appreciates the finer things in life. With his good taste, companionable nature and wide range of interests, he knows how to live well – and usually does!

However, for all his finesse and style, the Rabbit does possess traits he would do well to watch. His desire for a settled lifestyle makes him err on the side of caution. He dislikes change and as a consequence can miss out on opportunities. Also, there are many Rabbits who will go to great lengths to avoid difficult and fraught situations, and again, while few may relish these, sometimes in life it is necessary to take risks or stand your ground. At times it would certainly be in the Rabbit's interests to be bolder and more assertive in going after what he desires.

The Rabbit also attaches great importance to his relations with others and while he has a happy knack of getting on with most people, he can be sensitive to criticism. Difficult though it may be, he should really try to develop a thicker skin and recognize that criticism can provide valuable learning opportunities, as can some of the problems he strives so hard to avoid.

However, with his agreeable manner, keen intellect and shrewd judgement, the Rabbit does have a lot in his favour and invariably makes much of his life – and enjoys it too!

Advice for the Rabbit's Year Ahead

GENERAL PROSPECTS
A pleasing year, but the Rabbit will need to act positively. The support and goodwill of others can be an encouraging feature of the year.

CAREER PROSPECTS
The Rabbit can look forward to making steady rather than spectacular progress, but what he learns now can be of great value in the future. For those involved in communication or creative work, this is a time to promote ideas. Effort made now can bring rewards later on.

FINANCE

A year to be careful and thorough and to budget well. With some large expenses likely, early provision for these and other commitments can be of great help.

RELATIONS WITH OTHERS

The Rabbit will be in good form and in demand. Those keen to build up their social life or find romance should aim to go out more, as positive action can reap some exciting (and often long-term) rewards. An excellent year.

The Dragon

Enthusiastic, enterprising and honourable, the Dragon possesses many admirable qualities and his life is often full and varied. He always gives his best and even though not all his endeavours may meet with success, he is nonetheless resilient and hardy, and is much admired and respected.

However, for all his many qualities, the Dragon can be blunt and forthright and, through sheer strength of character, sometimes domineering. It would certainly be in his interests to listen more closely to others rather than be so self-reliant. Also, his enthusiasm can sometimes get the better of him and he can be impulsive. To make the most of his abilities, he should give himself priorities and set about his activities in a disciplined and systematic way. More tact and diplomacy might not come amiss either!

However, with his lively and outgoing manner, the Dragon is popular and well liked. With good fortune on his side (and the Dragon is often lucky), his life is almost certain to be eventful and fulfilling. He has many talents, and if he uses them wisely he will enjoy much success.

Advice for the Dragon's Year Ahead

GENERAL PROSPECTS

This is a year of considerable potential but the Dragon will need to put himself forward and seize his opportunities. With determination, commitment and perseverance, he can achieve a great deal.

CAREER PROSPECTS

A positive time in which the Dragon can make important advances. By drawing on his experience and keeping alert, he can further his career and move to more fulfilling duties. Skills and qualifications acquired now can have significant future value.

FINANCE

A much improved year, and with good financial planning, the Dragon will be pleased with what he is able to do. If he is able, he should consider making some savings, particularly for the longer term.

RELATIONS WITH OTHERS

A fine and enjoyable year, with the Dragon often benefiting from the support of those around him. However, he does need to watch his independent tendencies and be prepared to consult as well as listen. The input and advice of others can be particularly helpful. Socially, personal interests can be a good way to meet others and make new friendships. A time of considerable good fortune.

The Snake

The Snake is blessed with a keen intellect. He has wide interests, an enquiring mind and good judgement. He tends to be quiet and thoughtful and plans his activities with considerable care. With his fine abilities he often does well in life, but he does possess traits which can undermine his progress.

The Snake is often guarded in his actions and sometimes loses out to those who are more action-oriented and assertive. He also likes to retain a certain independence in his actions, and this too can hamper his progress. It would be in his interests to be more forthcoming and involve others more readily in his plans. The Snake has many talents and possesses a warm and rich personality, but there is a danger that this can remain concealed behind his often quiet and reserved manner. He would fare better if he were more outgoing and showed others his true worth.

However, the Snake is very much his own master. He invariably knows what he wants in life and is often prepared to journey long and hard to achieve his objectives. He does, though, have it in his power to make that journey easier. Lose some of that reticence, Snake, be more open and assertive, and do not be afraid of the occasional risk!

Advice for the Snake's Year Ahead

GENERAL PROSPECTS

This may be a mixed year, but it will not be without its value. The Snake should make the most of any chances to add to his skills and experience. While his progress in 2007 may be modest, what he learns can be to his future benefit. He would also do well to broaden his personal interests.

CAREER PROSPECTS

Progress will not be easy and the Snake will need to put in considerable effort as well as be adaptable in his approach. He would do well to work closely with others rather than on his own. However, what he learns now and can bear sizeable fruit, particularly in the more encouraging Rat year that follows.

FINANCE

A year for care and thoroughness and not one for the Snake to lower his usual cautious guard. He will need to watch his financial position and check the terms and implications of any major transaction. This is not a year for risk, carelessness or acting in haste.

RELATIONS WITH OTHERS

The Snake may have an independent side to his character, but he will gain a lot this year by liaising with others and discussing any decisions and problems. He should also make sure he spends time with loved ones and does not neglect his social life.

The Horse

Versatile, hardworking and sociable, the Horse makes his mark wherever he goes. He has an eloquent and engaging manner and makes friends with ease. He is quick-witted, has an alert mind and is certainly not averse to taking risks or experimenting with new ideas.

The Horse possesses a strong and likeable personality, but he does also have his weaknesses. With his wide interests he does not always finish everything he starts and he would do well to be more persevering. He has it within him to achieve considerable success, but to make the most of his talents he does need to overcome his restless tendencies. When he has made his plans he should stick with them.

The Horse loves company and values both his family and friends. However, there will have been many a time when he will have lost his temper or spoken in haste and regretted his words. Throughout his life, he needs to keep his temper in check and be diplomatic in tense situations. If not, he could risk jeopardizing the respect and good relations he so values.

However, the Horse has a multitude of talents and a lively and outgoing personality. If he can overcome his restless and volatile nature, he can lead a rich and highly fulfilling life.

Advice for the Horse's Year Ahead

GENERAL PROSPECTS

The Horse has an active nature and likes getting things done. He could, though, find the Pig year trying. Some of his plans could be subject to delay or possible alteration.

However, by adapting to situations, showing patience (not a Horse strong point!) and doing what he can, he can gain experience which will be useful in the future.

CAREER PROSPECTS
This can be a demanding year with the Horse sometimes facing a heavy workload and high expectations. However, by showing commitment and working hard, he can make progress that will be of great future value. The benefits of this sometimes challenging year can be considerable.

FINANCE
The Horse's earning abilities will be on good form this year, but with often high accommodation costs and good travel opportunities, the Horse needs to control his finances well and, if he is able, consider making some savings for the longer term. With good management, however, this can be a much-improved year.

RELATIONS WITH OTHERS
The Horse will particularly appreciate the positive relations he enjoys with his family, friends and colleagues. However, in view of the active nature of the year, he does need to consult others as well as set time aside for his loved ones, interests and recreational pursuits. It is important that he keeps his lifestyle in balance.

The Goat
The Goat has a warm, friendly and understanding manner and gets on well with most people. He is generally easy-

going, has a fond appreciation of the finer things in life and possesses a rich imagination. He is often artistic and enjoys the creative arts and outdoor activities.

However, despite his engaging manner, there lurks beneath his skin a sometimes tense and pessimistic nature. The Goat can be a worrier, and without the support and encouragement of others, can feel insecure and be hesitant in his actions.

To make the most of himself the Goat should aim to become more assertive and decisive as well as more at ease with himself. He has much in his favour, but he really does need to promote himself more and be bolder. He would also be helped if he were to sort out his priorities and set about his activities in an organized and disciplined manner. There are some Goats who tend to be haphazard in the way they go about things and this can hamper their progress.

Although the Goat will always value the support of others, it would also be in his interests to become more independent and not be so reticent about striking out on his own. He does, after all, possess many talents, as well as a sincere and likeable personality, and by always giving his best he can make his life rich, rewarding and enjoyable.

Advice for the Goat's Year Ahead

GENERAL PROSPECTS

This will be a fine year for the Goat and by making good use of his talents and opportunities, he can achieve a great deal. This is a time for taking the initiative. Fortune will favour the bold.

CAREER PROSPECTS

A year of considerable potential, with the chance to secure promotion and/or move to more fulfilling responsibilities. Again, though, this is a year for positive and determined action. The Goat should believe in himself and put himself forward.

FINANCE

The Goat's progress can bring some fine rewards, although to benefit the Goat does need to manage his money carefully. Without some discipline – and restraint – anything extra he receives could quickly be spent. If he is able, he should make some savings, particularly for the longer term.

RELATIONS WITH OTHERS

The Goat will be in excellent form and both his domestic and social life will bring pleasure. New friendships and romance can come to mean a great deal and there may be good cause for a personal celebration. This is a time to be with others and revel in the opportunities that the year will bring. Travel is also well aspected.

The Monkey

Lively, enterprising and innovative, the Monkey certainly knows how to impress. He has wide interests, a good sense of fun and relates well to others. He also possesses a shrewd mind and often has a happy knack of turning events to his advantage.

However, despite his versatility and considerable gifts, the Monkey does have his weaknesses. He often lacks persistence, can get distracted easily and also places tremendous reliance upon his own judgement. While his belief in himself is a commendable asset, it would certainly be in his interests to be more mindful of the views of others. Also, while he likes to keep tabs on all that is going on around him, he can be evasive and secretive with regard to his own feelings and activities, and again a more forth-coming attitude would be to his advantage.

In his desire to succeed the Monkey can also be tempted to cut corners or be crafty and he should recognize that such actions can rebound on him!

However, the Monkey is resourceful and his sheer strength of character will ensure he has an interesting and varied life. If he can channel his considerable energies wisely and overcome his sometimes restless tendencies, his life can be crowned with success and achievement. And with his amiable personality, he will enjoy the friendship of many.

Advice for the Monkey's Year Ahead

GENERAL PROSPECTS

A reasonable year, although the Monkey will need to be realistic. This is not a year to expect major breakthroughs. However, by planning activities and using his time well the Monkey can make useful headway and prepare the way for the upturn in fortunes he will enjoy in 2008.

CAREER PROSPECTS

This is very much a year for the Monkey to add to skills, experience and qualifications. It is also a year to remain thorough and patient and avoid acting too hastily. 'Slow and steady wins the race.' The Monkey's progress may be slow and steady, but it will help his longer-term prospects.

FINANCE

A reasonably good year, with the Monkey's hard work and enterprise often leading to a rise in income. However, he does need to be wary of haste and of impulse buying and would do well to keep watch over his general level of spending and take his time with his purchases.

RELATIONS WITH OTHERS

A generally pleasing year, with the Monkey valuing the support of those around him. However, he does need to be forthcoming and prepared to consult others. His interests can have a good social element and lead to new friendships.

The Rooster

With his considerable bearing and incisive and resolute manner, the Rooster cuts an impressive figure. He has a sharp mind, is well informed on many matters and expresses himself clearly and convincingly. He is meticulous and efficient in his undertakings and commands a great deal of respect. He also has a genuine and caring interest in others.

The Rooster has much in his favour, but there are some aspects of his character that can tell against him. He can be candid in his views and over-zealous in his actions, and sometimes he can say or do things he later regrets. His high standards also make him fussy, even pedantic, and he can get diverted into relatively minor matters when in truth he could be occupying his time more profitably. This is something all Roosters would do well to watch. Also, while the Rooster is a great planner, he can sometimes be unrealistic in his expectations. In making plans – indeed, in most of his activities – he would do well to consult others. He would benefit greatly from their input.

The Rooster has many talents as well as commendable drive and commitment, but to make the most of himself he does need to channel his energies wisely and watch his candid and sometimes volatile nature. With care, however, he can make a success of his life, and with his wide interests and outgoing personality, he will enjoy the friendship and respect of many.

Advice for the Rooster's Year Ahead

GENERAL PROSPECTS
A year of considerable potential, although the Rooster will need to act and *to persevere*. With determination and focus, however, much can be achieved.

CAREER PROSPECTS
A year for progress. By seizing his opportunities the Rooster can make important headway and also more effective – and satisfying – use of his talents. This is a year when he can really show his true worth and reap some fine and well-deserved rewards.

FINANCE
An improved year, but the Rooster still needs to keep a close watch on spending and budget carefully for his

commitments and any large purchases. By being patient and waiting for favourable buying opportunities he could save himself considerable outlay and make more appropriate purchases.

RELATIONS WITH OTHERS

The Rooster will value the support he receives, although to benefit he does need to be forthcoming. This is a year when the input of others can make a real difference to how he fares. The aspects are particularly favourable for new friendships and romance.

The Dog

Loyal, dependable and with a good understanding of human nature, the Dog is well placed to win the respect and admiration of many. He is a no-nonsense sort of person and hates any sort of hypocrisy and falsehood. With the Dog you know where you stand and, given his direct manner, where he stands on any issue. He also has a strong humanitarian nature and often champions good and just causes.

The Dog has many fine attributes, although there are certain traits that can prevent him from either enjoying or making the most of his life. He is a great worrier and can get anxious over all manner of things. Although it may not always be easy, he should try to rid himself of the 'worry habit'. Whenever he is tense or concerned, he should be prepared to speak to others rather than shoulder his worries all by himself. In some cases, they could even be of his own making! Also, the Dog has a tendency to look on the pessimistic side and he would certainly be helped if he were to view his undertakings more optimistically. He does, after all, possess many skills and should have faith in his abilities. Another weakness is his tendency to be stubborn over certain issues. If he is not careful, at times this could undermine his position.

If the Dog can reduce the worrying and pessimistic side of his nature, then he will not only enjoy life more but also find he is achieving more. He possesses a truly admirable character and his loyalty, reliability and sincerity are appreciated by all he meets. In his life he will do much good and befriend many – and he owes it to himself to enjoy life too. Sometimes it might help him to recall the words of another Dog, Sir Winston Churchill: 'When I look back on all these worries I remember the story of the old man who said on his deathbed that he had had a lot of trouble in his life, most of which never happened.'

Advice for the Dog's Year Ahead

GENERAL PROSPECTS

The Pig year will suit the Dog's temperament and give him the chance to make the most of his talents. To benefit, though, he will need to take purposeful action. He should also make sure he gives adequate time to his interests and looks to develop them in some way.

CAREER PROSPECTS

The Pig year will give the Dog an excellent chance t
his skills and strengths, and he will often find
more fulfilling than it has been for some ti

and encouraging year and one for the Dog to seize his opportunities.

FINANCE

A generally favourable year, with the Dog's successes often leading to a rise in income. However he would still do well to keep a watchful eye on his outgoings, and important financial paperwork and travel documents do need to be checked carefully if problems are to be avoided.

RELATIONS WITH OTHERS

The Dog's loyal, attentive and caring nature will be valued by many, and romantic prospects are also good. However, should problems arise it is important that the Dog is forthcoming and gives others the chance to help. Overall, though, a pleasing year.

The Pig

Genial, sincere and trusting, the Pig gets on well with most people. He has a kind and caring nature, a dislike of discord and often a good sense of humour. In addition, he has a fondness for ~ ; and enjoying the good life!

Th~ ~hrewd mind, is particularly adept at ~and financial matters and has a ~e. Although not all his plans may ~, he is tenacious and will often ~eriencing setbacks and difficul- ~aried life he can accomplish a ~e certain aspects of his char- ~. If he can modify these or keep them in check then his life will certainly be easier and possibly even more successful.

In his activities the Pig can sometimes over-commit himself, and while he does not want to disappoint, he would certainly be helped if he were to set about his activities in an organized and systematic manner and give himself priorities at busy times. He should also not allow others to take advantage of his good nature and it would be in his interests to be more discerning. There will have been times when he has been gullible and naïve; fortunately, though, he quickly learns from his mistakes. However, he possesses a stubborn streak and if new situations do not fit in with his line of thinking, he can be inflexible. Such an attitude may not always be to his advantage.

The Pig is a great pleasure-seeker and while he should enjoy the fruits of his labours, he can sometimes be self-indulgent and extravagant. This is also something he would do well to watch.

However, though the Pig may possess some faults, those who come into contact with him are invariably impressed by his integrity, amiable manner and intelligence. If he uses his talents wisely, his life can be crowned with considerable achievement and he will also be loved and respected by many.

Advice for the Pig's Year Ahead

GENERAL PROSPECTS

With this being the Pig's own year, he will often sense this is a time of opportunity and set about his aims with greater energy and resolve. As a result, he is set to do very well. This is a year for action and for making the most of the very good opportunities his own year will present.

CAREER PROSPECTS

A year of encouraging developments and significant headway. The Pig could find an enterprising idea rewarding him well. With commitment, determination and the support of his colleagues, he is likely to prosper.

FINANCE

The Pig's hard work and industry can reward him well, however with accommodation costs likely to be high, he does need to keep a watchful eye on his situation and budget wisely. This may be a year of good fortune, but it also requires prudent management.

RELATIONS WITH OTHERS

The Pig's personal skills will be on great form. In his work his ability to forge good working relations with others will certainly be to his advantage, while on a domestic and social level he will be in demand and romantic prospects are good. For the Pig, his own year is one of the best.